About to engage your sister in a difficult conversation? Have something important to discuss with your parents? Need to communicate with your child? If you've ever been in one of these situations, *Lifescripts for Family and Friends* tells you just what you need to say, no matter to whom you're speaking.

Your parents

- Announcing you won't be home for the holidays
- Revealing an impending move far away

Your siblings

- Telling them they can't bring their children to a social event
- Asking a brother or sister to repay an outstanding loan

Your children

- Informing them of a loved one's death
- Having a talk about sex

Your spouse

- Bringing up a pet peeve
- Debating household chores

Find the right **Life***script* in these pages.

Life*scripts*

for Family
and Friends

What to Say in 101 of Life's Most Troubling
and Uncomfortable Situations

Erik Kolbell
Edited by Stephen M. Pollan
and Mark Levine

POCKET BOOKS
New York London Toronto Sydney Singapore

An *Original* Publication of POCKET BOOKS

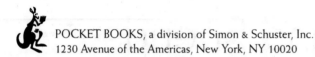

POCKET BOOKS, a division of Simon & Schuster, Inc.
1230 Avenue of the Americas, New York, NY 10020

Copyright © 2002 by Third Millennium Press, Inc., Erik Kolbell and Stephen M. Pollan

ISBN: 0-7434-0060-7

First Pocket Books trade paperback printing January 2002

10   9   8   7   6   5   4   3   2

POCKET and colophon are registered trademarks of
Simon & Schuster, Inc.

For information regarding special discounts for bulk purchases,
please contact Simon & Schuster Special Sales at 1-800-456-6798
or business@simonandschuster.com

Book design by Nancy Singer
Cover design by Regina Starace, front cover photo by James Stirling/The Image Bank

Printed in the U.S.A.

to my father and the memory of my mother,
who authored our family

Author's Note

This book was completed well before the September 11 terrorist attacks on the Pentagon and the World Trade Center, a day when everything changed.

At first blush, there is little or no correlation between world events of this magnitude and a book designed simply to help families talk more freely with one another. Still, I do think we can, both as individuals and families, be greatly informed by this tragedy.

If nothing else, the events of that day underscore—as we hope this book does—the need for families to be strong in the face of great uncertainties and cohesive in the face of forces that threaten to divide us.

It is a time for parents to be duly diligent with their children, spouses to be exceedingly attentive to their mates, adult children to be patient and understanding with their aging parents, and good friends to cement relationships that might otherwise wither and fade from a lack of attention. And perhaps most of all, it is a time to be demonstratively loving toward all those we care about.

I hope this book, in some small way, helps you with this. I say this because one true test of the power of love is our ability to be forthright with one another, to say what needs to be said instead of just what wants to be heard, and to do so in a way that conveys compassion rather than judgment.

Acknowledgments

While I take responsibility for every word you read in this book, I nonetheless want to thank a handful of people whose best efforts have only served to make it a better project than it would have been without them. In particular, thanks to: Mark Levine, who wields an editorial pen the way a fine surgeon wields a sharp scalpel; Stephen Pollan, whose genius gave birth to the idea in the first place; Dr. Cassandra Cook, Dr. Bernice Berk, and Dr. Amy Miller, for their brilliance in shaping the chapters on lifescripts for children; my daughter, Kate, who in the wisdom of her youth suggested chapters we adults overlooked and shouldn't have; and most especially my wife, Ann, my partner in life, for, well, being just that.

Erik Kolbell

Contents

part 1 **Life***scripts* for talking to parents

Contents

part 2 **Life**scripts for siblings

part 3 **Life***scripts* for talking to children

part 4 **Life***scripts* for talking to adult children

part 5 **Life***scripts* for spouses

part 6 **Life***scripts* for friends

The Secret of Lifescripts

I've been giving advice to people for most of my adult life.

Usually it's in my capacity as an attorney and financial adviser; but other times it's as a son, husband, father, or friend. Most often I'm being asked for help with vital legal, financial, career, and business matters. I suppose I've become a source of advice in these areas because of my long and varied experience in the law and business, my reputation as an effective negotiator, my notoriety as an author and media commentator, and the uniquely personal brand of service and attention I offer clients and readers.

I like to take people by the hand and lead them through a process, helping them plan and prepare for potential obstacles. Whether it's helping a young couple buy their first home, helping an experienced corporate executive negotiate an employment contract, or helping a widow complain to her insurance company, I try to break every project down into manageable steps. But despite my best efforts at explaining and coaching, there's always one last question: But what do I say?

Whether they're high-powered professionals, shy homemakers, or somewhere in between, all of my clients want to know what words they should use and how they should deal with possible responses.

To ease their anxiety, I tell my clients to telephone me just prior to the event so we can together create a lifescript for the whole conversation: an outline of the entire dialogue, including counters, responses, and rejoinders. Often the script is used verbatim; sometimes only the icebreaker is used; and other times the script just serves as the extra measure of confidence the person needs to face a difficult, unpleasant, or awkward situation. My clients are almost universally amazed at how effective these lifescripts can be, and how much better they fare using them.

I could claim that the reason my lifescripts work so well is that I'm the savviest negotiator in the world. But that would be boastful and probably untrue. While I am a very good negotiator, the secret behind lifescripts isn't my skill—it's that they're comprehensive plans for situations we usually don't plan for.

When a couple decides to have a formal wedding, they don't just wing it. They sit down, either with a party planner or on their own, and plan out the whole affair. They make sure there will be enough food, that the napkins match the centerpieces, and that Uncle Otto and Cousin Morty, who have been feuding for twenty years, are sitting at separate tables. By the day of the wedding, little is left to chance. The reason lifescripts work so well is that they bring the same kind of planning and attention to a conversation that is brought to a wedding party.

Plan out your business and financial exchanges, and they'll be easier to handle and more apt to work out the way you want. With a lifescript, either in your hand or your head, you'll never be surprised. You'll have a plan that leads inexorably to your goal, regardless of what obstacle is thrown in your path. You'll have an answer to every question, a comeback to every putdown, and a defense for every attack.

In the original volume of lifescripts (*Lifescripts: What to Say to Get What You Want in 101 of Life's Toughest Situations*, Macmillan, 1996), my coauthor, Mark Levine, and I tried to demonstrate that scripting worked not only in business, career, and financial matters but in personal dialogues as well. Our professional expertise, however, doesn't extend to family dynamics, so we were limited in the number of situations we felt comfortable tackling. The continuing enthusiastic response to *Lifescripts* over the past five years led us to look for someone with the expertise, insight, warmth, skill, and humor to fully extend the concept to personal situations involving family and friends. We found that man in Erik Kolbell, a psychotherapist and author who, in his private practice and his career as an ordained minister, has helped thousands of families through difficult, painful, and awkward times.

Far from being a sequel, *Lifescripts for Family and Friends* stands on its own as an unprecedented tool for effective interpersonal communications. Truth be told, it surpasses our original work by dealing with far more difficult and important matters. Finding the right words when asking for a raise is certainly valuable, but it doesn't measure up to the burden of finding the right words to tell a child that she's suffering from a serious illness. I think this book deserves a place on every family's bookshelf.

—Stephen M. Pollan

Why Is It So Hard to Talk to One Another?

One of the recurring themes I've come upon in my work as a psychotherapist is how difficult it can be for many of us to have frank conversations with people for whom we hold great affection. While a young man can tell his butcher he's selling him a lousy piece of meat, he can't tell his mother she doesn't know how to cook it. Likewise, a company president has no trouble negotiating the deal to take over another company, but getting his best friend to return his lawnmower is another issue altogether. And while a teacher can preach about the need for kids to be careful about sex, when it comes to talking with her daughter about the same subject, well . . .

I believe we hit these roadblocks in large part *because* we hold such great affection for these people; because the relationships mean something to us, because we value them, and because we want to maintain them with as little disruption as possible. If, for instance, I don't think it's safe for my father to drive his car any longer, how do I tell him this without him resenting me and treating me coldly every time I see him? How can I confront my best friend about his drinking problem and ensure that afterward he'll still *be* my best friend? How do I have a hard conversation without stirring up hard feelings?

The answer, I think, is to map out the conversation beforehand, from the words we need to use to the inflection, emotion, and even place and time we need to deliver them—to design the conversation in a way that does not disrupt but rather protects and maybe even enhances this relationship that means so much to us. To write, in essence, a *lifescript*. And to do so, there are four major principles we want to keep in mind.

What is my goal?

Your sister has decided she's had it up to her eyeballs with her old job. It's frustrating, demeaning, demoralizing, and debilitating. First thing Monday morning she's storming into the office of her dimwitted boss, upbraiding him with a well-deserved and long overdue string of invectives the likes of which would make a sailor blush, and then storming out again, leaving in her wake a letter of resignation and a lot of burned bridges. Clearly this is a woman who, at this moment in her life, is long on passion but short on perspective. She's giving no thought to what it means to quit her job in *this* way and at *this* time, and may soon find herself out of work, luck, and money. You see trouble ahead. So what do you do? How do you force her to rethink her strategy?

Well, you don't. That is to say, you don't enter a conversation thinking you have the power to *force her* to do anything. Your sister is an adult, a free agent who, like the rest of us, has the right to make her own choices and the responsibility to live with their consequences. What you *can* do, however, is construct a conversation that will help her clarify what is bothering her, what range of solutions are open to her, what pluses and minuses accompany each solution, and what you're willing to do to help her do what's in her best interest. Then, having done that, it's up to her to figure out whether she's going to accept some, all, or none of your advice.

How will I be heard?

Okay, so your sister is determined to quit, but she's willing to talk it over with you first. The first thing you want to keep in mind is not only what you want say but *how it will be heard.* For instance, an opening line like "I don't think you should quit your job" may be misconstrued as "I think you should stop whining, stay in that lousy job, and be grateful you have it." This, I assure you, will make for a very brief conversation. If, on the other hand, you say to her, "You know, that *is* a horrible job you're in, and I think you're absolutely right to want to find a better one. Let's talk about how best to do that," what she hears is that you have sympathy for her situation, agree that she needs to change it, and at the same time want her to focus on what's in her long-term best interest.

Anticipate responses

Now you know what you want to say to your sister, and you *think* you know how she'll hear it; but remember, she's no more predictable than the rest of us, so you also need to be thinking about the range of ways she might respond to your suggestions. Will she be angry ("I'm tired of people telling me what to do! I'll handle this myself!"), offended ("I don't think I *asked* for your advice, did I?"), receptive ("What a relief to have someone to talk this over with!")? The point is, you don't know *how* she'll react, so you need to stay one step ahead of her by anticipating the range of reactions and preparing responses that suit each one. So if, for instance, she does react angrily, you can be ready for her by telling her, "I know how frustrating it is to have people trying to tell you what to do all the time, so I hope you understand that all I want is to help you decide *what you want to do*." Now she hears you're on her side, you're her ally, and you're not out to try and force-feed her a solution she doesn't want to swallow.

With this in mind, as the dialogue progresses, you gently, consistently direct your sister toward the goal you want her to consider.

Last things first

As you're thinking about how to talk with your sister, begin with where you want the conversation to end. What do you want the last word to be? What is the big broad rhetorical ribbon you're going to tie around this whole conversation?

This is important because your conclusion is also an introduction; *your closing thoughts define the first thing that's going to happen.* So you and your sister have had a good talk about her predicament. You've spoken heart to heart, and you now see eye to eye. She's decided, say, to keep her cool, obey her boss, and begin setting up interviews for other jobs at other companies. You reinforce her thinking by summarizing the understanding the two of you have reached: "This is great. You'll avoid your boss as much as possible on Monday, we'll both start looking for other job leads that might suit you, and I'll give you a call first thing Monday morning just to see how things are going." What this does is bring you full circle by giving substance to the initial goal you set for yourself; you're helping your sister extricate herself from a bad environment and situate herself in a good one.

How is this book organized?

This book takes 101 of these difficult topics and in each case offers you five tools for "scripting" them.

First, having identified a topic, I offer an overall *strategy* in which I discuss the goals you might reasonably set for yourself, the pitfalls you might face in trying to achieve them, and some general thoughts about how to maintain a steady course from your opening line to your closing thoughts.

Second, I suggest more specific *tactics* you may want to keep in mind that can maximize the effectiveness of the conversation: When should this conversation be conducted? Under what circumstances? What should I think of ahead of time? What should my body language convey? What kind of attitude do I want to exhibit, and why?

Third, I present a hypothetical conversation in *script* form, starting with an "icebreaker" (your opening line), then taking you through a variety of responses the other party might make to you and you to them (all the while trying to trim their options and navigate the two of you toward your stated goal), and concluding with your closing statement/summation of how the two of you will proceed from here.

Fourth, I offer variations on the theme; *adaptations* of the script in which, with minor modifications, you can apply the same thinking to a similar situation.

And finally, each chapter closes with *key points* that serve as a kind of "crib note" for you to keep in mind as you prepare to enter into the dialogue.

Whose words do I use?

Perhaps the most important thing to keep in mind as you read these lifescripts is that they are *guidelines*, not blueprints. I don't expect you to regurgitate them word for word any more than I expect your friend or family member to respond exactly as I've scripted them. How you ask your brother to repay an outstanding loan, for instance, will in large measure be determined by such variables as the nature of the relationship the two of you have built up over the years, the ways in which your respective personalities either mesh or collide, and the circumstances surrounding his resistance to pay. I can't know any of that, but I can give you a sense of how to take all of that into consideration when engaging him around your need to have him repay his debt.

To put it another way, lifescripts are designed to help you get through some of the most difficult conversations you can have with some of the most important people in your life by defining and anticipating three things:

- The general tone you want a conversation to take and how you can create it.
- The possible directions the conversation could go in and how you can guide it.
- The wisdom of defining a reasonable goal for that conversation and how you can arrive at it.

I believe you'll find them useful.

A Word on Gender

Rather than fill the texts and scripts in this book with such well-intended but clunky phrases as "his or her," "your son or daughter," and "mother or father," scripts have been written for single genders. Except for one or two exceptions (which are explained in the text), genders have randomly been assigned to scripts. Obviously, the lifescripts in this book are intended to be used for either males or females.

part 1

Lifescripts

for talking to parents

Suggesting to a Parent That He Shouldn't Drive Anymore

strategy

No parent wants to hand over the keys to the car once and for all. To do so not only limits their mobility but serves as a not-too-gentle reminder that as they age they will have to depend more and more on others to do the things they used to be able to do for themselves. It can leave them feeling demeaned and demoralized, as if they're little kids who have just had their favorite toys taken away. So when you think it might be in a parent's best interest to stop driving, try to do so by emphasizing three things. First, you're not drawing your own conclusion about his ability to drive, you're simply asking that he consult his doctor. Second, you're not accusing him of driving poorly, you're merely observing that it may be getting more difficult to steer clear of drivers who do. And third, you're acknowledging his need to maintain his active life and reinforcing the idea that there are other ways to ensure that he'll always be able to get around town with ease.

tactics

- **Attitude:** Be exceedingly respectful while at the same time stressing that this is something that needs to be looked into.
- **Preparation:** Numerous articles have been written on the subject. Read one or two, and if possible be prepared to cite an authority who is your parent's age or older. Also, research transportation alternatives that include shuttle buses for older adults, mass transit, and volunteers (including family members).
- **Timing:** Try holding this conversation just prior to your parent's next scheduled appointment with his physician.
- **Behavior:** Remain calm and firm, and keep the conversation from getting personal. Stress that this is a fact of life that all of us will face at some point, and the real issue is not whether or not the parent should drive but how best he can now get to wherever he wants to go.

1. Suggesting to a Parent That He Shouldn't Drive Anymore

Icebreaker: Dad, I read an article the other day written by a man about your age, who explained how as we get older our reflexes gradually slow down. He was recommending older adults see their doctors regularly to determine how much driving they should still be doing. I'd like it if you and I would go see Dr. Kessler and discuss it with him.

Acceptance: Well . . . maybe it wouldn't hurt just to talk to the doctor.

Fear: But if I stop driving I'll never be able to get around. I'll be stuck here at home all day.

Allay fears: Actually, I've been doing some investigating into transportation alternatives. Not only can we kids set up a schedule to get you where you want to go, but there's a shuttle service run by the county that can pick you up and take you anywhere in town. We could also pitch in for cab fare when you need it.

Anger: Look, no one's gonna tell me when I can and can't drive. I'm just fine behind the wheel!

Absorb anger: I can understand why you'd be angry at me for suggesting this; I just know that as safe a driver as you are, a lot of people aren't, and the last thing I want is for you to get into an accident because someone is being careless and you can't avoid them in time.

Indifference, avoidance: Well, I'll give it some thought. Maybe.

Persist: I know this is a lot to consider and it's probably something we're not going to figure out on our own. That's why it'll be useful to get the doctor's read on this.

Reluctance: I don't know. I've driven all my life. I need to think about this.

Continued anger: I tell you, I can take care of myself!

Softens (just a little): Well . . . are you kids really willing to help out if I need it?

Show support: I've actually spoken with the others about this, and we're all agreed that whenever it's time for you to curtail your driving or stop altogether, we promise we won't allow you to become housebound.

Gently nudge: I understand. Why don't we just call the doctor, sit down with him, and simply hear what he has to say? He may well tell you you'll be driving for another twenty years, and that'll make both of us feel better. I'll even set up the appointment.

Deflect anger: The doctor may well say the same thing. All I'm saying is that it's smart for us to speak with him.

Deeply skeptical: Well . . . I'll speak to the doctor. But that's all. And this is no guarantee that even if he does suggest I stop driving I'll do as he says!

Close: You've always made smart, courageous decisions, Dad. And I think talking to the doctor about this is one of the smartest things you've done. I'll call today and set up an appointment for next week and go with you.

adaptations

This lifescript can be adapted to suggest to a parent that he should no longer be preparing his own meals, or that he should consider having part-time home health care.

key points

- Don't make this a referendum on your parent's driving ability.
- Stress your concern for his safety in the face of reckless drivers on the road.
- Affirm his need to be mobile and as independent as possible. Offer to help with this.
- Don't let him defer the question to some vague time in the future.
- Remember you're not yet asking him to give his keys up; you're merely asking him to speak with his doctor.
- Try to go with him when he sees the doctor.

Revealing That You Have a Drinking or Drug Problem 2

strategy

Parents can receive this news with a swarm of feelings and a host of misconceptions. Initially, many will see it as their own failing. They will feel guilty, ashamed, and embarrassed. Others will get angry because they'll see it as a moral weakness on your part. They'll want to punish you, just as they did when you were a child, for doing something foolish and destructive. And some may react with shocked disbelief, convincing themselves this can't be happening in *their* family. Regardless of how your parents greet the news, however, there are three things you want to stay focused on: Make it clear to them that this is an illness for which you need treatment, not a moral failing for which you need punishment. Also, make it clear that it is ultimately your responsibility to remain clean and sober. And finally, tell them you need to know they will continue to love and support you as you try to straighten out your life. Keep in mind also that after this initial conversation they may remain highly skeptical of your commitment to sobriety, so you may need to have follow-up conversations to impress upon them how seriously you're treating this.

tactics

- **Attitude:** Be remorseful for the pain you may have caused them, but also show resolve in your determination to remain sober.

- **Preparation:** Begin seeking a substance abuse therapist. Attend AA meetings. Read literature that explains the nature of your illness and have it available to give to your parents. Have a list of Al Anon meetings to give to them.

- **Timing:** This conversation is best held on a weekend, when your parents aren't consumed with weekly concerns and responsibilities. It's also best to have it in the morning before the day's distractions set in. If possible, have it when no one else is around.

- **Behavior:** Be patient and persistent. Answer all of their questions. Continually stress you have a problem and you're working on it. Reinforce the notion that this is yours to deal with, but there is a positive role for them to play as well.

2. Revealing That You Have a Drinking or Drug Problem

Icebreaker: Mom and Dad, I have a serious problem that I need your help with. I'm an alcoholic, and I really need your support as I fight this disease.

Minimizes the situation: Oh, c'mon! You have a few beers now and then. We all do! That doesn't mean you have a problem.

Shock: This can't be true! I just don't know what to say. I'm stunned.

Anger: What?!? You come in here and tell us you've become a good-for-nothing drunk, and you ask us to *help* you?

Self-blame: This is all our fault, isn't it? We must've done something wrong when we were raising you.

Faulty thinking: That's what I thought for the longest time, too. But my behavior isn't that of a social drinker. The truth is, I was drinking every day, often heavily, often during the day, often blacking out, and sometimes forgetting what happened the night before. The hard fact of the matter is, I'm an alcoholic, and I need your help.

Acknowledge the shock: I know this is a lot to take in at one time, because it took me a long time before I could face it myself. I want to answer any questions you might have about it, including how I'm treating it, but right now I just need to know that you're still there for me; that you'll help me cope with this.

Absorb anger: You certainly have every right to be angry with me. I've made a real mess of things with my drinking. I'm angry with myself too. I don't want to be this way any more than you want me to. That's why I'm getting help, and why I need your help as well.

Relieve them of blame: I understand how you might think this is somehow your fault—lots of parents react that way. But I think the more you learn about this disease, the more you'll understand, as I have, that I need to be held solely responsible for whether or not I drink.

Looks to the past: Surely there was something we could've done to prevent this.

They can't make any promises: You've really broken our hearts. I don't know that we *can* help you.

Overwhelmed; want to deflect responsibility: Look, this is bigger than us. You need to see a doctor.

Unrealistic alternative: So you cut back on your booze. We can help with that. We'll make sure you don't drink too much or too often.

Focus on the present: What really matters now is that I stay sober. I'm seeing a counselor (or, if need be, "I'm going to spend some time in a hospital and then see a counselor") once a week, I'm reading a great deal about alcoholism, and I've begun attending AA meetings. I need to focus on how to deal with this, stay sober one day at a time, and it will really mean a lot to me to know I have your moral support.

You acknowledge the pain: The hardest thing about facing my alcoholism is the pain I've caused you with it. I've had a terrible past, and the only thing I can offer beyond my apologies is to tell you I'm working very hard to set myself straight again.

Agree, and assure them the responsibility for your sobriety doesn't lie with them: I am seeing a doctor, and a counselor, and I'm going to AA meetings. The responsibility to stay sober rests solely on my shoulders. But in addition to the care I'm getting from professionals, I simply need to know that you can help me as well.

Educate them: I appreciate your wanting to help, but alcoholics can't drink in moderation. We have to avoid alcohol entirely. I don't need your help in cutting back, I need it in making sure I never take another drink.

Capitulates, but with reservations: So if we help you, what do you want us to do that your doctors can't do for you already?

Close: I need to know I'm still welcome in your home. Beyond that, it would be an enormous help if you wouldn't serve liquor when I'm here, at least for now. Also, it would mean a lot to me if you would read some of the literature I've brought you about the nature of alcoholism so you can come to a better understanding of my disease. You may also want to consider attending an Al Anon meeting, which is a support group for families of alcoholics.

adaptations

This lifescript may be adapted to inform parents that you have an eating disorder or that you are addicted to gambling.

key points

- This is not their fault.
- It will not go away on its own.
- You are as angry with yourself as they are with you.
- You are not asking them to "fix it."
- You are doing everything in your power to address the problem.

Announcing Plans to Have a Child   **3**

---

strategy

Many parents wait with great anticipation to learn they're going to be grand-parents. Some, however, meet the news with concerns about whether their child is mature enough, well enough established in his or her profession, or financially secure enough to enter parenthood. Some just wonder if the whole task will be too daunting for their child. If you anticipate this kind of reaction from your parents, you want to underscore that you're not expecting it to be easy, that you know it will be full of surprises, and that you've begun to look at the prospect of parenthood with more than giddy excitement. You also want to reinforce their role. Let them know there will be questions you think only they might be able to answer. Make them feel a part of the process. Also, remind them they went through this once themselves, and were no doubt no more prepared than you for what was about to ensue.

---

tactics

- **Attitude**: Show excitement but at the same time show that you're thoughtful about this; that you are weighing the enormity of parenthood quite seriously.

- **Preparation**: Make a financial plan; estimate expenses and income after the baby is born and show how you'll be able to meet your obligations. Also, spend some time with new parents and have them tell you a little about their experiences, especially the difficulties. You may want to begin interviewing pediatricians as well.

- **Timing**: Have this conversation after you and your spouse have spent a day or evening with your parents, and it's gone well. Let your parents see the solidity of your relationship.

- **Behavior**: Hear them out. When they raise an objection, don't answer it right away. Give it a few moments' thought. Above all, behave like an adult—something we sometimes find exceedingly difficult to do when we're with our parents.

3. Announcing Plans to Have a Child

Icebreaker: Mom, Dad, we want you to be among the first to know that we're planning to have a baby. We're not pregnant yet, but the doctor says we should have no trouble conceiving.

Shock: I . . . I just don't know what to say. Do you *really* think you should?

Positive spin: We're actually pretty stunned ourselves, when we think about it. A baby's an enormous amount of responsibility, and we really have an awful lot to learn before it's born about caring for it. That's why we're going to be attending classes, and why we're reading a couple of really good books on the subject. We also want to feel as though we can come to you if we have questions we think you can help us with.

Financial concerns: I know it sounds romantic and all to have a baby, but do you have any idea how much it costs to raise a child in this day and age?

Allay fears: Boy, do we ever! A pediatrician we met with gave us some figures. We took them home, and the first thing we did was lay out a budget for ourselves based on our income and projected expenses. As a matter of fact, we'd like it if you would take a look at it.

Lack of confidence: Are you sure you two are ready for this? It's an awful lot of responsibility, and you're still pretty young.

Acknowledge anxieties: You're right, it is a tremendous amount of responsibility, which is why we've been talking with other young parents about their experiences, and why we're hoping the two of you will be able to share your wisdom with us as well.

Caution, skepticism: Well, I think I still have some misgivings. You really can't know what you're getting yourselves into until you actually experience it.

Cautious optimism: Well, I don't know . . . but it sounds like you're looking at it pretty carefully.

Reinforce your position: I'm sure we're feeling some of the same things you were when you started our family. It all makes us quite excited, and a little scared. We know this is going to be the most important thing we ever do in life, and we're confident that with the help of our families and friends, the wisdom of a good pediatrician, and our own common sense, we'll be good parents. We're really grateful for your support.

key points

- Acknowledge your own fears and concerns.
- If need be, remind them they've been down this road themselves.
- Tell them you're counting on them and, if need be, flatter them. Tell them they'll make wonderful grandparents.

Announcing a Religious Conversion   **4**

strategy

This is a conversation that requires kid gloves to handle, and one in which you don't want to set your goals too high. There is nothing quite so personal to an individual or a family as religious belief, and when a son or daughter abandons the religion of their youth to join another faith community, it can leave parents—even if they're not terribly observant—confused and heartbroken. You'll want to keep two things in mind when you have your first conversation on the subject. First, you want them to be somewhat prepared for it, meaning that for some months prior to this talk you have shared with them the yearnings and questions that have been stirring inside you. This demonstrates the seriousness you are applying to the subject. And second, you don't want this conversation to be their conversion experience. By this I mean that if you want them to accept this new path you've taken, you have to allow that it will take them time, just as it took you time. All you want to accomplish at the outset is to show that you care about them, that this is something you've labored mightily over, that you feel anchored in it, and that you hope the three of you can continue to talk about it in subsequent conversations. Finally, in this script I have chosen to give an example of a Christian converting to Judaism. This is arbitrary, and is easily adaptable to any religious conversion.

tactics

- **Attitude:** You don't want to be bubbling over with enthusiasm; they'll think you've made a rash decision based on emotion alone. Instead, you want to be sober and straightforward, and you want to *tell* them how happy you are without bending over backward to demonstrate it.

- **Preparation:** Talk with your family's clergy, and see if you can't get them to appreciate the decision you've made. Often ministers and rabbis are more open-minded than laypeople on this subject. Also, if you're comfortable with it, pray before you meet with your parents.

- **Timing:** Avoid holiday seasons, and don't have this conversation on either your "old Sabbath" or your "new Sabbath." Make sure you talk at a time when none of you will be interrupted, and when no other family members might walk in on you.

- **Behavior:** Continue to emphasize that this feels right to you, that you've spent a lot of time examining the issues behind it, and that you take their feelings very, very seriously.

15

4. Announcing a Religious Conversion

Icebreaker: Mom, Dad, as you know, over the past several months I've been working very hard to deepen my faith life. It's been a wonderful experience for me, and I think I'm a better person for it. What I need to tell you now is that through all my explorations and study, I've decided to convert to Judaism.

Skepticism: You do a little reading, and suddenly you're a Jew. Have you even spoken to a minister about this?

Assurance: That's a good question. Actually, I've been exploring this for some time now. I've read a good deal, spoken with friends and counselors, and prayed daily about it. I've also spoken with a minister about it. We had a very good, very frank discussion, and while he's sorry to see me leave the church, I think he respects my decision.

Fear: My God! What will our friends think?

Deflect concern, refocus: I honestly don't know, and I hope their reaction doesn't cause you any grief. But I guess I also hope they'll be happy that I've found a way to draw closer to God.

Fear: And what do you suppose your grandparents will say?

Caution: I've thought about that, and if it's all right with you, I'd like to hold off on telling them anything until after you and I have come to some sort of understanding of what all this means.

Hurt: Oh, this really breaks our hearts.

Acknowledge hurt: I knew this would be an awful lot for you to come to grips with, and the last thing in the world I want to do is see the two of you in any kind of pain. That's why I wanted to have this talk, and why I hope we can have more talks about this in the future.

Anger: What?!? How could you do this to us?

Absorb anger: I know you're angry. After all, I'm leaving the religion you brought me up in. But I hope you'll understand this is not something I'm doing *to you*, it's something I'm doing *for me*.

Follow-up: In fact, I wouldn't ask you to accept this right away; all I'm asking for today is that you keep an open mind, and that we can agree to have some more conversations about this. I think you might want to come to terms with this slowly, as I have.

Continued fear: It could really break their hearts.

Personal concern: Well, it *may* indeed cause us grief. This has never happened in our circle of friends before.

Resentment: You talk to other people, but you don't discuss it with us?

Making a plan: I know that. It could really break their hearts if they weren't told in such a way that they could understand how good this is for me. This is a complicated experience for all of us. I think it's going to take us time to get used to it. That's why I wanted to speak to the two of you first, so that I might be able to begin to explain to you what this means to me.

Empathy: I know this may make for some uncomfortable situations at first, but I believe that over time whoever has any doubts or concerns about it will come to accept it when they see that I'm serious, and that it makes me a happier person.

Show concern for their feelings, and implicate someone else: It may feel like I'm dropping this on you out of nowhere, but I think I've tried to be pretty upfront about the fact that I've been exploring what other faiths have to say. I waited until now to begin this conversation because our minister thought it a good idea to make my decision and then come and share it with you. That makes sense to me, too.

Continued on page 18.

4. Announcing a Religious Conversion *(Continued)*

Resignation (perhaps with some residual anger): So you've made up your mind. What do you want from us?

Still overwhelmed: We're just too overwhelmed to know what to say. I can't promise you anything right now.

Rejection: I'm sorry, but we just can't accept this right now.

Offer to talk: I would never ask you to accept something like this so quickly; after all, it's taken me months of skepticism and searching to come to this decision. Because this is so important to me, and because you're so important to me, all I'm asking is that you keep an open mind to the possibility that this might be good for me, and agree that we can talk some more about this over the next few weeks. I want to answer any questions you might have, and allay any fears you might have.

adaptation

This script can be adapted for any conversion, and could also be adapted for someone who is simply *considering* converting to a different religion.

key points

- Emphasize that this is a deliberate process; that you don't approach this decision lightly.

- If possible, in this or subsequent conversations, let your parents know you don't feel as though you're "rejecting" the religion of your youth. You still have faith in God, as they have taught you, and you've simply found a new way to express that faith.

- Tell them how grateful you are that you have been raised with an appreciation for the importance of religious faith.

Revealing Your Sexuality 5

strategy

As a gay man or woman who has chosen to "come out" to your parents, the things you want to communicate are that you know who you are sexually, that you've come to this realization on your own, and that you're comfortable with it. You don't want your parents to misinterpret this as a problem you want their help in solving. In addition, you want to reinforce for them the idea that you are the same son or daughter they've always known. Your sexuality doesn't entirely define who you are, so you are not asking them to get accustomed to a new child. You're simply asking that they get acquainted with a part of that child they didn't know existed. Finally, remember that most gay women and men come to understand their sexuality gradually; so afford your parents the same patience you afforded yourself. This may take time, not because they reject you, but because it's something they've probably never considered before.

tactics

- **Attitude**: Don't be defiant or defensive. Be matter-of-fact, patient, and calm. If there is any taunting, don't respond in kind.

- **Preparation**: Talk to other gay women and men who have come out to their parents. Ask them what surprises the experience held for them. Also, have a list of support groups that your parents might find helpful.

- **Timing**: Have this conversation when you and your family have spent a sizable amount of time together, doing the things that have long defined you as a family. By doing this, you reinforce a sense that you haven't somehow mysteriously "changed."

- **Behavior**: Speak slowly, establish eye contact, listen attentively to everything your parents have to say, and be courteous. And show strength; show that this is not something you will be "talked out of."

5. Revealing Your Sexuality

Icebreaker: Mom and Dad, there's something I want to share with you about myself. I am a gay man, and I'm hoping I'll be able to help you understand what this means to me.

Disbelief: I can't believe this. It can't be true.

Empathy: You know, I really don't expect you to believe this right off the bat. It actually took me time to realize and accept that it's who I am. But you've both always been so good at accepting me for who I am that I'm sure you'll be able to understand this part of me as well.

Ignorance: Maybe it's just a phase you're going through.

Educate: Some people go through phases when they experiment with their sexuality. In fact, for quite some time I wondered if I was "supposed" to be straight, like the majority of people. But I am now quite sure that this is who I am.

Blame: Oh, my gosh! Where did we go wrong?!?

Absolve of blame: I understand a lot of parents have that same reaction. Actually, my sexuality has nothing to do with how you raised me; it's simply who I am. Like being left-handed or blue-eyed. And that's why I like to believe there's nothing "wrong" with being gay.

Anger: No son of mine is gonna be some freak!

Absorb anger: I'm awfully sorry you think of me as a freak. I know this news comes as quite a shock, but I hope you'll be able to understand that I'm still the same son you've always said you were proud of, and still believe I'd never do anything to hurt or embarrass you.

Concern: Aren't you afraid? You know, AIDS? Prejudice?

Prejudice: But it's not normal! It's perverted!

Ridicule: So, you gonna start wearing dresses now?

More anger: No way am I gonna accept this!

Absorb anger, toss in a little guilt: I know you can't fully accept this right now, and you don't think you'll ever be able to. But you've always taught me to be honest with you, and that's what I'm trying to do. You might be interested to know that an awful lot of parents feel the way you do when they learn their son or daughter is gay, but in time they come to feel differently. Your love means everything to me and all I'm asking is that you leave an open mind to the possibility of coming to accept me for who I am. I think if we keep talking, we may be able to grow into an understanding.

Stay cool, debunk prejudices: I think there are a lot of popular misconceptions about being gay. I know I certainly held some before I realized that this is who I am. Gay men and women are really just everyday folk; we're doctors and ditch diggers and football players and lawyers. We vote in elections, raise children, and mow our lawns on Saturday. In other words, we do all the stuff straight folks do. The only difference is that we feel the same love for a person of our own sex as a straight person feels for a member of the opposite sex.

Acknowledge your fears: I am concerned. I think AIDS should be a concern for all people, gay and straight. Fortunately, if and when I were to get involved with someone, I would be exceedingly careful. As far as prejudice is concerned, it worries me, too. It's sad, but in many communities gay people often have to be more discreet about their relationships than straight people, and while that's not fair, it's something I'm learning to deal with. Fortunately, though, you two have always taught me to take good care of myself, and I'm grateful for that.

Seek help: Have you thought of going to a counselor about this?

Continued on page 24.

Despair: I don't think I'll ever understand this. I'm sorry.

Reluctance: Look, it's gonna take some time for all this to sink in. You're going to have to be patient here.

Resistance: Forget it! I'll never understand this sort of thing, I'll never accept it, and that's that.

5. Revealing Your Sexuality (*Continued*)

Bottom line: Okay. I know you can't accept this now, so here is what I want you to hear from me: If you ever come to have a change of heart, I want you to know my door will always be open. I'll always be ready to talk this out some more. Our relationship is important to me, as it is to you, so I'm prepared to wait until you're ready to talk. I love you both.

Acceptance: I understand. Let's keep talking about it. Also, if you're ever interested, there are education and support groups for the parents of children who are gay. You might find it helpful to hear from other parents who've had to take time to accept their children's sexuality. I've brought some phone numbers for you.

Assurance, a little humor: I felt the same way about physics when I was in school! It does take time, but I can help you learn to understand. In the meantime, just remember that I'm the same son you've always loved. I have the same job, same hobbies, same values and beliefs, same personality. All the good stuff you instilled in me since I was a child—it's all still there.

Reinforce that you know who you are: I might have gone to a counselor if I felt uncertain abut my sexuality, or if I was disturbed by it. But fortunately I don't have either of those burdens; I know who I am, and I'm comfortable with it.

Accepting: You are our son, and we love you. This is going to take some getting used to, but we support you.

Warming up just a little: Well, give me some time. I'll need to think about all this.

Close the conversation: I'm really grateful that you're my parents, and that you're willing to have open minds about this. Let's talk again next week, but let me also say that if you have any questions I can answer, any at all, please ask them. Maybe you'd like to give it some thought before we get together again.

adaptations

This script can be adapted to reveal your sexuality to other family members. It can also be adapted to reveal a friend's sexuality to your parents.

key points

- You want to stress that this is a part of who you are, and you're certain of it.
- You want to tell them gay men and women lead perfectly normal lives.
- You want to be prepared to debunk any myths and stereotypes they might hold.
- Be prepared for them to reject you. If this happens, leave the door open for them to return to the conversation when they're ready.

Revealing That Your Marriage Is Breaking Up

6

strategy

As much pain as this may cause you, remember that the news can also be very hard on your parents. Rightly or wrongly, they may feel guilty you're going through this, as though it is somehow their fault. Add to this the hurt they'll feel for you and, perhaps, anger toward your ex, and you begin to realize they're not going to take this easily. With this in mind, you will do well to let them know that this was a long time coming, that the two of you have explored it from every conceivable angle, that your minds are made up, and that although you are in pain, you believe this is the right thing for your family. But because parents can feel so helpless at a time like this, you do yourself *and them* a favor if you can come up with something to ask of them to make this transition as easy as possible.

tactics

- **Attitude:** Be forthright and calm, but at the same time don't hide your pain (they'll see right through this).

- **Preparation:** You should both see a marriage counselor. Assuming that doesn't resolve your problems and you still agree to separate, try to agree on what the next steps should be. Agreeing to see a mediator can prevent a messy court fight. Agreeing to involve the children (if you have any) as little as possible is also good. This will show your parents you're both thinking clearly.

- **Timing:** Avoid all holidays or family celebrations (birthdays, anniversaries, etc.). Also, don't talk to them shortly after you and your ex have had a quarrel. Finally, have this conversation on a Saturday morning or afternoon, so there's plenty of free time for them to digest it.

- **Behavior:** Emphasize your commitment to this; speak with conviction and stress that this is not a matter of who's right or who's wrong, but of incompatibility.

6. Revealing That Your Marriage Is Breaking Up

Icebreaker: Mom and Dad, I'm afraid I have to deliver some sad news. Bob and I have been having a very rough time for quite a while now, and after trying very hard to straighten things out, we've both decided that the best thing to do is dissolve our marriage.

Finger-pointing: What did he do to you?

Minimizing: Look, all couples have their rough spots. You two just stick to it and work it out.

Disbelief: This can't be! You've always struck us as completely happy with one another.

Ill-directed pragmatism: I'm sorry you two aren't happier, but you have to stay together for the sake of the kids.

Avoid blaming: There's really no one to blame here. We've both been unhappy for quite some time, so this is something we both decided needed to do.

Acknowledge their argument: You're quite right; all couples do hit rough times. As a matter of fact, when we first started noticing we were having problems, we thought we'd be able to work them through. When that didn't happen, we tried working them out with a counselor, but that didn't work either. Things got much worse, and we had really exhausted all of our options, and that's when we decided we had to do this.

Defend your privacy: We both thought it wise to keep our problems between ourselves until we had a clearer sense of how we were going to resolve them, and our counselor supported us in that. We didn't want to burden you or Bob's parents because we knew you'd both worry and because this was something we had to work through on our own.

Acknowledge kids' needs: That crossed both of our minds as well, but the truth is, the kids see our unhappiness, and it makes them miserable too. Common sense tells us, and our counselor assures us, that although a separation can be very rough on them in the early going, if we handle it properly, they'll be able to adjust to it. And most importantly, they'll come to learn that we both love them and we'll always be there for them.

Warning: What do you do next? This can get very ugly, you know.

Paper over the problems: Maybe what the two of you need

Curiosity: But what happened to make things go so bad so quickly?

Support: This is all very disturbing, but we love you and

Reassure: We know couples who have had very ugly separations and those who have done this very civilly. Bob and I both feel we've endured a great deal of pain already, and we want to make this as easy as possible on all of us. We've decided that Bob will get a place to live so the kids can stay in the house with me, and we've agreed to a visitation schedule. We're also going to ask a mediator to help us divide our property, and we've agreed that if either one of us feels the need, we'll both go back to our counselor to help us separate as cleanly as possible. What we need now is to know we can count on you for emotional support.

Explain that it's not so simple: I wish it were that simple, believe me. We wouldn't be doing this if we hadn't exhausted every option open to us, including going away for a few days. I'm afraid the problems were still there waiting for us when we got back. But we feel alright about the way we're dealing with this, and now all we ask is for your support.

Protect your privacy: You know, I don't really want to get into specifics just now. Bob and I think we both might give slightly different answers to that question, so we've agreed to hold off on answering it. What's important to know is that we respect each other immensely, we love the kids immeasurably, but we simply can't live together and be happy. What's also important is that we feel as though you can find it in your hearts to support us in this.

... is to get away for a couple of days, a romantic vacation. Get to know one another again.

... we'll do anything we can. You tell us how we can help.

Support: So tell us what you want from us.

Be clear about what you do and don't want: I knew I could count on you. What I need is three things: I need you to make sure you don't say anything to the kids that would prejudice them against either Bob or me; I need to know that you'll offer advice as you see fit, and you'll leave it up to me as to whether or not I heed your advice; and I need to know your door is always open to me, and that you're there for emotional support when I need it.

adaptations

This script can be adapted to inform parents that you're thinking of leaving your spouse or that you and a longtime lover are calling it quits.

key points

- You're both more sad than you are angry; both of you feel responsible, but neither of you feels guilt or blame.
- You've both tried every avenue to make it work.
- Your minds are made up, and you are in complete agreement on this.
- You want your parents' help, which may or may not include their advice.

Confronting a Parent about His Drug Problem

7

strategy

It's extremely difficult to confront anyone about a drug problem, let alone a parent. Not only will he be resistant to the news, he certainly isn't going to want to hear it from his child. For this reason, you want to gather a small circle of close family members and confront the parent as a unified block. Together, you need to persist in insisting that the parent get treatment, and get it immediately. You want to reinforce the fact that what he's grappling with is a serious illness and not a moral lapse, and you want also to emphasize that this is something he will not be able to solve on his own. Above all, you do not leave the room until your parent has capitulated to getting help.

tactics

- **Attitude:** Be firm and forceful, but don't preach at him. And don't present treatment as an "option," but rather as something he absolutely must do.

- **Preparation:** Arrange for the parent to have a bed at a local rehab center (you may want to consult your physician for a recommendation). Meet with a staff member to discuss your intervention and what the treatment regimen will consist of. Discreetly arrange for him to miss work for a month or two. Meet among yourselves prior to the confrontation and agree that you will all say the same thing; namely, that this is an illness, that it must be addressed immediately, and that you are there to offer support.

- **Timing:** If possible, do this when the parent is lucid, so as to decrease possible belligerence. Also, doing it on a Friday after work will allow him to get situated in the rehab center without "mysteriously" disappearing from work midweek.

- **Behavior:** The parent might display a wide range of intense feelings. All of you must be prepared to answer him calmly and coolly. Remind him that he is loved and that he has an illness that must be treated.

7. Confronting a Parent about His Drug Problem

Icebreaker: This is the most difficult thing we've ever had to do, but we're here to tell you that you have developed a serious drug problem, and you'll need to go to a hospital for a while to get the help you need.

Denial: So I take a couple of pain killers for my back; it's no big deal.

Anger: How dare you accuse me of being some kind of drug addict! Now all of you get out and leave me alone.

Bargaining: Well, I'm just fine, but if it'll make you happy, I'll cut down. I'll do it on my own.

Absorb anger: You can get as angry as you want at all of us. I know I would. But we're telling you this because your health is in real danger. You need help in fixing this problem, and we're here to support you as you get that help.

Explain why it is a big deal: It's not that simple. You're taking these pills every day, and with greater frequency each day. You're missing work. Your speech is slurred. And you're having trouble driving your car. The pills you're taking can be addictive, so the longer you take them, the harder it is to stop. That's why you need some help.

Explain why this isn't an option: We've discussed this with experts, and they tell us that because of the nature of the drug and the way it works in your body, it's impossible to cut down on your own. Your body simply won't let you. That's why you need professional help.

Stereotyping addiction: That stuff's for winos and derelicts. I'm a professional. I make good money. I have a family, a house. I'm no junkie.

Fear: Okay, I know I *may* have a problem, but the idea of going to a hospital really scares me. Isn't it a little much? Can't I get treatment without having to go to such extremes?

Resistance: Look, I'll tell you what. Tomorrow I'll give my doctor a call and make an appointment with him, see what he has to say about all this.

Assurance: There's nothing to worry about because nothing drastic will happen at the hospital. You'll meet with a specialist who will answer all your questions and give you a very clear understanding of your course of treatment and how long it should take. And we'll be looking in on you whenever we're permitted. The thing to keep in mind is that you're sick, and this is the place for you to get better. It's time to go now, and I'm wondering if there's anyone you want to ride over to the hospital with us.

Alleviate concern: We've looked at your employee manual, and you're entitled to this time off as sick leave. No one outside of human resources needs to know why you're out, and we'll be sure to tell your friends and colleagues that you'll be out sick for a while and we'll let them know when you're feeling better. We need to be getting over to the hospital now. We've packed you some things, and I was wondering if there's anyone you'd like to go along with us on the ride over.

Debunk stereotype: The truth is, there are a great many people such as yourself who are very successful but who've been hit with this illness. People from all walks of life are susceptible to it. You're not alone.

Concern about missing work: But how long will this take? I have responsibilities, I have to get to work. What will people think about where I am?

Insist: I'm afraid putting it off will only make it harder for you. That's why we've gone ahead and told the hospital you'd be coming today. We're going to take you over there now. You'll meet with a substance abuse specialist and be on your way to recovery before the day is out.

Annoyance at feeling "set up": Geez, you've ambushed me, done all this behind my back.

Close in: You're right, we did, because this is the only way we could be sure you'd get the help you need. We're sorry we had to do it this way, but I think you'll feel a whole lot better when you don't have to worry about taking these pills anymore. We need to go now; the car is ready, and we've packed you a bag. Is there anyone besides me you'd like to go in the car with you?

adaptations

This script can be adapted to confront a parent with a drinking problem, a gambling problem, or other addictive behavior.

key points

- Do this as a family.
- Be unified; speak as if with one voice.
- Emphasize that drug addiction is an illness.
- Insist on taking the parent to the hospital/rehab center.
- As best as you can, tell him what to expect when he gets there, and when he might be able to expect to come home.

Announcing That You Won't Be Home for the Holidays

8

strategy

There are three factors that can make this script prove either a piece of cake or tough sledding. First, the better your reason for not coming home, the less difficult it will be for your family to accept your decision. If—as I have suggested here—you and your spouse are simply too exhausted to make the trip and you've decided to stay at home for a little R&R, chances are a reasonable family will understand. If, on the other hand, you've decided to go out on a blind date instead of sitting at the family's annual Thanksgiving dinner table, be prepared for some fireworks. Second, the meaning your family ascribes to the particular holiday will figure in how intensely they react. Labor Day, for instance, might not be as big a deal as, say, Christmas or Passover. Finally, your load will be lighter if you can propose an occasion after the holiday season when you all might get together, reinforcing your affection for them.

tactics

- **Attitude**: Show this isn't an easy decision for you; that you truly enjoy the holidays at home, but this year something simply had to give.

- **Preparation**: If possible, speak to your siblings first and see if they will support your decision. They may be easier to persuade than your parents. Also, think of when after the holidays you might be able to visit your family and be prepared to suggest this.

- **Timing**: Do this at a time when you've been attentive to your family (phone calls, visits, etc.) as opposed to a time when you've been out of touch for a while. Also, do it as far in advance of the holiday as possible.

- **Behavior**: Don't be apologetic for a decision you've made of your own free will. By the same token, don't be defiant, as though you dare them to find fault with your decision. Stress that you see this as a necessity, and you hope they'll understand. Also, don't rise to the bait of sarcasm or veiled anger. Stay cool.

8. Announcing That You Won't Be Home for the Holidays

Icebreaker: Mom and Dad, there's something you need to know about this holiday season. Karen and I have decided we really need to spend this holiday by ourselves, so I won't be coming out.

Anger: What, you don't love us anymore? We'll never see you now? Fine! Have it your way.

Deflect anger: This was a hard decision for us to reach, and it has nothing to do with my feelings for you or for our family. In fact, one of the things I wanted you to be thinking about was when it might be convenient for us to pay a visit some time after the holidays. It's just that right now we're both so exhausted that the one thing we really need this holiday season is a little quiet time alone together.

Blame: This is Karen, isn't it? She never thought much of us, did she? She's doing this!

Hurt: Gosh, this really hurts. I don't know what to say.

Redefine the situation: I don't want you to feel this is something either one of us is doing *to you*. It's something *we're* doing *for us*. We've both had an extremely stressful year, and we've seen so little of each other, that we feel it's best to stay at home alone and enjoy some quiet time together.

Guilt: But we've always done the holidays here at home. You'll be breaking up a family tradition.

Deflect guilt: And it's a tradition that means a lot to me, which is why it was so hard to make this decision. But we've both had such a stressful year, and we've seen so little of each other, that we feel it's best for us to stay home alone and enjoy some quiet time together.

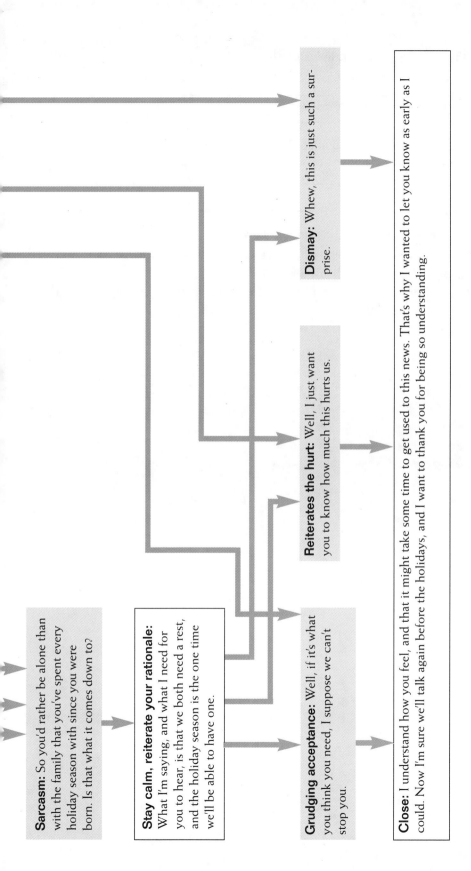

Sarcasm: So you'd rather be alone than with the family that you've spent every holiday season with since you were born. Is that what it comes down to?

Stay calm, reiterate your rationale: What I'm saying, and what I need for you to hear, is that we both need a rest, and the holiday season is the one time we'll be able to have one.

Grudging acceptance: Well, if it's what you think you need, I suppose we can't stop you.

Dismay: Whew, this is just such a surprise.

Reiterates the hurt: Well, I just want you to know how much this hurts us.

Close: I understand how you feel, and that it might take some time to get used to this news. That's why I wanted to let you know as early as I could. Now I'm sure we'll talk again before the holidays, and I want to thank you for being so understanding.

adaptations

A college student could adapt this script to announce he or she wishes to change holiday traditions or won't be home for summer vacation.

key points

- You're not doing this _to them_ but _for you_.
- This is not something you came by lightly; acknowledge there will be things you'll miss about not being there.
- You hope and expect to see your family at the first opportunity that works for all of you.

Revealing an Impending Move Far Away

9

---

strategy

How this conversation plays itself out depends on at least two things. First, are you being relocated because of work, in which case you have little choice in the matter, or are you looking for better opportunities and a different lifestyle, in which case you do have some choice? And second, do you and your parents now spend a good deal of time together, so this move will significantly change the frequency of your getting together? Let's assume the worst: this is a decision you don't have to make but choose to, and you'll be going from seeing your parents on a regular basis to seeing them only a few times a year. With this in mind, you want to let them know that although you're "choosing" to do this, you saw precious few options; if your career is going to advance, you need to go. Also, continually remind them leaving is hard for you, and you didn't come to this decision blithely, but after a great deal of thought and research. And finally, remind them you have every intention of getting together with them as often as is practical. This will not take away their disappointment so much as it will keep them from feeling rejected by you.

---

tactics

- **Attitude:** You want to show excitement over the opportunity this move affords you but also sorrow about having to leave home.

- **Preparation:** Do your homework. Get as clear a picture as possible of what it will be like to live in your new home state. Be prepared to show your parents it offers better work opportunities for you and is better suited to the kind of life you want to live.

- **Timing:** It's not a bad idea to have this conversation at a time when work hasn't been going particularly well for you; when the hassles are piling up and the savings are winnowing down.

- **Behavior:** Have this conversation in your home, particularly if the home is too small for your family. Let your parents see how inadequate your lifestyle currently is. Also, use this conversation as a "heads-up," meaning you're letting them know now about a move that will not happen for several months. This gives them time to adjust.

9. Revealing an Impending Move Far Away

Icebreaker: Mom and Dad, I want to let you know I've decided to move out to the coast. I've researched it pretty thoroughly, and have found the job opportunities will be much greater for me out there, and I think I will like the kind of lifestyle it offers.

Anger: So what's the big hurry to get away from us, your own parents?

Deflect anger: I can see why you'd be angry, but I hope you can understand that I'm in no hurry to get away from you, but I have to go where the opportunities are. I'd love it if you decided to move out with me, although I know you're settled here.

Fear: But it's so far away; we'll never see you.

Assurance: Actually, I've looked into flights, and the way I figure it, we can probably afford at least three visits next year, maybe more. I'm certainly hoping you'll want to come out and visit, and I want to get home at least for the holidays.

Anger: We'll go from seeing each other every week to seeing each other a few times a year. That's a better lifestyle?

Surprise: But we always thought you were happy living here.

Nostalgia: But this is your home. You've lived here all your life. Your roots are in this town.

Gratitude for having been raised there: I love this town, and I'm so grateful you raised us here. It was a wonderful place to grow up. Unfortunately, the opportunities I need to make a life for myself are no longer here like they were ten or twenty years ago, so as difficult as it is, I need to go where I can find them.

Doubts: What opportunities? What do you think you'll do out there that you can't do here?

Acknowledge need for adjustment: It won't be the same as it has been, and that's the hardest thing I'm facing. I'm going to miss seeing you with such frequency; that's an adjustment we'll all have to make. But even though we won't see each other as often as we do now, I have no doubt we'll remain as close as we are now. I know I'm really going to appreciate the times we *do* get to spend together.

Hurt/guilt: This is a lot for us to accept, especially at our age. . . .

Address the hurt, not the guilt: It is. It's a lot for me too. That's why I wanted to tell you now, even though I don't plan to leave for another six months or so. It's also why one of the things I want to do before I leave is make sure we know when we're going to visit one another, either here or on the coast.

Uncertainty: I just don't know how this is gonna work out.

Assurances; you've done your homework: Actually, I've researched it pretty thoroughly. I've been reading newspapers from the coast, talking to representatives of the Chambers of Commerce, and looking at job postings on the Internet, and I've been very encouraged by what I've found. I even had a session with a career counselor here in town who thinks this may be very good for me. There are a number of opportunities for someone with my qualifications.

Curiosity/anxiety: So you've got this thing thought out. It sounds like you're getting ready to leave tomorrow.

You're not in any hurry: I've thought this through because it's such a big step. But I'm not planning to leave for another six months. And one of the things I want to do before I go is agree on a time when we'll visit—either here or out on the coast.

Acceptance: Well, if you really need to do this, I suppose we can't stand in the way.

Close: I think we'll all be a little curious about how this works out, but it feels very much like the right thing for me to do at this point in my life. I hope we all adjust to it without too much difficulty, but thankfully you've always taught me not to shy away from difficult situations.

adaptations

This script can be adapted by parents who need to tell their adult children they are planning to move far away.

key points

- You need to make this move because you're at a dead end in your career.
- Acknowledge that this will be painful for your parents, but let them know it will be painful for you, too.
- Acknowledge how wonderful it was to have grown up in your hometown, and your debt of gratitude to them.

Announcing Plans Not to Have Children

10

---

strategy

This is a classic example of reason bumping up against emotion. You and your spouse have agonized over this, talked it out, talked it out some more, and finally, courageously, come to your decision. Now it's the parents' turn to digest it, and it doesn't go down well. No matter how much they raised you to be your own boss and abide by your own decisions, a good many parents are going to be troubled by this. Not only might they think you're losing out on one of life's pleasures, *they'll* be losing out as well. In anticipation of this conversation, there are a number of things you want to be clear about. First, if you are going to be biologically capable of bearing a child for a few more years, you *may* want to tell your parents that, as remote a possibility as it is, you will remain open to a change of heart. Second, especially if the biological clock has almost run its course, you may want to spend a few sessions with a counselor just to be absolutely clear in your own mind that this is what you want. Third, keep in mind that although your parents might resist, chances are, when they are talking about this among themselves one of them will look upon your decision with more understanding than the other and will encourage the other to accept your decision. And finally, remember that there will be greater pressure put on you if you're the only one in the family who can deliver up grandchildren; if you have siblings, the weight won't be so enormous, because your parents can still realize their dreams of becoming grandparents, if not through you, then through your brother or sister.

---

tactics

- **Attitude**: Be quite clearheaded about this. Remember that you're not likely to convince them of the rightness of your decision; but if you show yourselves to be resolute, they will be forced to concede they're not going to change your minds, and they will have to accept this.

- **Preparation**: Talk to other couples who have made the same choice, and ask if there are any unanticipated consequences. Talk with one another to be clear that neither is pressuring the other to accept a child-free home. And if you're uncertain, see a counselor, on a short-term basis, to explore your ambivalence.

- **Timing**: This is a good conversation to have when your parents will have plenty of time to digest it. Also, have it at the end of a day or a weekend that you've all spent together, when they've been able to observe how happy you and your spouse are with each other.

10. Announcing Plans Not to Have Children

Icebreaker: Mom and Dad, I suspect this news will disappoint you, but Karen and I felt we should tell you that after a great deal of thought, we've decided not to have children.

Judgment: It's just so unnatural. This is why people get married—to raise kids.

Confusion: How can anyone possibly not want kids? We just don't get it.

Hurt: Oh, and we so looked forward to grandchildren!

Anger: Well, that's a pretty selfish attitude to take!

Deflect judgment: Even though many couples can't or choose not to have kids, I know that having them is certainly a big part of most marriages. We're not judging what's best for other couples. Our concern is merely for what seems right for us.

Clarify your thinking: I know it's certainly harder to understand the decision *not* to have kids than to have them, but Karen and I feel fulfilled in our relationship with one another, and so happy with the lives we lead that we simply want to continue to nurture what we already have.

Acknowledge hurt: I know that. That's why it's difficult to be telling you this. I think we all recognize that no one should create a family just to please the grandparents. I also know how much you looked forward to having grandkids, and how wonderful you would be with them.

Absorb anger: I can understand why it might seem selfish to you, as though kids would just get in the way of a comfortable lifestyle. But that's not what led us to this decision. We're so grateful to have one another that what we really want out of our relationship is to continue to allow it to fulfill us. We certainly understand how for other people marriage alone may not be completely fulfilling, but for us it is.

Warning shot: I tell you, you'll both live to regret this.

Full-court press: You don't know how wonderful it is to have kids. You *can't* know. You should go ahead and have them; then, you'll see.

"We know better": You just think that now. You'll change your tune, though. I just hope it's not too late.

Dodge the warning shot: I don't know that that's true, but I do know we were both brought up to accept responsibility for the decisions we make, and we're prepared to do that now.

Acknowledge the difficulty of your decision: Perhaps you're right; perhaps we can't know. But as difficult as this is, we had to make this decision based on what we *do* know.

Press your point: We talked about that, because we know couples who did change their minds. But we feel very strongly about this, and think it's wise to act in accordance with those feelings.

Entrenched resistance: Well, if you're asking us to be happy about this, you'd best forget it.

Acceptance: It's certainly not what we want, but if it's your choice, we'll support you in it.

Leaving a wedge of hope: At least promise you'll keep an open mind.

Reluctance: You have to understand how hard it is for us to accept this.

Show empathy, sum up: We know this is a hard thing for you to hear, and I think you know it is not something we came by lightly. We don't want to hold out any false hope, but if for some reason we do change our minds, believe me, we'll tell you. In the meantime, it means a great deal to us to know that you accept us even when we make choices that you don't necessarily agree with.

- **Behavior**: You're not asking permission; you're asking only to be understood. Acknowledge their hurt feelings (if there are any) but stress that this is the result of a long period of conversation and discernment on your part, and it's something you're both committed to.

key points

- The decision to have a baby or not to have one is a personal one; there is no "right" or "wrong." You have nothing to apologize for.
- You have the utmost respect for couples who do choose to start families. What you have in common with them is the fact that you're both doing what your heart tells you is right for you.
- You appreciate the fact that your parents taught you to make your own decisions, even if they're not always the most popular ones.

Revealing That You've Lost Your Job

11

strategy

In today's workplace, there are any number of reasons why we lose our jobs. Companies merge, dissolve, or downsize. Automation claims some jobs. Products become obsolete. And, of course, a worker can simply displease his boss to the point where he gets fired. Whatever the reason, it's difficult news to break to your parents, who often take great pride in knowing their children are gainfully employed. When they receive the news, they're more than likely to experience many of the same feelings you experienced when *you* received it—anger, disbelief, shame, puzzlement. What you need to do is get beyond those feelings about your *old* job and start strategizing for how you're going to secure a *new* one. This way you can demonstrate control over the situation. When your parents see you've begun to take positive steps, they'll be less disposed to dwell on what's happened and more apt to support your job search efforts. The example we use here will be the most difficult to navigate: someone who has been fired on the grounds of poor performance.

tactics

- **Attitude:** You want to exude confidence. You've hit a rough spot, but you're on top of the situation, and everything will be all right.

- **Preparation:** Either consult an outplacement agency or set up an appointment to do so. Your old firm may even offer you this service. Also, write a six-month budget so as to alleviate your parents' fears about you running out of cash. Finally, if possible, speak with others who have been in your situation and have secured new jobs.

- **Timing:** This is a good conversation to have the day before you are to see a job counselor or outplacement specialist. This way, your parents will be able to see your immediate effort to find a new job.

- **Behavior:** Be calm and self-assured. Anticipate their anxiety and speak to them in soothing tones so as to quiet their fears. Show them you want their support but not their pity or their judgment.

11. Revealing That You've Lost Your Job

Icebreaker: Mom and Dad, I want you to know the company let me go last week; I'll be looking for a new job. And while this isn't as bad as it might sound, it's still a bit of a jolt to the system.

Blame: So, what'd you do wrong? How'd you screw up?

Shame: You should be ashamed of yourself. Nothing like this has ever happened in our family

Pity: Oh, my poor baby. Why don't you come home and live with us? We'll take care of you.

Anger: Well, that's just great! So, what the heck are you gonna do *now*?

Support: Oh, we're so sorry this happened. How can we help you?

Look ahead: I don't believe I did anything to warrant this, and I even considered challenging it. But that's not important right now. What is important is that I develop my strategy for landing a new job, and I've already made an appointment to speak to a counselor at a very reputable outplacement agency here in town.

Clarify your feelings about what happened: I really appreciate your sympathy, but to tell you the truth, I don't feel too bad about this. I wasn't happy in my work, and while I didn't want to be let go, I'm seeing it as an opportunity to start over. It's a little frightening, but it's exciting too.

Absorb anger: I understand your anger; I'm probably angrier about this than you. But I've thought a good deal about it, and I've decided that what's important now is to devote my energies toward landing my next job rather than stewing about the old one.

Doubt: So what do you think some agency's going to do for your money?

Anxiety: But what'll you do? Where will you go? How will you live? How will you find another job?

Derision: What makes you think you'll do any better in your next job, now that you've blown this one?

You're one of many: One of the things I've learned is that today's workplace is very different from the one you were a part of when you were my age. Today, almost everybody changes jobs at least a few times; there's nothing uncommon about employee impermanence. What I plan to do with *this* job hunt is look for a position that plays to my strengths—my interests, skills, and aptitudes—because the experts tell us that one key to job security is to do something you find fulfilling.

Show you're prepared: Losing a job is not at all uncommon in this day and age, so there's no need for me to panic. I've looked at my finances, and I've managed to write a budget for myself that will take me through the next six months, even though I don't anticipate it taking that long to land my next job. And in the meantime, I intend to treat looking for a job as a full-time job in and of itself. I'll be plenty busy writing my resume, searching the Internet, setting up appointments, going on interviews, and the like.

Warning: Well, all I know is you'd better get yourself something. You need to work.

You've done your homework: This is an extremely reputable agency, recommended to me by a number of people, including the human resources adviser at my old job. Their rates are reasonable, and I've already budgeted for them. If you can think of other resources or advisory agencies that might be helpful, I'd certainly welcome your suggestions.

Doubting: Well, you lost your job, so I have my doubts about what you'll be able to do next, but I guess we'll see what happens.

Close: I'm confident, and with good reason. I'm better equipped and better qualified to land a good job today than I was when I landed my last one. I'll supply the hard work and discipline, and all I ask of you is your encouragement and support. And if you have any advice, I'm eager to listen.

adaptations

This script can be used by someone who has lost a job through attrition or other reasons over which he or she had no control. It can also be adapted to be used by someone who is simply looking to get out of a bad job situation.

key points

- Be looking to the future, not to the past.
- Don't be paralyzed by anger or self-pity. Make searching for a new job a full-time job in and of itself, and let your parents know you are doing this.
- Remind your parents that losing your job can have an upside; you can land a better one.
- The rules are different today than they were when your parents first went to work; job loss is much more commonplace.

Revealing That You Have a Serious Illness

12

Parents harbor no greater fear than the death of their child, so what makes this script tricky is that your folks will have a hard time hearing it as solely *your* problem. Their natural inclination—perhaps unconsciously—will be to feel the threat to their own well-being as well as to yours, because they won't be able to bear the pain of losing you. In addition, they may well experience and express irrational guilt because parents desire to protect their children from pain and suffering. Finally, when such a grave threat as serious illness descends upon you, your parents will be exceedingly uncomfortable with their own sense of helplessness. With this in mind, be ready for a whole host of reactions. They may minimize or deny there is a problem, in which case you must be firm and straightforward with them, and impress upon them the reality of the situation. In addition, they may feel they need to somehow take over the situation, in which case you will need to give them meaningful ways of helping you while at the same time deciding for yourself how you want to handle your illness. In some instances they may react with panic and uncontrollable weeping, in which case you need to allow room for their emotions without letting those emotions overwhelm the situation and prevent them from being of service to you.

tactics

- **Attitude**: There's no need for stoicism here; let your feelings show. But by the same token try to maintain a sense of calm and control. You have a serious problem, and you're doing everything imaginable to take care of it.

- **Preparation**: Make sure your doctors give you as clear a picture as possible, so you can show your parents there's a plan of action. You will also want to make sure that you're comfortable with your doctors, and with their treatment strategy, so you can convey your confidence to your parents.

- **Timing**: The nature of your illness may be that you need to tell your parents immediately. Otherwise, you will want to wait until you have a fairly clear picture of what you're dealing with. You may also want to tell them the news a few days prior to your next doctor's appointment, so they can accompany you (if you wish) and get answers to any lingering questions they may have.

12. Revealing That You Have a Serious Illness

Icebreaker: I have something very serious to discuss with you. I haven't felt well for a few months now, and doctors have detected a trace of cancer in my stomach.

Blame: You know, you should've taken better care of yourself. I don't know how many times we've told you that.

Panic: Oh, my God, no. You're too young! This can't be true! It's not true! Not my child!

Denial: Oh, that's ridiculous. Probably a little acid indigestion. No way you have anything more serious than that. You're strong as a tree!

Taking over: Nonsense. You'll go to *our* doctors. We won't have you looked at by a bunch of strangers. I'll call them first thing in the morning.

Deflect blame: This is one of those cancers that's totally unrelated to the way people care for themselves. The doctors explained to me how it was simply something wrong with my internal workings that was waiting to get triggered.

Calming: Obviously, I was terribly upset about this when I first learned of it too. But I'm beginning to understand it better now, and two of the things that are clear to me are that we need to be as calm as possible about this, and we need to understand that while there are no guarantees, this cancer is treatable. And my doctors intend to go after it with everything they have.

Gently force the issue: I wish it were nothing too. I wish it would just go away magically. In fact, I wish I had never gotten cancer in the first place. But we need to face that this is what I have, it's serious, but it's treatable as well. So while I have no guarantees, my doctors are going to go after it with everything they have.

Take control: Boy, that's very generous of you, but I have the utmost confidence in the doctors I'm seeing, and I think you'd agree that is awfully important when you're getting ready to be treated for a serious condition like mine.

Skepticism: Yeah, so what else did these guys have to say?

Continued disbelief: I still can't believe this. No one in our family has ever had cancer, and you're too young. There must be some mistake. Someone made a big mistake.

Still panicking: I can't be calm. This is cancer! I don't know what to do! You need to promise me you're going to be all right!

Curious/a little skeptical: So what do these folks intend to do to you?

Tell them what you need for them to do: I need you to face this with me and help me get through it. It may be difficult, and I can't promise you anything, but I do know I can draw a great deal of strength if I have your support.

Explain what you are facing: Let me tell you what I know so far. First, I will be scheduled for surgery early next week. The surgery will take a few hours, and you'll be able to visit me the next day. The doctors will remove the tumor. After that, they will examine it and, based on that examination, will discuss with me what kind of ongoing therapy would work best for me. If all goes well, my hospital stay shouldn't last more than a week or so, and my treatment would begin shortly thereafter. About six weeks later, they'll examine me again to gauge what kind of improvement I'm making.

Continued on page 54.

12. Revealing That You Have a Serious Illness *(Continued)*

Still looking for encouragement: When will we know you're in the clear?

Take it one day at a time: Everything will become gradually clearer to us, first after the operation, then after the biopsy, and then after my treatments have had a chance to work. My doctors and I both agree that the best way to take this is one step at a time. What we know now is I have a treatable form of cancer, I need the surgery, and I will need further treatment.

Wanting to help but not knowing how: It sounds like it's pretty much out of our hands. What can *we* do to help?

Close; make them useful: I'm glad you asked, because while nothing concrete comes to mind right now, just knowing you'll be there for me is worth a great deal. When the time comes, of course, I'll want you to come to the hospital to visit. I also may need assistance with meals, visits to the doctor, and other day-to-day chores. I'll have a better idea of that sort of thing a little ways down the road.

- **Behavior**: Show you're in control of the conversation by keeping a steady voice and constantly reinforcing that you are coming to terms with the reality of your situation. Call your illness by its name. Speak matter-of-factly about what is ahead. Don't raise false hopes, but by the same token don't communicate despair.

adaptations

This script can be adapted to inform your parents of the illness of a close friend or extended family member.

key points

- You want your parents to see this situation realistically.
- You want to demonstrate your need and ability to control your own course of treatment.
- Your parents will want to know things they can do to help you; encourage this.

Asking a Parent for a Substantial Loan

13

The key to getting a parent to grant you a loan is for you to communicate to him that this represents responsibility as opposed to irresponsibility on your part. If he feels you need the money simply because you've squandered your assets or lived well beyond your means, he will be understandably reluctant to float you any cold cash. If, however, you can show him it's wise for you to have this money now because it will benefit you substantially in the long run, he's more likely to look upon it as a way of helping you help yourself. Money to pay off a gambling debt will be a lot harder to come by than a partial down payment on your first home. Also critical to closing the deal is your emphasis on the word *loan*. This is not a gift. You're simply asking for a fair business transaction, and you're willing to sign papers, pay the money back on a regular schedule, and pay interest. Treat the exchange more like an application than a supplication. Finally, be prepared to show you're also putting up as much of your own money as you can. The example we use here is that of a son or daughter unable to purchase a first home without a little help.

tactics

- **Attitude:** You want to present this with excitement, as an excellent opportunity that awaits you if only you can raise some front money.

- **Preparation:** Consult a financial adviser who can help you lay out a reasonable payment schedule and personal budget so you can show your parent you'll be able to meet your expenses.

- **Timing:** If possible, make this presentation at a time when you are doing well at work and when you can show that your job is secure and your company is happy with your performance. This makes you less of a perceived risk.

- **Behavior:** Don't appear in too much of a hurry to walk out the door with a check in your hand. Be patient, and be prepared to answer any and all questions he may have.

13. Asking a Parent for a Substantial Loan

Icebreaker: Dad, I need your help. I'm hoping to buy my first home, but I'm afraid I can't come up with all of the down payment. If you can help out with a loan—with interest, of course—I think I'd be able to swing it.

Pass the buck: Why me? What about your in-laws? They have money, don't they?

Doesn't see the value: I dunno, it sure seems like a luxury to me.

Skepticism: If you can't afford the down payment, what makes you think you'll be able to afford a mortgage *and* pay me back?

Anger: What do I look like, a bank? If you can't afford a home, you don't have a home! Nobody lent me money when I was your age, I can tell you that!

Flattery: Frankly, I've always considered you to be much more generous than they are, not only with your money, but with your time and advice as well.

Reassurance: That's what I thought at first, too. But real estate values have gone steadily higher over the years, so the investment I make in the house today could be worth about double that amount in about ten years. It's more like putting my money into a savings account, instead of just spending it in rent each month.

Provide the data: Actually, I've done some research on that. With the thirty-year mortgage I can obtain at today's rates, I could pay the bank *and* you for just a little more than what I'm paying in rent right now. And I'll be building equity at the same time.

Generosity: I know you've always been more generous with me than your parents were with you, and I really appreciate that. I like to think that buying a house is a more responsible investment than paying rent every month.

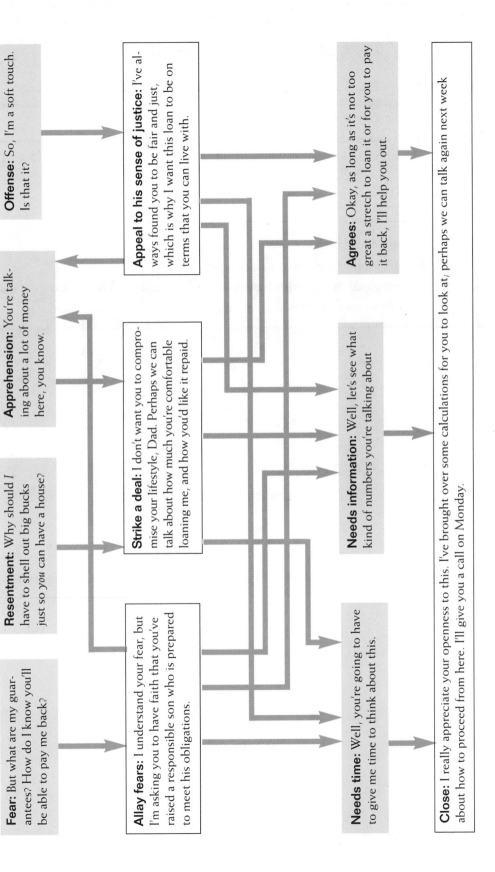

Fear: But what are my guarantees? How do I know you'll be able to pay me back?

Resentment: Why should *I* have to shell out big bucks just so *you* can have a house?

Apprehension: You're talking about a lot of money here, you know.

Offense: So, I'm a soft touch. Is that it?

Appeal to his sense of justice: I've always found you to be fair and just, which is why I want this loan to be on terms that you can live with.

Strike a deal: I don't want you to compromise your lifestyle, Dad. Perhaps we can talk about how much you're comfortable loaning me, and how you'd like it repaid.

Allay fears: I understand your fear, but I'm asking you to have faith that you've raised a responsible son who is prepared to meet his obligations.

Agrees: Okay, as long as it's not too great a stretch to loan it or for you to pay it back, I'll help you out.

Needs information: Well, let's see what kind of numbers you're talking about

Needs time: Well, you're going to have to give me time to think about this.

Close: I really appreciate your openness to this. I've brought over some calculations for you to look at; perhaps we can talk again next week about how to proceed from here. I'll give you a call on Monday.

adaptations

This script can be adapted to request a loan guarantee from a parent or from a close friend or relative. It can also be adapted—with some effort—to ask for an outright gift of money.

key points

- This can benefit both you *and* your parent.
- You don't want to leave him strapped for cash.
- You're prepared to make this transaction as businesslike as he wants.
- You don't necessarily want to do anything more than give him something to consider.

Asking to Temporarily Move Back 14 into Your Parents' Home

The attitude you take into this conversation will go a long way in determining how your parents will react. If you come in looking like a beaten puppy, you can engender either scorn or pity, neither of which will help you in the long run. If you come in cocky and self-assured, as though this is just a minor snafu and everything will be worked out in no time, your parents may sense you're not being totally forthcoming. What you want to show is you have been living responsibly, but unforeseen circumstances have conspired to pull the rug out from under you. You also want to let them know that you are much the wiser for it, and will build safeguards into your budget to ensure this won't happen again. You are smart to emphasize the word *temporary* when asking to come home, so they don't think you're simply trying to re-create the carefree comforts of childhood. And finally, be prepared for your parents to be of two minds on this. One might be protective and the other scornful or suspicious. You may need to address two sets of conversations at the same time. The example I've chosen here is of someone who has lost an apartment because of a steep rent hike, but any unexpectedly steep increase in expenses or decrease in income can be the cause.

tactics

- **Attitude**: You're sorry this has happened, but chastened by it. You're looking for a little help, but you expect to pull your weight while you're at home, so this will be a short-term proposition.

- **Preparation**: You've already begun to reorganize your budget so you can save more money and prevent this from happening in the future. You've also begun to look at alternative living arrangements.

- **Timing**: Have this conversation well in advance of the time you'll actually need to vacate your apartment. This way your parents won't feel ambushed.

- **Behavior**: Repeatedly show your appreciation for all they've done for you. Also demonstrate an eagerness to get back on your own again. You want to come across as someone who has had a surmountable obstacle put in his way.

14. Asking to Temporarily Move Back into Your Parents' Home

Icebreaker: Mom and Dad, I've come upon an unexpected emergency. My landlord is raising my rent considerably, and I'm afraid I'll have to move out of my apartment. It's going to take a little time to find a new place, so I'd like to move in with you just until I get squared away again.

Skepticism: Well, what do you mean, "just until I get squared away?" What's the real story here?

Clarify: I see no reason why this should take any more than eight weeks. I've already begun looking for a new place, and if need be, I can always get a roommate.

Pleads poverty: We're not made of money, you know. Having you home again is going to cost us.

Anger: Well, what the heck are you doing with that paycheck you're supposedly bringing home each week?

Absorb anger: Yeah, I'm angry at myself too. I've been saving money out of each of my paychecks, but it's simply not enough to cover this much of a hike this quickly. I guess I should try to set aside even more each month.

Distrust: And what makes you think this won't happen again?

Pity: Oh, my poor child. You move back home with your mom and dad. I knew it would be too tough for you out there.

Show your strength: I really appreciate your concern. But this will only be for a few months at most. I've already started looking at new rentals, and I don't think I'll have any problem securing a place.

Overly protective: Maybe it's just too soon for you to be trying to make it on your own. You come live with us; we'll know when it's time for you to leave the nest.

Derision: Can't even live out there alone, huh? And you call yourself an adult?!?

Confess naïveté, but deflect blame: This was a real eye-opener to me. My landlord gave me every reason to believe the rent was set for another year, and then pulled a fast one on me. I never knew they could be so unscrupulous!

Opportunistic browbeating: So exactly when are you gonna learn? You expect us to bail you out every time you get in a fix like this?

Offer to pay: I certainly understand that, and I'm prepared to pay my share of the expenses. What do you think would be a fair amount?

Show what you've learned: I thought the same thing, and next time I plan to get a one-year lease with a sixty-day notification requirement so when it's two months short of expiration, I'll know where I stand.

Reassure but reassert: I know we'll always be in each others' lives, and we'll always be looking out for each other. But living on my own has been a real education for me, and it's where I need to be at this stage in my life. That's why I plan to make this short-term. But you can be sure that when I get resettled, you'll be the first ones over for dinner!

Turn the tables (just slightly): I don't ever expect to be in this predicament again, and I plan to be sure of that. In fact, I like to think of the time when I'm older and a little more established, and I'm in a position to give a little back to you for all the generosity you've shown me over the years.

Conditional approval: Okay, but I want daily reports on what you're doing to find your own place. And the two of us (parents) will discuss whether or not you should help out with the expenses.

Unconditional approval: By all means, come home. And stay if you wish.

Cautious approval: Well . . . as long as we're clear this is a one-time-only arrangement.

Express gratitude: I'm very grateful we can do this, and I hope there are ways I can show my gratitude while I'm living here. In the meantime, you can be sure I'll be making this arrangement as temporary as possible, and I'm confident it won't last long at all.

adaptations

This script can be adapted to ask a sibling or friend for temporary shelter.

key points

- You've analyzed what led to this situation, and you've developed safeguards for preventing it from happening again.
- You're not looking for a handout; you're more than willing to pay rent.
- Finding a new place to live is now a second job for you.

Requesting That a Parent Move Out of Your Home

15

strategy

Parents who live with their children and grandchildren may begin to feel as though they're perceived as useless, as though they can no longer take care of themselves. On the other hand, when a parent is asked to leave and find her own place, she may well feel shunted aside, discarded, no longer of any use to their kids. The key to making this script work is threefold: Explain how there is no choice but to do this, reinforce your need to maintain regular contact with your parent after she settles into her own place, and do everything you can to ease the transition for her. Still, after she agrees to move, you can expect some lingering skepticism on her part. Only after she's been on her own for a while and you make good on your promise to keep in touch will she begin to feel securely rooted in two worlds—yours and her own.

tactics

- **Attitude**: Show remorse, not for asking her to leave, but for the situation. You want them to know this was by no means an easy decision for you to reach.

- **Preparation**: Explore living alternatives for your parent. Talk to leaders of senior citizen programs, social workers, clergy, and local officials who oversee senior activities. Be prepared to present your parent with the kinds of living options you think would most appeal to her.

- **Timing**: Have this conversation well in advance of her need to move out. Also, avoid holidays, birthdays, etc. It's a good idea to broach this subject at a time when she and your family have been actively doing things together, so as to assure her of her importance to you.

- **Behavior**: Be quick to listen and slow to speak. Hear her reservations and acknowledge their legitimacy. Let her come to terms with this at her own pace.

15. Requesting That a Parent Move Out of Your Home

Icebreaker: Mom, these past few years that you've been living with us and the kids have meant a great deal to me. Unfortunately, though, I'm afraid our house is just too small to accommodate all of us now, and I think we need to talk about another living arrangement that will keep you close by but in your own home.

Resentment: For twenty years you live scot-free under my roof, and now there's no room for me under yours?! Boy, that's some gratitude!

Anger/sarcasm: Well, excuse me for being such a burden to you! If I'd known this was how you felt, I never would've moved in in the first place.

Hurt: Never mind, I'll find my own living arrangement, and I don't need to be close by to someone who doesn't care about me.

Fear: But I haven't lived alone in a long time; I don't know how I'll do out there.

Reframe her assumption: I've always felt that having you here was a way I could give a little something back to you for all you've done for me. But our family's grown, and we can't afford more space than we now have. What I want to do now is find other ways for us to stay close that won't force my own kids to go without the room they need to grow up. I do have some ideas.

Absorb anger, place blame elsewhere: You've never been a burden. Not being able to afford a bigger home is my burden. That's why we want you to remain close by.

Empathy: I think I know how you feel; this hurts me deeply too. But I want to believe that you'll allow me to express my love for you in other ways. I have some ideas.

Assuage fears: I understand that the thought of going out on your own again can seem daunting, but I think we can discuss it with each other and with counselors who specialize in this sort of thing, and we can find a way to transition into a new arrangement.

Skepticism: Ideas, huh? What sort of ideas can you have for an old woman who isn't used to living on her own?

Continued anger: What do you care where I am or what I do? You've made your intentions quite clear.

Fear/resistance: But I'm too old to make a change. I'd rather stay put.

Ideas to soften the blow: I've done some casual looking in the paper and seen a number of ads for condominium residences, retirement villages, and the like that can offer a whole array of services and activities that we can't, but would keep us close to one another, maybe even in the same neighborhood. I'm also hoping you'll want to come over for dinners, spend the night with us on occasion, and maybe have the kids do the same at your place as well.

Reiterate the bind you're in: Maybe I haven't. What I'm trying to do is strike a balance between your needs and the needs of my kids, so that you remain a big part of our lives and the children have the room they need here at home.

Flattery: We wish this could've worked for a few more years, but by making this move at this relatively early point in your life you're giving yourself a lot of years to enjoy your self-sufficiency. I certainly hope I'm as fit and independent as you when I reach your age.

Insecurity: But how often will we really see each other if I'm not here? You'll probably forget about me.

Resentment: You're just putting me out to pasture; you're trying to get rid of me.

Anxiety about the future: But where will I go? I've never lived by myself before.

Continued on page 68.

15. Requesting That a Parent Move Out of Your Home *(Continued)*

Promise your time: I want to assure you that we'll see a lot of each other. When we get ready for the actual move, I was thinking that we might want to take our calendars out and mark off several dates over two months' time that we can set aside to get together.

Deflect resentment: I'm sorry you feel that way. I see your getting your own place as a way of expanding your social circle to more easily include other people *as well as* us. I certainly hope *you* won't try to get rid of *us!*

Concrete proposals: I can understand why you might be nervous. I've done a little research, though, and there are a number of ways you can live that won't make you feel as though you're out there by yourself. Retirement communities here in town are staffed with social workers, doctors, counselors, and social directors. They have a number of the activities you enjoy, and they really create a sense of community. Or, if you didn't want that sort of arrangement, there are condominiums populated with people such as yourself who are no longer working but still very active. Also, I'd be happy to set up an appointment for you and me to meet with the town's director of senior services, who, I understand, has a very good sense of all the activities and support services that can be made available to you if you want them.

Begrudging resignation: Well, I don't know how I feel about all this, but I guess it's gonna be.

Acceptance: Well, I'm not crazy about the idea, but I guess it can work out all right if you're really serious about keeping in touch.

I'm not not crazy about the idea, but I guess it can work out all right if you're really serious about keeping in touch.

Close: It's meant a great deal to all of us that you've lived with us all these years, so I think we'll all have to go through a period of adjustment. But we love you very much, and I speak for the whole family when I say you're a big, big part of our lives, and you always will be.

adaptations

This script can be adapted to encourage a parent or other relative to consider moving to an assisted living community.

key points

- Transition is often difficult in older age; don't lose sight of what a monumental move this may be for your parent.
- Reinforce her importance to your family, especially to your children.
- If possible, bring other siblings into the discussion as well.
- Emphasize your willingness to help her get resituated.

Suggesting That a Parent Get Psychological Counseling

16

---

strategy

Because there's still so much unnecessary stigma around the idea of seeking counseling, you have to choose your words for this script very carefully. Words like *unstable, psychiatrist,* or even *troubled* can really make your parent recoil in defense. This is why, regardless of the behavior that leads you to believe he needs counseling, it's safer to use words that connote his mood or emotion rather than his psychological state. You want to point out to him that he may not be happy with the way he's feeling right now, and that talking it out with a professional might do him some good. In doing this, try to inform him that this is quite common today; people often get things off their chest in short order, and they're back to feeling like themselves in no time. Also, keep in mind his possible reluctance to unburden himself to a stranger, and be prepared to encourage him to speak with his doctor or a trusted member of the clergy, both of whom can then make a referral to a psychotherapist. And finally, remember that the point of this script is to *suggest* counseling. This is something that can't be imposed, but even if you are rebuked, you have at least succeeded in planting the thought in his mind, perhaps to germinate at a later date.

---

tactics

- **Attitude:** You don't want to minimize the problem, but you don't want to be alarmist either. Speak calmly and reassuringly with him, but be firm and stress that in your opinion this is a wise move for him to make.

- **Preparation:** You may want to describe to a professional counselor the behaviors you think are troublesome. This way you may be able to get a clearer picture of what your parent is experiencing, and how serious it might be. In addition, be prepared to point out—gently—specific behaviors you've witnessed in the past few weeks that support your concern.

- **Timing:** You'll want to have this conversation in a private moment when you know you won't be disturbed. Sunday is a good day because calls to the professionals can be made the next day.

- **Behavior:** You want to show that this comes from your love and concern for him. Don't be patronizing. Look him in the eye, establish contact with him, perhaps put an arm around him or hold his hand.

16. Suggesting That a Parent Get Psychological Counseling

Icebreaker: Dad, you've seemed awfully unhappy lately, not really yourself, and I'm a little concerned. I'd like you to give some thought to talking to someone about how you've been feeling.

Anger: What, you think I'm crazy? Like I need to see some shrink or something? Forget it.

Denial: What are you talking about? I'm fine, just fine.

Minimizes it: Oh, don't you worry about me. I'm just a little blue. I'll be fine.

Vagueness: Huh? Oh, uh-huh. Um, maybe I'll talk to someone. I'll think about it.

Absorb anger: I'm sorry if you feel I'm suggesting you're crazy, because I don't think that at all. I do think you may be going through a rough time right now, like a lot of us do, and that you'd benefit from being able to talk about things with an expert.

Point out symptoms: I'm sure there's nothing serious going on, but I have noticed that you haven't been sleeping well lately, and you've been in tears a few times in the past few weeks. I think sitting down with an expert and talking over how you're feeling might do you some good.

Reinforce: I thought you might be agreeable to seeing someone, and I'm glad to hear you have an open mind about this. I'd like to make an appointment for you to see a counselor, and I think we should call your doctor for a recommendation. If you'd like, I'll accompany you to the appointment.

Resistance: I said I'd think about it, and that's what I'll do. Don't rush me.

Respect their hesitation: I understand, and I appreciate that. Let's leave it alone for now, and I'll give you a call early next week so we can talk about what to do next.

Reluctance: I really don't want to talk to some stranger about my personal life.

Make it easier: I can appreciate your reluctance. Instead of seeing a stranger, perhaps we should make an appointment with your doctor, or maybe your minister. Who would you like to see about this?

Cautious capitulation: Well, I'll tell you what I'll do. Maybe I'll have a word with my doctor. But if he says I'm fine, I don't want to hear another word about this, do you understand?

Reinforce the decision: I think that's a great idea. In fact, let's call his office right now. What days next week are you free to see him?

Deflecting your overture: Oh, I've just been a little tired and distracted lately, that's all.

Reinforce your point: Yes, and that's what concerns me. We're used to seeing you a good bit sharper, so I'd like you to talk with someone just to see what it is that might have you feeling so tired and distracted. I'm sure you want to get back to your old self.

Clarify, and stand your ground: I don't mean to imply anything. I'm merely saying I've observed you to be unhappy for some time now, and I want to encourage you to talk with someone about it.

Resentment: Look, I'm not some nut case, and I don't appreciate your implications!

Skepticism: Well ... I'm not crazy, I can tell you that!

Reassurance: Of course you're not! You're just like anyone else; when we're not feeling on top of our game, it's good to just sit down and talk it through with someone.

---

adaptations

This script can be adapted to suggest counseling to a friend or spouse.

---

key points

- You're only suggesting that he see someone.
- You believe he would be happier if he could unburden himself of some feelings or thoughts that seem to be troubling him.
- He needn't see a stranger; he can begin with his own doctor's appraisal.
- You're *not* suggesting he's "crazy."
- Don't push him in one conversation; give him time to mull over what you're saying.

Confronting Actions That Undermine Your Parental Authority

17

strategy

We're grateful to our parents when they look after our children, when they shower them with love, and even when they offer us advice on how to handle them. On the other hand, we don't want them treating our children decidedly differently than we do. When our sons or daughters get one message from Mom and Dad about, say, whether or not it's okay to eat a couple of candy bars before dinner, and another from Grandma and Grandpa, the kids are bound to be confused as to which message is meant for them. And in all likelihood, they'll choose to obey the one more suited to their desires than their needs. So how do you gratefully encourage your parents' access to their grandchildren while at the same time getting them to agree to play by your rules? You do it by keeping three things in mind. First, you want to reinforce your gratitude for their involvement in your kids' lives while at the same time reminding them that you need to be in charge of how they're raised. Second, you want to define this issue in terms of *what is in the best interest of your child*, not simply what you or your parents "want to do." And third, you want to encourage them to discuss differences of opinion they might have with you regarding how you parent your children, because while the final decisions are yours, you welcome the benefit of their experience.

tactics

- **Attitude**: Speak with a slow and steady voice. Don't raise your voice or show either anger or weakness. It's important to convey that *you* are the ultimate arbiter of how your children will be raised.

- **Preparation**: Virtually all of the prevailing literature in this field supports a parent's need to set the rules for her children. Read some articles and/or books, and, if it's convenient, sound out a family counselor or child psychologist about what he thinks.

- **Timing**: Don't have this conversation immediately after your parents have shown a great deal of generosity toward your child(ren). Choose a neutral time, when the kids aren't around, when you're all free to air out your feelings.

- **Behavior**: Don't behave like your parents' child. Behave like your child's parent. Be strong and sure of yourself.

17. Confronting Actions That Undermine Your Parental Authority

Icebreaker: Dad, there's something I want us to talk about. Last week when you and Mom were looking after Jack, you let him come home past midnight, even though you knew his curfew was 10:30. We can't have him getting mixed signals like that.

Minimizes the issue: Oh, it's no big deal; he was just a little late, that's all.

Plays the "grandparents" card: Oh, c'mon, lighten up. That's what grandparents are for, to spoil their grandkids a little from time to time.

They know better: Ten-thirty is simply too early for a responsible boy like Jack. Besides, he didn't get into any trouble by being out late now, did he?

Resentment: We come over and take care of your son while you two go away, and this is the thanks we get?!?

The real issue: The real issue here is that like all kids, Jack needs to have a consistent set of rules to follow because that's the only way he'll understand what's right and what's wrong.

Discriminate between small and large issues: If you want to treat him to small indulgences from time to time, I have no problem with that, provided we agree on them ahead of time. But when it comes to rules of behavior, it's only fair to him if we're consistent in what we all enforce.

Who's in charge: I know that we differ on this issue, but I'm responsible for setting out the rules for my son, and I need to have anyone who looks out for him—a sitter, a teacher, whoever—abide by those rules. He needs to get a consistent message from all of the authority figures in his life.

Show appreciation, deflect resentment: I think you know how much I appreciate your looking after him; it's a great favor, and I know it means a lot to him too. The only issue I'm trying to raise here is that he get a consistent message of what he can and can't do, regardless of who's watching out for him.

Hurt/anger: Well then, perhaps next time you should have someone else watch Jack when you want to go away.

Absorb anger: I can certainly understand how you might resent my bringing this up, especially in light of all you do for me and for Jack. The truth is, I love to have you look after him, and so does he. All I'm trying to do here is be sure he's not getting confused by hearing two different sets of rules and thinking he can choose between them.

Disagrees with your rules: But we happen to think a responsible kid his age should be allowed to stay out later than 10:30, and I think he proved that to you.

Acknowledge difference of opinion: I know we disagree on this point of when he should be home at night, and I don't think we can say one of us is right and one of us is wrong. But because I'm his parent and I take my parental responsibilities very seriously, I need to be the one who sets the rules, and I need to depend on you and everyone else who loves him to support me with this.

Challenges you: So you're saying it has to be your rules and nobody else's. Is that it?

Disagrees with you: Oh, kids can play by "different rules" with different people; there's no harm in them getting away with a little more when we're around.

Cite experts: I used to think the same thing, and I wish I still did. But I've done a good deal of reading on this. I've also discussed it with his teacher and the school counselor. I'm now convinced that when a child is given one clear, fair set of rules and those rules are applied evenly by all of the adults who look out for him, the child feels much more secure and has a much clearer sense of what's expected of him than when he's getting mixed messages. This is why I need to insist on this.

Resentment: So you think your "experts" know more than your father and mother, is that it?

Continued on page 78.

17. Confronting Actions That Undermine Your Parental Authority (*Continued*)

You've made up your own mind: The people I've spoken to and the books I've read have made a great deal of sense to me, and that's why I've decided to handle the rules for Jack in this way.

Wish it could be simpler: I wish there was an easier way, but nobody knows better than you how hard it is to raise a kid, and I feel it's in his best interest to learn that I'm in charge of our family, that I know what's best for him, and that he's responsible to abide by what I say.

Surrender: Well [*unconvincedly*], he's your child. That's what you want, you won't get any more argument out of us.

Parting shot: I still think you're too protective of him, but you'll do what you think you need to.

Close: I suspect parents will always disagree about what's best for their particular kids, but I'm glad you're willing to let me do what I think is best for Jack, and I'm very grateful that you look after him when you do.

adaptations

This script can be adapted to confront the parents of your child's friend when you feel they're undermining your authority. It can also be adapted to confront your child's aunt or uncle if you feel they're doing the same.

key points

- You don't necessarily want to discuss a particular issue regarding parenting (e.g., how late the child should be allowed to stay out, whether she can have a sleepover on a school night, etc.). Instead, you want to discuss who is in charge of making the rules.

- You accept the fact that you and your parents might not agree on how to parent, but you need to have them play by your rules, not their own. They need to do this for their grandchild(ren)'s sake.

- All the literature and popular wisdom supports you on this.

- Play to the one shared experience you can both identify with—the difficulties of raising healthy, happy kids. It's no small bond.

Confronting a Parent's Inappropriate Treatment of Your Spouse

18

strategy

This script is a real table-turner, because in it you are expected to reprimand a parent. You're used to the shoe being on the other foot, but if you plan to stay married to your spouse and you don't want to write your parent out of your life, you have to stop this behavior as soon as it rears its head. In discussing it with the offending parent, be prepared for him to dismiss you as being too sensitive; you're "getting upset over nothing." You want to respond to this by telling him that while it may be insignificant to him, it is hurtful to you. Simply put, "When you say this, I feel that." You don't have to justify your feelings, you only have to make them plain. Also, stick to the subject at hand, which is how you and your spouse feel when your parent behaves a certain way. We say this because the parent might use the conversation as a forum to discuss why it is he behaves the way he does, rather than how it makes you feel. In the example given here, a father ridicules his son-in-law for his low salary and wants to engage his daughter in a discussion about what constitutes a decent wage. The daughter, on the other hand, keeps the conversation focused on how her father's behavior affects her and her husband. And finally, watch to see if your parent's behavior is symptomatic of a generalized disrespect for or disregard of your spouse. Your mother may make fun of your wife's clothes because she doesn't like her personality, values, etc. In this case stick to the issue at hand; just try to get the behavior to stop. Their broader feelings about your spouse constitute a conversation that will need to happen another day.

tactics

- **Attitude:** Be firm in your resolve to stop the behavior but at the same time be willing to allow that it might not be perceived as offensive by your parent.
- **Preparation:** Note specific instances when the behavior has been exhibited so that you'll be prepared to cite them as evidence.
- **Timing:** Hold this conversation in private with the offending parent, and do it without your spouse present.
- **Behavior:** Show through your words and actions that your primary allegiance in this matter is to your spouse, not your parent.

18. Confronting a Parent's Inappropriate Treatment of Your Spouse

Icebreaker: Dad, there's something we need to speak about. You seem to enjoy poking fun at Joe's salary, and while you don't mean to be hurtful, you need to know it bothers us a great deal.

Ridicule: Oh, you two shouldn't be such babies about my just having a little fun with him.

Dismissive: Well, I don't see anything wrong with a little harmless ribbing.

Defensive: Well, it's true, isn't it? He doesn't make much money now, does he?

Dislike: You know I never really liked Joe, and I guess his measly salary is just part of that.

Make your case: I understand you're just trying to have fun, but it strikes us a little too close to home to make jokes about it. Surely there are other ways we can kid around with each other.

Focus: What's important is that Joe works very hard and we're both proud of what he's accomplished so far. What we're asking is for you to respect that.

Address underlying issue: What matters to me is that Joe and I are very, very happy together, and even though you might not approve of the man I've chosen to marry, I expect you to treat him with respect.

Agreement: Neither do we; we both love your sense of humor. But this particular topic does bother us, which is why I'm asking you to stop bringing it up.

Not buying it: Oh, c'mon, how can a few words spoken as a joke really hurt someone?

Aggressive: So if he works so hard, how come he isn't making more money?

Won't respect the spouse: Well, I hate to say it, but it's awfully hard to respect someone I don't like.

Gives in, begrudgingly: Well, it really *is* no big deal, but if you're gonna be so sensitive about it, I'll leave him alone.

Give him an "out": You've always struck me as a strong man, so I'm sure these jibes wouldn't hurt you. But you and I are different in that way, which is why I wanted to call this to your attention.

Focus again: We're not discussing Joe's salary; we're discussing how he and I feel when you make fun of it. I don't believe you mean to hurt us, which is why I wanted to call it to your attention.

Must respect you: Because I'm your daughter, what's important is that I like him, which is why you need to stop doing something that you know hurts me.

Shoulder a little responsibility, close: Perhaps we are both sensitive to this issue; so I'm very grateful you've agreed to stop kidding us about it.

Agrees to do this for you: Look, if I let up on him, it's gonna be because of you, not him. I'm not about to change my opinion of him.

Accept his terms: That's fine. I wish you would like him better, but if this is all you're willing to concede, I can at least appreciate your agreeing to leave us alone about this.

Harps on the subject: Look, I don't mean to hurt you by anything. But you gotta admit, he really doesn't make much money.

Begrudging, stubborn: Well, it sure feels as though you're being awfully sensitive about a little kidding.

Come down a little harder, and throw in a veiled threat: What I need to do is have your assurance that you'll leave us alone about this. I'm afraid that's the only way I can be comfortable if we're going to continue to get together as a family.

Apology: Look, I never meant to hurt you.

Give ground: You may be right, but thanks an awful lot for respecting this request, even if you don't necessarily agree with us.

Close: I understand that you just meant to have fun; thanks for respecting our feelings on this.

adaptations

This script can be adapted to ask a friend to stop treating another friend inappropriately, or to ask a business colleague to do the same. It can even be adapted to ask someone to treat your pet the way you want it treated.

key points

- This is something that bothers not only your spouse but you too.
- If your parent is going to want to continue to spend time with you, he will have to cease the offending behavior.
- Give the parent a chance to save face; let him feel that he's capitulating to a trivial request.
- Stick to the presenting problem, i.e., his behavior and how it makes the two of you feel.

Expressing Fears about a Parent's Health

strategy

We're often more attentive to the health of those we love than to our own, and this script is designed to encourage an obstinate parent to seek help for what appears to be a presenting medical problem. Because stubbornness is often a sign of latent fear, you will do well to consider that your parent's resistance to seeing a doctor about her problem is related to a fear that there is something seriously wrong with her, that she will be told to curtail her life's activities, or that her condition presages the end of her days. These fears, however overblown they may be, should be assumed, respected, and gently allayed. The thing you want to emphasize is that there is something presenting itself that is affecting her health and well-being, that a doctor will be able to tell her exactly what she's dealing with, and that together they can devise a game plan for coping with it, all the while assuring her that the final say over what kind of treatment—if any—she will accept is hers.

tactics

- **Attitude:** You want to show concern but not alarm. You want to define this as a real but surmountable problem, something for which there's no need to panic but for which there *is* need for information.

- **Preparation:** Speak to other members of the family so that you can be sure that their sentiments are in sync with yours; you may need to remind your parent that you're not alone in your concerns. Also, speak with your own doctor about your parent's symptoms. This will allow you to say that a professional has encouraged you to pursue this.

- **Timing:** If possible, have this conversation shortly after the parent has exhibited symptoms of a problem, recently enough so that it's fresh in her mind but with enough distance that she can discuss it clearly and rationally, without being overwhelmed by fear. Also, have it at a time when the doctor's office can be contacted and an appointment can be made.

- **Behavior:** You want to show the right balance of concern and cool, levelheaded thinking. Sit back, speak slowly, with little affect in your voice, and don't rush the conversation. Don't be in a hurry to push against your parent's resistance.

19. Expressing Fears about a Parent's Health

Icebreaker: I had my annual physical today, and I want to tell you about a conversation I had with my doctor. We spoke about the shortness of breath I've noticed in you, and she recommended you see your own internist and have it checked out.

Rationalizes it: Ah, it comes with age. The old body's just slowin' down, that's all.

Emphasize an active life: You've always been a very active woman, and I have to believe you'll want to resume some of your old interests, which is one reason we need to get this thing cleared up right away.

Dismisses doctors: Ah, doctors don't know anything, I've always taken care of myself, and I'll take care of myself now.

Sidesteps it: Well, I'll see to it one of these days. Don't you worry about it.

Stay on the subject: My concern is that it doesn't seem to be improving, so I think we want to make an appointment right away and find out what you might be able to do to clear it up.

Conversation stopper: Look, I'm fine, and I'll take care of myself. I promise.

Shrugs it off: It's nothing really, just a little pollen in the air.

Don't disagree, but press your point: You may very well be right; that's exactly what your internist might tell us. If so, I know that'll make me feel better and I suspect you and Dad will rest easier knowing it, too.

Anger, resentment: You discussed *my* condition with *your* doctor? How dare you invade my privacy that way!

Deflect anger (even if you have to tell a little lie): No, no. I never mentioned you by name, and I never said it was my mom I was speaking about.

Continued anger: Well it's still none of your business!

Play to a larger audience: I think you know I've never wanted to compromise your privacy. But I think you also realize your health is all of our concern, because you have a husband, children, and grand-children who want to be secure in know-ing that what you're experiencing isn't anything we need to be concerned with.

Endorse the place of the physician in her way of thinking: I have no doubt you'll take care of yourself, you always have. But just like you and Dad have taught me, that includes seeing a doctor regularly, especially when something doesn't seem quite right.

Give a little credence: You know, I agree with you that doctors don't always know everything, but you've always had a frank and honest relationship with yours, so when you see him, you may want to tell him that even with this shortness of breath you're pretty sure you can take care of yourself. Maybe he'll agree with you.

Begrudging acquiescence: Well, look, if it'll calm your father's jitters, I'll go ahead and see him. But only to make *him* feel better, understand?

Fear; bottom-line feelings: Look, what if, just *if* I get in there and he tells me my heart's all screwed up or something? What if I need an operation? What if he tells me to stop playing tennis on Sundays, or bowling on Tuesday nights? Then what am I supposed to do with my life?

Halfhearted cooperation: Well, I can tell you one thing. I may go see him, but that doesn't mean I have to agree with him!

Continued on page 88.

19. Expressing Fears about a Parent's Health (*Continued*)

Express appreciation: It will, and it'll make me feel better as well. Let's give the doctor's office a call right now. I bet it'll make Dad feel good just knowing you've gone ahead and scheduled an appointment. Here's the number.

Give credence to her feelings: I can certainly understand your concerns; you've been so active all your life, and you don't want to be told to give up some of the things you love. That was actually one of the reasons I wanted us to have this conversation. I was afraid that if you continued to have trouble, you eventually might not feel up to doing those things. By getting on top of this now, with the doctor's help, I figured, you'd be able to get your old energy back.

Half a loaf: That's a good place to start. You're looking at this as a kind of fact-finding visit, and the final decision as to what you'll do with the information your doctor gives you is yours.

Agrees to see doctor, if not to obey him: Well, okay. No harm in seeing what he has to say. But after that, I'm gonna do what *I* need to do.

Close: Like I said earlier, you've always taken good care of yourself, and I know you'll do as you see fit. I suspect we're both eager to hear what he has to say, though. Here's his phone number; I'm sure Dad will be as delighted as I am that you've gone ahead and made an appointment.

adaptations

This script can be adapted to express fears about the kind of medical treatment you feel your parent is receiving.

key points

- Remember that obstinance is often a sign of repressed fear.
- Reinforce the notion that she is ultimately in charge of whatever health regimen she will follow.
- If need be, remind her that she needs to care for herself not only for her own sake but for the sake of her wider family.
- A visit to the doctor's office can be treated simply as an occasion to gather information.

Bringing Up a Parent's Bad Hygiene

20

Hygiene is such a private issue that there may be no more ticklish subject to broach with a parent than this. If it is done the wrong way, she can be made to feel like a little child, as though you're suggesting there is nothing she can do for herself, or that she ought to be in diapers. To avoid this, you will need to approach the topic as a natural part of the aging process, and as a problem that has the kinds of solutions the parent can easily incorporate into her life. With this in mind, you will want to have this conversation early, as the situation first rears its head. By getting to it while your parent is still capable of caring for herself, it will make it less difficult for her if, down the line, she needs to take more drastic measures. Also, you want to play up the fact that you're coming to her in part because she has always encouraged you to be honest with her, regardless of how personal the topic. And finally, if possible, this conversation should be conducted by a member of the same sex as the parent.

tactics

- **Attitude:** Be very soft-spoken but at the same time discuss this as something quite natural. This is not a comment upon your parent's habits as much as a recognition of one part of aging.

- **Preparation:** Speak to geriatric specialists, who can be found at your local hospital. Also, gather any reprints they might have. Put them in envelopes to give to your parent, so that she might open them when she is alone.

- **Timing:** Have this conversation early enough that the problem is in its nascent stages. Also, speak with her in her own home, when no one else is around, and when she can be assured of privacy for a time after you leave.

- **Behavior:** You want to exude love but not sympathy, understanding but not pity. Encourage any question she asks, and above all else respect her privacy. If she does nothing more than agree to give this some thought, leave knowing you have accomplished much.

20. Bringing Up a Parent's Bad Hygiene

Icebreaker: Mom, I'm glad we can confide in one another, because there's something rather personal I want to discuss with you. Mom, you've always taken such great pride in your appearance, and I think you may need to devote a little more attention to your personal hygiene.

Confusion: Whatever do you mean by that?

Clarification: Apparently, as we age our sense of smell diminishes, and we become less aware of our own bodies' natural odors, so we need to bathe more frequently and more thoroughly than we might think.

Embarrassment: This is so embarrassing for you to bring up. I don't what to say.

Make her feel more comfortable: Please understand that there's no need to be embarrassed. What you're experiencing is just a natural part of aging, not unlike finding a few new gray hairs or a wrinkle or two. What's important is that you can manage this, and if you'd like, I'd be happy to help.

Rejection: I'll have you know I take very good care of myself, and always have.

Discuss aging: Your personal habits have always been impeccable. But I've been doing a little reading about this, and I've learned that one of the things that happens as we age is that our sense of smell actually decreases, so sometimes we might not always realize when we have a need to shower or bathe. Also, apparently our bodies give off different odors than they do when we're younger, so our hygiene habits need to change.

Anger: What?!? How dare a child of mine come into my home and speak to me that way!

Absorb anger: I understand your anger; this is not an easy subject for either one of us. But I know how important this is to you, and I decided I needed to risk mentioning it. I certainly mean no disrespect by it.

Slightly indignant: Well, what in the world do you mean by "devote more attention," anyway?

Sarcasm: And what do these so-called experts say about *how* my habits are supposed to change at this stage of my life?

Self-protective: I really cherish my independence, you know. I'd rather work this out myself.

Fear: But . . . what am I supposed to do? How should I know how often to bathe if I can't detect any problem?

Helpful response: That's a good question. The people who have studied this recommend that you set up a schedule for yourself that includes at least one shower or bath every day, and two on days when you get a lot of physical exercise. They also recommend you do this at the same time each day, preferably in the morning but at night if that's more to your liking. In fact, I have some literature on this that I'm happy to leave for you to look over.

Respect the self-protection, offer some suggestions: I understand. I know you can work this out for yourself too. In fact the experts I've read on this subject have some very useful suggestions on how to handle this in complete privacy.

Reluctant agreement: Well, I'll look this stuff over, later. But I'll handle this, understand?

Curiosity, hesitation: You mean I don't have to involve anyone else if I don't want to? But how can I do this?

Close: I certainly do. I've always admired your ability to look after yourself and handle anything that comes your way. And thanks for being so understanding.

adaptations

This script can be adapted to discuss a parent's disheveled appearance (hair not cut or combed, fingernails not clipped, etc.) or inappropriate attire.

key points

- This is not slovenliness on her part; it is a matter of aging.
- You would be happy to help her get started in the development of new routines, but you respect her wishes if she chooses to do this herself.
- You're grateful to her that she invites such honesty.
- Some weeks later, you want to discreetly mention to her how good she looks.

Turning Down a Parent's Request for a Loan **21**

---

strategy

It's often difficult for a parent to ask something of his child, so when the child has to reject that request, it can put a real strain on the relationship. The parent feels wounded pride and resentment; the child feels inadequate and guilty. In an effort to soften these hard-edged feelings, you must impress two things upon your parent: First, you are not choosing to turn him down. Rather, as you can demonstrate, the money simply isn't there. And second, you do want to help him, and so to that end you will make yourself available to him so that together you can explore other options. Be prepared to take a couple of personal hits before your parent is ready to believe you or take you up on your offer, but each time he lays into you, keep reminding him that this is a decision dictated by the limits of your finances rather than his perceived limits of your compassion.

---

tactics

- **Attitude**: You are extremely disappointed that you aren't in a position to help, but you're equally determined to see to it that he gets his money.

- **Preparation**: Speak with a financial adviser who is willing to meet with you and your parent, and if need be, be prepared to pay for his or her services. Also, be prepared to show in black and white why your own finances make it impossible to float a loan at this time.

- **Timing**: Have this conversation as soon after your parent makes his request as possible. This way he knows where he stands and will have ample time to pursue other options. Also, have it at a time when you and your parent are generally getting along well with one another. Finally, it is good to have this talk at a time when you are displaying your generosity toward him in other ways (doing chores around the house, chauffeuring him somewhere, having him over for dinner, etc.).

- **Behavior**: You want to steer the conversation away from personal hurt and innuendo. Be patient, don't rush the conversation, and keep it focused on how to fix the problem, not how to fix the blame.

21. Turning Down a Parent's Request for a Loan

Icebreaker: Dad, we've looked awfully hard at our finances, and I'm afraid we're not in a position to give you a loan. I came by today because I want to explain why and because I want to help you find other means to get this money.

Anger: Save your speech, I don't need to hear your excuses for why you won't even help out your own father!

Guilt: Wow. After all I've done for you, you can't see yourself clear to help me out when I need you?

Pleading: But it's just a loan; I'm not asking to have the money, just to borrow some. And you know I'll pay you back, with interest.

Absorb anger: I can certainly understand your anger at our not being able to come through for you. I'm angry that we don't have the money! I wish business had been better this year, but it just wasn't. Still, I do think that if we put our heads together, we can come up with some ideas as to where you might be able to get your loan. I've even found someone who can help us.

Argue from logistics, not emotion: I've been wracking my brains for the past few nights looking for a way to come up with the money for you, but business was so bad this year that we may be looking for loans ourselves. Still, let's talk about some alternatives that might work out for you.

Panic: But I just don't know if I'll be able to get by right now without some more money.

Zero in on how to get a loan: I'm confident we can find a way to get the money you need. In fact, I've found a financial adviser who has agreed to look at your finances and discuss what your options might be.

Get him thinking clearly and strategically, not emotionally: I know how important this loan is to you, which is why as soon as I realized we didn't have the money, I got in touch with a financial adviser who's willing to help us look at options.

Resentment: Never mind! I'll take care of myself. As if you care.

Surprise: But I always thought you were loaded! That's certainly the impression I got.

Suspicion: Yeah? And what's *that* supposed to cost me?

Despair: Nah. You were my last hope. I'm sunk.

Make your case, briefly, and then reiterate your offer to help: You need to understand that the only reason we can't do this is because we don't have the money. However, the financial adviser I've contacted is eager to sit down and help us figure out how you can get the loan you need.

Clarify your own financial position: I'm so sorry if that's the impression you got. The truth is, our income is just barely sufficient to cover our expenses and service our own loans. In fact, in trying to come up with the money to loan you ourselves, we wrote up our budget. I made a copy for you. You can see for yourself what we're up against.

Absorb the cost (and lie a little): It won't cost you anything; he's doing this as a favor to me.

Take charge: I'm quite certain there's a way out of this, so I think we all need to keep a clear head right now. The fellow I want us to meet with assures me he's been able to help a number of people who didn't think they'd be able to get the money they needed, and I have a great deal of faith in him.

Resistance (but weakening): I don't like talking to some stranger about my personal finances.

Extremely doubtful: Well . . . I don't know. It just seems so futile.

A little doubtful: Well, I don't know what good it'll do, but I suppose it's better than nothing.

Acknowledge need for privacy: I can certainly respect your desire for privacy, and I think he will too. What he told me is that he only needs enough information to be able to steer us in the right direction for securing this loan.

Close: It's easy to understand your reservations about this, but on the other hand it certainly won't hurt us to talk with him and see what comes of it. I'll give him a call right now.

adaptations

This script can be adapted to reject the loan request of a sibling or close friend. It can also be adapted to refuse a parent's request to help guarantee a loan he is securing elsewhere.

key points

- You've been trying to find ways to give him the money he needs.
- You're financially unable—not personally unwilling—to do this.
- You want to work together with your parent to help him secure his loan.
- You've identified at least one resource who will help you.

Bringing Up a Parent's Bad Manners

22

strategy

This is a difficult script to broach with a parent without him feeling embarrassment or wounded pride, so one of the things you want to do right off the bat is set your expectations low. There's a better than even chance you won't get your parent to admit to what you're raising with him, let alone agree to change. At best you might do nothing more than give him something to think about. Even so, that's no small accomplishment, so know when to draw the conversation to a close. Watch for him retreating into a defensive posture from which he refuses to come out, and if this happens, wrap things up by saying something along the lines of, "Dad, I simply wanted to raise this with you as something for you to consider; let's leave it alone now." Also, if your parent takes the position, "I'll behave any way I want to behave; that's my right," gently remind him that while you agree with him, he needs to realize that he must bear the consequences of his behavior. This might mean that those around him might attenuate or even sever the relationship. Finally, let this be a conversation about a specific behavior, not an indictment of the person. Couch your criticisms in what communicators call "plus arrow plus" statements: begin with an affirmation of his goodness, follow with a critique of the particular behavior, and then close with another affirmation, such as "I love your wit, but I wish you wouldn't tell such off-color jokes, because you can be so funny without having to do that sort of thing."

tactics

- **Attitude:** Be gentle but not apologetic. Convey the fact that this is something you're raising for the parent's good. Treat it as the passing along of information rather than a private flogging.

- **Preparation:** *Discreetly* check with others around you to make sure that the behavior you're critiquing is in fact bothersome to others.

- **Timing:** Have this conversation at a time a day or two removed from an incident of offensive behavior. This makes the topic fresh and relevant but doesn't make it appear as if you are reacting to the emotion of the moment.

- **Behavior:** Keep both of you focused on the individual behavior; don't let your parent hear this as a referendum on his character. Be supportive of him on the whole. And don't shy away if he reacts with indignation.

22. Bringing Up a Parent's Bad Manners

Icebreaker: Dad, I think there's something we need to talk about. I need to tell you how uncomfortable it makes me when you get on my friends' cases about their political views. I sometimes find your tone to be aggressive, and I'd like to ask you to ratchet it down a few notches.

Defiant: Look, if your friends can't take my honesty, then they should just stay away!

Plays the "values" card: I'm only stating my convictions. So what's wrong with that?

Shows aggression: Well, they're nothing but a bunch of whiny liberals who don't know what the heck they're talking about!

Hurt/angry: Well, maybe you just don't want to be seen with your old man, then. Maybe I embarrass you. Maybe we should just stay away from one another.

Stay on your topic: I'm not interested in arguing politics with you right now, Dad. I'm simply trying to point out that when you express yourself the way you do, I'm left feeling very uncomfortable because I believe my friends feel belittled by the way you make your case. It's as though you build your argument up by tearing them down.

Challenge the tone, not the content, of the message: I respect your views *and* your right to voice them, Dad, but I think you may not realize that you sometimes express them in a way that makes those of us who don't necessarily agree with you feel disrespected. You clearly give a great deal of thought to what you say, which is why I'm asking that you give a little more thought to how it's heard.

Support the relationship: I have a great deal of respect for you *and* for your opinions. I'm not always happy with the way you express them when we're with my friends because I believe it makes them feel belittled. Still, I love your company and the time we spend together, and I hope we'll always be able to speak with one another so frankly.

Dodging responsibility: I shouldn't be held responsible for how someone else feels about what I say. I'm not gonna sugarcoat my opinions!

Wants to be "true to himself": How can I be any different than I am? I need to be me!

Agree with premise, not with execution: You need to be yourself, and you needn't be held responsible for how your words affect other people, but I think it's helpful for you to know what my reaction is to these matters, because I *do* want to spend time with you in the company of others, but I *don't* want to subject myself or others to situations where we're going to be made to feel uncomfortable. What I'm saying is that I want to be with you publicly, but I also want you to be sensitive to how you're experienced by others. You can attract people to you because of the passion of your beliefs, but you can drive them away if you express them in a hurtful way.

Bottom line: So you're saying that if I don't handle myself differently, I can forget about spending any time with you and your friends?

Rephrase: I'm saying if you show a little more sensitivity to me and to my friends, we'll continue to welcome and enjoy your company.

Relenting: I'm not going to change what I believe in. If your friends don't like the way I say things, I can respect their feelings. But don't expect me to change my beliefs, understand?

Close: Not only do I respect the passion of your convictions, I really admire the fact that you and I can sit down and have this conversation.

adaptations

This script can be adapted to bring up the issue of a parent's expressed prejudices toward others.

key points

- Define the offensive behavior as clearly, concisely, and particularly as possible.
- Admit to your own discomfort when you experience this side of your parent.
- Affirm his essential goodness and your pleasure in being in his company.
- Allow him a graceful exit; if you can do no more than plant a seed of thought for him to ponder, you've done your job.

Asking about a Parent's Estate/Living Will Plans

23

It's never easy to discuss mortality with anyone in the waning years of middle age or the waxing years of old age. This is not something people want to think about, let alone talk about or make provisions for. With this in mind, accept the fact that there's no way to sugarcoat this conversation—no way to make it seem anything it's not. It is not a cheery topic. But by the same token, it needn't be a morbid one either. What you want to be able to do is speak matter-of-factly about the need to prepare now for an eventuality that won't need to be faced until well into the future. You want to emphasize how helpful it is to simply "have it out of the way" and how anxiety-releasing it can be for your parent's spouse to not have to face difficult decisions at a critical time. You also want to make clear that this is not for your benefit, that you stand to gain nothing from it other than peace of mind, and that you hope your parent gains the same.

tactics

- **Attitude**: You want to discuss this topic with as little emotion as possible. Treat it as something inevitable but by no means imminent.

- **Preparation**: Have your own living will drawn up first and, if possible, ask your parent to accompany you to your lawyer's office when you go to discuss it.

- **Timing**: You certainly want to have this conversation when your parent is relatively young and certainly healthy. Don't broach the subject when there has been a recent illness in the family, or near the time a close friend of your parent's may have died.

- **Behavior**: Meet resistance with persistence. If this topic is important enough to you to have broached it, it is important enough to at least secure a promise that your parent will call his attorney.

23. Asking about a Parent's Estate/Living Will Plans

Icebreaker: Dad, you've always taught us kids to be prepared for the future, and I know you've always operated that way yourself, which got me thinking the other day when my doctor and I were talking about living wills. I'm wondering if that's something you've ever given any consideration to.

Denial II (humor): Hah, no problem for me; I'm not gonna die!

Denial I (shutting the door): I don't want to talk about it, okay?

Conversation stopper: It's really none of your business, you know.

Anger: You just want to make sure I don't end up costing you an arm and a leg when I die, that's all you care about!

Resentful: What's this? You've got me dead and buried already?

Acknowledge the humorous undercurrent: You and me both; I'll see you in the next century! But I've had my lawyer write one up anyway, if for no other reason than simply because I don't want to think about the prospect of my family having to make tough decisions on my behalf.

Empathize: I just had my lawyer draw one up for me, so I can appreciate that it's a difficult thing to think about. But I also found that once it was done, I felt much better knowing I could spare my family the trouble of having to make any hard decisions on my behalf in a time of crisis.

Define the need: It is my business insofar as I want to be certain your needs are met and respected, and that Mom doesn't have to worry about making any tough decisions on your behalf.

Deflect anger: I want to be sure all your needs are met and all your wishes are respected in terms of whatever care you might need to receive. I also want to be sure Mom isn't faced with any hard decisions.

Deflect resentment: Actually, I'm like you. I see you living a long, long time. The idea here is simply that this is something you want to get out of the way early in life, just so it's done with. I've just had my lawyer draw one up myself.

Sees it as distasteful: Why should I be in so much of a hurry to be mapping out my own death? That's morbid!

Sees it as frightening: Gee, it all seems kind of ghoulish. I don't think I'm ready for this conversation right now.

Defers conversation: Your mother and I will discuss this when the time comes.

Wants to cut you out: Look, this is too private a thing for us to be talking about; I'll deal with it when I need to.

Reinforce the need for preemptive action: My doctor had a good line about this. She said it falls into the category of, "It wasn't raining when Noah built the ark," by which she meant I was smart to get it out of the way before I had to. I guess that's why I think this is so important for you to take care of now, well before you'll ever have to consider such things.

Sees the logic: Well, it's certainly not the most pleasant thing I've had to think about, but I suppose it makes some sense.

Affirm the need to push ahead: I think it's wonderful that you want to get on top of this. I procrastinated until my doctor finally nudged me to go ahead and get it out of the way. I guess that's what encouraged me to come over and discuss it with you. So what do you say we give your lawyer a call?

Needs time: Give me a little while to think about this. It's a big deal to me.

Reinforce the decision: You've always done the smart thing, even when it's difficult. I think this is wise of you, and I know it'll ease any anxieties Mom might have. And if you would like, I'll be happy to go to your lawyer's office with you when you go to have the will drawn up. Maybe we can go out and have some lunch afterward.

Grudging acceptance: Well, if it'll get you off my back, I'll give him a call in a couple of days.

Meet him where he is: I think it's wise of you to consider doing this. I'll give you a call early next week, say, Tuesday, and see if you're ready to go ahead and set up the meeting with your attorney. And if it'd be of any use to you, I'll be happy to go to that meeting with you. I'll even let you buy me lunch afterward!

adaptations

This script can be adapted to discuss the writing of a parent's will. It can also be adapted to discuss medical options in the face of serious, life-threatening surgery.

key points

- A living will gives the parent decision-making power that he otherwise might not enjoy.
- It relieves a spouse of the burden of facing hard and perhaps morally ambiguous choices.
- This is something every adult, whatever his age, is wise to have.
- It must be seen as both a private matter *and* a family matter.

Discussing Funeral Planning with a Parent

24

When you look at the diagram of this script, you'll see that to have this conversation with a parent or parents, you're going to have to be ready for any number of responses to our overtures. This is because if you're old enough to discuss funeral plans with them, they're old enough to want not to think about it, and they may say anything they can think of to stop this conversation. This is why you have a leg up on them if you go ahead and make your own plans first, with the rationale that this unburdens your kids some time down the road. By doing this you shift emphasis from the unpleasant task of anticipating one's demise to the noble goal of making life a little easier for those you leave behind. In addition, you show your parents that this is a concern not merely of older folks but of any of us who want to soften the burden for our survivors.

- **Attitude**: Don't be afraid to show your own reluctance; admit that this is something you didn't want to do, but having done it, you're glad it's behind you.

- **Preparation**: Make your arrangements and be prepared to present some explanatory literature to your parents.

- **Timing**: This conversation should be conducted in extreme privacy, at a time when both parents are feeling healthy and optimistic. Avoid birthdays, anniversaries, and holidays.

- **Behavior**: Don't be afraid to moralize to your parents. Let them know you need for them to do this for your sake as much as for theirs. Be firm and unambiguous about this.

24. Discussing Funeral Planning with a Parent

Icebreaker: Dad, Mom, Sue and I just did something I thought I would hate. We drew up plans for our funerals because we wanted to spare anyone the hassle and grief of having to see to it after we were gone. I'm wondering, have you given any thought to doing this?

Wants to defer: We'll deal with that when the time comes, not before.

Correct them: Actually, if you don't take care of it, *we'll* be the ones dealing with it, and that's precisely what we wanted to spare our kids.

Somewhat disposed to the idea: Well, I see your point, I suppose.

Reluctant: Well, it might make some sense, I suppose. But I find the whole thing rather depressing.

Acknowledge the reluctance: I wasn't crazy about it either, but Sue persisted, and I'm glad she did, because now that it's out of the way I don't have to give it a second thought. And when the time comes, the kids won't have to hassle themselves with it either.

Unwilling, resentful: But what's the rush? Why the hurry, for Pete's sake?

Horrified: What?!? I don't even want to think about that! I'm interested in living, not dying!

Agree, but clarify: I agree, and I'm glad you feel that way. Actually, that's precisely why we went ahead and took care of it now; this way we don't ever have to worry about burdening ourselves or the kids with it sometime down the road.

Somewhat disengaged: Well, we'll look into it one of these days.

Press the point: I think you'll feel better—as I did—for having gotten it out of the way. Let me leave you with some of the information we gathered so the two of you can look it over. I'll give you a call in a few days and see if you have any questions.

Guilt trip (gently): The only hurry for us was in gaining the security of knowing we'd done a big favor for our kids and one another.

Gently nudge and affirm: I'm glad you do. Let me leave some information with you so you can read up on this a little bit, and I'll give you a call in the next week or so to see if you have any questions.

Makes no promises: Well, we'll look this stuff over, but we're not promising anything, understand?

Close: All we ask is that you give this consideration, because it will spare others a lot of unnecessary cost and grief. I think you'll be as happy to get your arrangements out of the way as we are to have taken care of ours.

adaptations

This script can be adapted to encourage a sibling to make his or her funeral plans.

key points

- Be prepared for them to try to appease you with lip service. Press your point.
- Make it clear that this is not simply the domain of the elderly. Rather, it is something anyone with kids should give thought to.
- Emphasize the practicality of funeral planning. It's cheaper, it's simpler, it honors your wishes, and it avoids undue burdens for your survivors.

Trying to Stop a Parent's Foolish Action   **25**

Smart people do dumb things for good reasons. We often have a hard time distinguishing what we want from what we need, and our parents are no different. As they get older, they sometimes grow tired of waiting to satisfy those needs and may choose to do something that's not in their long-term interest. They might blow their savings on the car they've always wanted, only to discover they can't afford to pay the insurance on it, or refuse to see a doctor about a nagging cough because they're determined to go on that vacation, only to end up in the emergency ward of a South Seas hospital. In short, when we get older, we very often don't want to be denied what we feel is our just reward, and when this happens, it's incumbent upon the children to step in and ensure their parents that gratification deferred is not necessarily gratification denied. To demonstrate this, I've created a fictitious situation in which a fairly recently widowed woman has accepted the wedding proposal of a man several years younger whom she has taken little time to get to know.

tactics

- **Attitude:** You cannot be punitive, moralistic, or parental toward your own parent without being met with hostility and resentment. Instead, appeal to the wisdom *she* imparted to you when you were faced with monumental decisions.

- **Preparation:** Prepare in two ways: First, interview two or three professional counselors, ideally near your parent's age, and be prepared to make a recommendation. And second, if possible, gather your siblings together and present this as a shared concern. If you *are* able to do this together with your brothers and sisters, rehearse what you're going to say ahead of time.

- **Timing:** Have this discussion sooner rather than later, so the momentum of your parent's action isn't so great that it's nearly impossible to stop. Also, have it at a time when your parent is feeling neither particularly high nor particularly low; the more lucid and rational, the better.

- **Behavior:** Don't bully her, but persist in making your point that you're acting out of love and concern, and that you see potential problems here that she might be missing.

25. Trying to Stop a Parent's Foolish Action

Icebreaker: Mom, there's something that concerns us as a family. We couldn't be happier that you're dating Michael, but we also think your decision to get married may be hasty. We don't want to discourage you, but we do want you to consider waiting a little while.

Resentment: I'm a grown woman, not a little child. I can make my own decisions, thank you!

Anger: Why don't you kids just mind your own business? I'll thank you to stay out of my personal life!

Wants to relieve sadness: I've been so miserable since your father died; this is like a second chance for me.

Impatience: I'm seventy-five years old. Frankly, I don't know how much longer I have to live, so I don't want to wait for anything.

Absorb anger: We certainly understand your anger at our butting into your affairs this way, and we hope you understand that we're only doing it because your happiness means everything to us, and we want you to be sure you've given this decision all the attention it deserves.

Acknowledge the pain: We know how unhappy you've been since Dad died, which is one of the reasons we're hoping you'll give this decision the kind of thought and attention it deserves. I think we all want to be sure that it's not just a good thing for you to do right now, but the *best* thing for you in the long run.

Counsel patience: Aside from the fact that you're going to live a long, long time, we want to be sure they're really happy years for you. That's why we're hoping you'll just give a little more consideration to a decision this big.

Curious, somewhat amenable: What sort of things do you think we need to consider that we haven't already talked about?

Pushes ahead: Look, for your information, I have thought about it. We both have. Michael makes me happy. We have a good time together. As far as we're concerned, that's all that matters!

Raise pertinent issues: All we ask is that you consider some of the things you and Daddy gave us to think about when we got serious with someone. Do you have similar values, religious beliefs, aspirations? Do you have the same interests? Where do you both want to be in, say, five years? Michael is considerably younger than you, so do you think his interest in the relationship will keep up? You know how it is in marriage, Mom. You and Dad loved each other but we all go through ups and downs, and will you and Michael be ready for them?

Interested, but uncomfortable: Well, what you're saying makes some sense, I suppose. But I can't bring up questions like that without making Michael feel as though I don't trust our relationship. After all, I've already agreed to marry him.

Insist that these questions aren't important: Believe me, Michael and I have talked about everything. Take my word for it, there are no problems.

Continued on page 114.

25. Trying to Stop a Parent's Foolish Action *(Continued)*

Be firm: Mom, you've known each other for six weeks. You've had great times together, but you don't know what it'll be like to live with each other, day in and day out. You don't know how you'll settle disagreements because you haven't had any yet—but you will. You don't know if he balls his socks up and throws them at the foot of the bed, or whether he leaves the toothpaste cap off the tube. Marriage is the stuff that goes on after the infatuation wears off. You simply need to know one another better.

Make it easy: You're right, that could be awkward. What we would recommend is that you tell him you think premarital counseling would be a good idea for the two of you, just so you can explore some of the questions that make for a good marriage. I have the names of a couple of very good counselors right here.

Fearful: But . . . what if we find out we're *not* compatible? I can't stand loneliness any more.

Reassure: We love you too much to ever want to see you unhappy, and that's why we want you to be sure this is the right thing for you to do. I know you don't want the loneliness of an unhappy marriage, so it's worth you taking a good hard look at your decision now. In fact, the easiest way to approach it might be for you to tell Michael you want the two of you to go for some premarital counseling, just to explore some of these questions. I have the names of a few very good counselors right here.

Agrees: Well, okay. I'll talk with him about it. It can't hurt for us to just look at these questions.

Close: We know the two of you will do what's best for you, and you know we'll always be here for you.

adaptations

Although this script demonstrates how to prevent a parent from precipitously entering a marriage, it can be adapted to stop them from engaging in any action that might cause them harm or unhappiness.

key points

- You don't necessarily want them not to do what they're planning to do; you merely want them to think it through more clearly.

- You are respectful of the pain or unhappiness in their life that may have given rise to this rash behavior.

- Provide reasoned, logical arguments for why they need to take a harder look at what they're proposing to do.

Announcing the Adoption of a Child

26

strategy

There are adoptions, and then there are adoptions. By this I mean that the circumstances and particulars that surround a couple's decision to adopt will play a huge part in how well their decision is received by their parents. Is the couple unable to conceive their own child? Are they adopting a baby of a race or nationality other than their own? Is it in fact a traditional couple doing the adopting, or is it a prospective single parent or a same-sex couple? Are you adopting a baby, a toddler, a pre-adolescent? These sorts of questions are certain to have an effect on how parents react to the announcement, but one thing is certain: This is an enormous decision that may take time for your parents to process, so while you want to convey enthusiasm about your decision, at the same time you may need to wait for *their* excitement to catch up to yours. For this script, I have chosen a couple who could have their own children but instead have decided to adopt a newborn baby from mainland China.

tactics

- **Attitude**: You're excited about this, but also rational. You appreciate the weight of the decision you've made and the uncertainties that go along with it. Yet you are deeply committed to seeing it through.

- **Preparation**: Speak with adoption counselors first. Also, speak (and spend time) with families who have adopted children and are aware of the unique difficulties and blessings that ensue from it. Ask them if they'd be willing to have a conversation with your parents, should the opportunity arise.

- **Timing**: Impart this news to your parents soon after you've made your decision so that they have time to warm to the idea and begin to share your sense of anticipation as you await delivery of the child.

- **Behavior**: Speak slowly and deliberately. Emphasize the research and thought you've put into this. Discuss it with a sobriety befitting such a profound decision.

26. Announcing the Adoption of a Child

Icebreaker: Mom and Dad, Brian and I have some exciting news. We've given this a great deal of thought and we've decided to start a family by adopting. We're making arrangements through an agency that will help us provide a home to an orphan, a baby girl from China.

Urge caution: Isn't this kind of hasty? I mean, it's a noble idea and all, but this is a decision you have to live with the rest of your lives. Have you really thought this thing through?

Acknowledge the legitimacy of their concern: Boy, I couldn't agree with you more about how momentous a decision this is. That's why we've really taken our time with it. We've spoken with counselors, done a good bit of reading on it, and spent quite a bit of time with parents who've done this and can speak from experience.

Concern about differences: Aren't you concerned about the differences in culture? Why not adopt a child from our country, and our race?

Respect the question: That's actually something we gave a great deal of thought to. We feel good about deciding to adopt from China for three reasons: First, adoption from other cultures and races is much more common today than it was a few years ago. Second, we wanted to adopt a child who would otherwise be likely to face a life of deprivation if we hadn't interceded. And third, we plan to raise her with an appreciation of the culture of her origin.

Don't understand: But why, why adopt? I mean, why not kids of your own?

Explain your thinking: We know we could have children of our own, and we may decide to do that some day. But I guess we see this decision as an outgrowth of something you taught me when I was growing up—to do well by doing good. We give a good home to a child who would otherwise grow up without parents, and in return we receive all of the love and affection that child has to offer.

Disappointment: But what about having your own kids? I always looked forward to the day that I'd be a grandparent. A *real* grandparent. Why take some stranger's kid into your home?

Calm their fears: First of all, we haven't eliminated consideration of having our own children one day. And second, I think you'll make a wonderful grandparent. We're really counting on you to help us bring a lot of love to this little girl.

Concern about uncertainties: But what do you know about this kid? How is her health? What was her mother's health? Her father's health? What do you know about her genes?

Reassure: That was a concern of ours too, and as the counselor at the agency told us, we'll receive a full medical report on the child, which we will then bring to a pediatrician here to assess. It's a lot like having your own child insofar as there's always risk involved, but you do what you can to minimize it.

Plays a race card: I dunno . . . I guess I just don't like the idea of some foreign kid, some Asian kid, coming into our family.

Eschew the race card; don't rise to the bait: I guess that's one area where you and we are different. I can certainly understand how this is a decision you wouldn't make, but I hope you will respect it as a decision we've chosen to make.

Concern about problems later on down the road: But what happens when she starts to grow up? When she gets confused about who she really is? I mean, a Chinese kid with white parents?

Show that you have a plan: That's a real good point, and we've already begun to think about it. As she grows up, she'll be exposed to a whole variety of family arrangements—single parents, adopted children, mixed marriages—and we think this can give her a deeper appreciation for the fact that where she came from is of less importance than the fact that together we constitute a family.

Disconcerted by it: Well, nobody in our family's ever done anything like this. I, I just don't know how I feel about it.

Willingness to give it a try: Well, I can't say I approve of the whole thing, but you're our child, so I'll support you in your decision. Even if I think it's a lousy one.

Close: This whole thing is going to be strange for all of us for a little while. I think we'll all grow into it as we go along. All we need to know is that—despite any misgivings you have—you'll be there to help us be as good a set of parents as you've been.

adaptations

As mentioned, this script can be adapted to be used by single parents choosing to adopt, gay parents choosing to adopt, or couples who have decided to become foster parents.

key points

- You've given a great deal of thought to the potential pitfalls of such an endeavor.
- Even having your own children carries the prospect of risk.
- This is probably not as unusual an occurrence as your parents think it is.
- You're acting out of a desire to enrich your own lives _and_ to do something good for a less fortunate child; your motives are therefore not only self-serving but altruistic as well.

Asking a Parent for Child Care Help

27

You might be walking a delicate balance if you need to ask your parents for help watching your children while you're at work. We want the grandparents to be involved, but we also want to be the primary authority figure in our child's life. We want to be able to depend on our parents, and we want them to feel useful, but we don't want them to interpret our inability to secure child care as a sign of incompetence. We want to let them know they're useful to us but we don't want them to feel taken advantage of. Impress upon them that you're turning to them because you have faith in them and because circumstances beyond your control have forced you to scramble for child care. Finally, be prepared to explain when and how you expect to secure full-time professional child care.

- **Attitude**: There's no room for pride here; you're making this request because, despite your best efforts, you're really in a pinch and you need their help.
- **Preparation**: You've already begun looking for a permanent arrangement.
- **Timing**: Have this conversation at a time shortly after your parents have had an enjoyable afternoon with you and your child or children. Also, try to have it well in advance of your actually *needing* them to step in and watch the kids.
- **Behavior**: Be solicitous. Ask them how you can make this easier for them. Ask if they have any alternative solutions. Let them *feel* like your rescuers.

27. Asking a Parent for Child Care Help

Icebreaker: Mom, Dad, Jack and I are going to be in a bit of a child care pinch for the next four or five months, and we were wondering if you might be able to watch the kids a couple of days a week.

Skeptical: Well, what exactly do you mean? Every day? How long each day? And how do you know you won't need us after four or five months?

Set limits: I'm glad you asked. Right now, we've been able to secure coverage two days a week, and between Jack and I we can cover one more day. We need help the other two days. Meanwhile, we're in touch with child care agencies, and we'll be interviewing candidates until we find someone we can feel comfortable with.

Resentment: Oh, you just assume we have no life! You don't think we have other things to keep ourselves busy with?

Acknowledge their busy schedule: As a matter of fact, that's one of the reasons we didn't want to come to you with this. We know how full your lives already are. We're just hoping you can help us out a little—temporarily.

Sarcasm: What do we look like, baby-sitters? You think you can call on us just like that whenever you need something, and we'll jump at the chance to bail you out?

Be contrite and flattering: I hope you don't feel as though we're trying to take advantage of you, especially in light of all the generosity you've shown us so far. We wouldn't even think of coming to you now if it weren't an emergency. It turns out that at the last minute the woman we planned to hire told us she couldn't take the job.

Scolding: Why didn't you two have this thing figured out before now? You knew you were going to need child care! Why didn't you make plans? It's just like you not to be prepared!

Absorb the scolding, explain your position: I know it looks like we haven't been giving this any consideration. That's because we thought we had something worked out with a child care provider, but at the last minute she told us she couldn't take the job.

Begins to soften: All right, so, what's your plan, anyway?

Other in-laws: But what about Jack's parents? Why can't they pitch in?

Resistant: Boy, I don't know. I wasn't planning on this. You've really caught me off guard.

Needs assurances: So what makes you so sure you'll have someone in four or five months?

You only have faith in them: To be perfectly honest with you, we're much more comfortable with you; we have a lot more confidence in you.

Enlist their thinking: Us too! We had every reason to believe we had this covered. Maybe you have other ideas of where we can turn to help, or perhaps you can help us out for some of the time, if not all of it.

Allay fears: That's the first thing we were concerned with, so when we went back to the agency, we asked the director how long it would take to find someone. We were told it usually takes no more than a month or two, so we're just trying to play it safe by saying four months, tops.

Will consider it: Well, we can't make any guarantees. Give us some time to think about it.

Consents: Well, I think we can work it out. But we need to be assured this is very short-term.

Close: I can't tell you how much we appreciate this. Let's talk again next week; I'll give you a call on Monday. And if you think it will make you feel more comfortable, maybe you'd like to sit and talk with our child care counselor and be reassured that this shouldn't be for too long.

adaptations

This script can be adapted to ask a parent to provide full-time and/or permanent child care assistance.

key points

- You're at their mercy.
- You're coming to them because you don't believe anybody else can pitch in and help out quite as well as they can.
- You want to impress upon them that this is a short-term arrangement.
- You welcome any alternative ideas they have to solve this dilemma.

part 2

Life*scripts*

for siblings

Announcing That You Can't Attend a Sibling's Wedding

1

---

strategy

The first assumption we need to make with this script is that you really *can't* attend; that some intruding issue is *so* compelling, *so* overriding, *so* impinging, that you have no choice but to renege on your promise to be there. That said, there are degrees of excuses. A sick child or the death of a spouse's parent, for instance, is pretty hard to argue with. But what do you do when it *appears* as though you have some choice in the matter, when your brother or sister perceives that you're electing to do something other than involve yourself in the biggest day of their lives? The only way to assuage hurt feelings and avoid lingering bitterness and family enmity is to make your case as persuasively as possible: You tried to find a way out of the problem, you ultimately had no choice (your fate was sealed by others), and you feel as sick about this as they do. The example I use here is of someone who has literally been forced by their boss to either travel to a business meeting or lose their job.

---

tactics

- **Attitude**: You are contrite over what has happened; you feel horrible about this, but you *don't* feel guilty. This was an imposed decision.

- **Preparation**: Do whatever you can to amass "evidence" to prove you've explored every alternative and now *must* do something other than attend the wedding.

- **Timing**: Strike as quickly as possible. This shows your sibling that you haven't been avoiding telling him, keeps him from accidentally hearing it from someone else, and gives him time to make emotional adjustments to your not being there.

- **Behavior**: If possible, tell him face to face. Go to his home, sit down with him, and don't be too quick to offer reasons *why* this conflict is unavoidable. Instead, put more effort into showing how terrible you feel, then press your defense.

1. Announcing That You Can't Attend a Sibling's Wedding

Icebreaker: Sam, my boss just told me I have to go on a business trip next weekend, and he's made it clear that if I turn him down, I'll lose my job. I feel just sick about this, but I'm afraid I can't go to your wedding.

Irrationally angry: Jeez, you have to choose between your career and your family, and you choose your career?!?

Rationally angry: Man, that makes me furious! I know, I know, there's nothing you can do about it. But wow! That's just not fair. You've really nailed me with this one!

Hopes for a reprieve: Oh, surely there's someone else he can send. Or maybe delay the trip a day or two. Just go reason with the guy.

Hurt, but understanding: I've looked forward to this day my whole life. I understand the jam you're in, but I gotta tell you, it's just not going to be the same without you there.

Put it in proper perspective: I certainly understand your anger, Sam. I'm angry too. But this is my livelihood. It's what feeds *my* family. Believe me, I wish I had a choice.

Agree: I couldn't agree with you more. It's not fair, and that's what I tried to tell the boss. The guy just refused to cut me *any* slack.

Explain your predicament: I was thinking the same thing. In fact, as soon as he told me I had to do this, I tried to come up with alternatives. But he wouldn't hear of them.

You do what you can: There's nowhere in the world I'd rather be that day than at your wedding. I'm hoping to at least be able to call you some time that evening, and before I leave, why don't we pick a time we can all go out and celebrate? We'll save your gift until then.

A minor guilt trip: Well, it's still not going to be the same.

Empathize, but don't accept responsibility: I guess we both feel pretty horrible about this. But the last thing I want is for my boss to ruin the biggest day of your life.

Desperate: Nothing?! How about if I talked to him? Do you think he'd listen to me? It's my wedding day, after all.

There's nothing to be done: Unfortunately I've been with this guy long enough to know that when he puts his foot down, there's no way to reason with him.

Doubtful: I have a hard time believing any boss would be so inflexible.

Offer proof: It is incredible, isn't it? In fact, here's the memo ordering me to go.

Resigned, if a bit bitter: Well, this stinks. But I guess there's nothing you or I can do about it. I'm gonna miss having you there.

Close: All we can do is make the most of it when I get back. You two decide where you want to go for dinner, we'll find a night that works for all of us, and the whole evening's on me.

adaptations

This script can be adapted to tell a sibling you won't be able to attend a niece or nephew's baptism, naming, bar or bas mitzvah, confirmation, or graduation ceremony.

key points

- You've looked at this problem from every angle, but you have absolutely no way out of your conflicting commitment.
- You want to make clear to him who (if anyone) or what is the real culprit here.
- You know you can't "make it up to him," but you do want to do something to commemorate their wedding at the earliest opportunity.

Confronting a Sibling about His Drinking or Drug Problem

2

strategy

In lifescript 7 in part 1 we offered a script for confronting a parent about his drug or alcohol abuse, and we outlined a script for a family confrontation, in which the power of so many people confronting the addict with the same complaint becomes so overwhelming that he has no choice but to relent and agree to treatment. Here we suggest an alternative that can be used with a sibling, with the understanding that if it doesn't succeed in getting him to seek help, a broader confrontation is possible. In order to make this work, be prepared for the rage of unmitigated anger, the cunning of deceit, and the shoulder-shrugging indifference of complete denial. Be as patient as water on a stone. Wear him down gradually, but don't give up. If all else fails, if he absolutely refuses your assistance, at least let him know that you won't let the topic die, and that you'll enlist as much help as you need to get the sibling into rehab.

tactics

- **Attitude**: You want to exude concern, affection, anger, and determination. You're not "suggesting" the need for help, you're insisting on it.

- **Preparation**: Have a confidential conversation with a professional substance abuse counselor and discuss what you see as your sibling's symptoms. This way you can rely on expertise that goes beyond your own hunches and fears.

- **Timing**: This conversation shouldn't wait, but if at all possible, hold it at a time shortly after there's been an episode of drug or alcohol use. Hold the conversation in the morning, to allow for professional intervention later that day.

- **Behavior**: Keep your voice strong but not strident. Don't yell or point fingers. Stress the problem and the threat it poses to the sibling's health. Don't moralize.

2. Confronting a Sibling about His Drinking or Drug Problem

Icebreaker: I love you, Steve, which is why I wanted to meet with you this morning. I believe you're abusing cocaine, and I want you to get some professional help.

Anger, resentment: Who do you think you are, accusing your *older* brother of something so ridiculous?!?

Minimizes, deflects: I appreciate the concern, but it's just a little recreational habit. I have it under *complete* control.

Denial: As a matter of fact, I don't even use the stuff anymore.

Anger, defiance: And what makes *you* the expert on drugs?

Pretends to be in control: I don't have a problem. I can stop any time I want, and if I think it's getting out of hand, that's exactly what I'll do.

Absorb anger: I understand your anger. After all, I'm butting into your personal life here. But I'm doing this because I'm worried about you.

Disagree: I don't think you do. I spoke with a professional drug counselor who told me the behavior I described to him sounded like that of a habitual user.

Confront: I'd like to believe that, but I'm certain you were high the other night when we met for dinner.

Defer to an expert: I don't consider myself an expert, which is why I consulted one. When I described some of your behavior, he told me it sounded like you had a serious problem that we need to address right away. That's why I came to see you.

Don't let him get away with it: I'd like to believe that, but you give every evidence of being a habitual user.

Pushes you away: Look, just keep out of my life, okay?!?

Furious: What right did you have to discuss my life with some stranger?!?

Thinks you're overstating the problem: What makes you think I have a problem, anyway? There's a difference between drug use and drug abuse, you know.

Justify yourself: I've spoken—in complete confidence and without using any names—to an expert in drug abuse. I told him what I've seen. You use the drug regularly. You've asked to borrow money. You show up late for work. You miss appointments. You're losing weight. And your eyes are bloodshot. You need help. All I'm telling you to do is speak with a professional, and see what he or she says.

Relents: Well, all right, I'll talk to someone, but that's all I'll do.

Tries to put it off: Look, I'll call somebody, if it'll make you feel better.

Continued defiance: No way! I'll take care of myself!

Stay in control of the situation: I appreciate your intentions; that's a great first step. But we need to do it right now. Should I call the person I spoke with, or do you have someone else you want to see?

Threaten: I'm hoping we can work this out between the two of us, and not involve anyone else in it.

Continued on page 134.

2. Confronting a Sibling about His Drinking or Drug Problem *(Continued)*

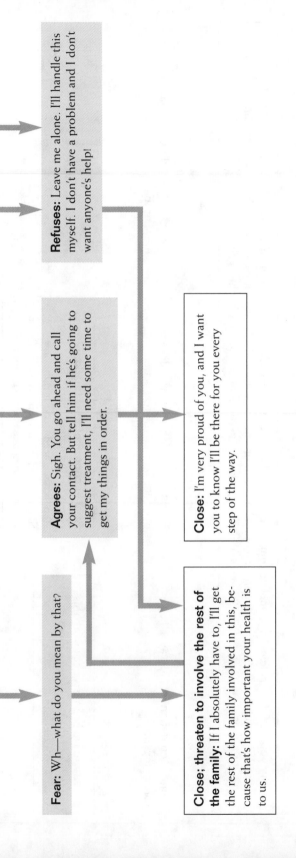

Fear: Wh—what do you mean by that?

Close; threaten to involve the rest of the family: If I absolutely have to, I'll get the rest of the family involved in this, because that's how important your health is to us.

Agrees: Sigh. You go ahead and call your contact. But tell him if he's going to suggest treatment, I'll need some time to get my things in order.

Close: I'm very proud of you, and I want you to know I'll be there for you every step of the way.

Refuses: Leave me alone. I'll handle this myself. I don't have a problem and I don't want anyone's help!

adaptations

This script was designed to address the problems of a drug addict but can be adapted to confront an alcoholic as well. It can also be adapted to confront one's spouse.

key points

- You are motivated to do this because of love and concern for your sibling.
- Should he consent to getting help, you must be prepared to follow through immediately.
- Don't accept excuses, explanations, or defenses. These are the tools of the addict.
- Don't ask for anything more than that the sibling speak with a professional.

Asking a Sibling to Drive More Safely

3

The trick to penetrating your sibling's psyche when it comes to their driving is to focus on the need for defensiveness behind the wheel instead of coming across as though you're critiquing their *ability* as a driver. In essence, you can be saying, "Look, you're a talented driver, but there are an awful lot of folks out there who aren't, and there's no point in taking risks with their safety *or* yours." Many of us have an awful lot of ego tied up in our driving ability, and we're unwilling to listen to criticism of it. But if we're told we need to be more careful for the sake of others who may not be as slick as we are behind the wheel, we'll be more apt to listen. Finally, if all else fails, be prepared to issue an ultimatum.

tactics

- **Attitude**: Don't be preachy or moralistic, but don't back down if you're ridiculed; derision is a defensive front masquerading as an aggressive posture. When confronted by it, stand up to it and press your point.

- **Preparation**: Arm yourself with statistics that bolster your case. Call the National Highway Safety Administration for information about accidents and fatalities in your state.

- **Timing**: Have this conversation when you are alone with your sibling on a long drive. And make sure you are doing the driving. By doing this, you demonstrate what it is you're asking for.

- **Behavior**: Drive safely but not too cautiously. Don't overcompensate. Point out unsafe practices you see *other* drivers engaging in.

3. Asking a Sibling to Drive More Safely

Icebreaker: Jack, I know this is a ticklish topic for a lot of us, but I've noticed that when you drive you take some unnecessary risks. You're one of the most talented drivers I know, but I think you need to be a little more cautious behind the wheel.

Irrational anger: You don't like the way I drive? Then don't drive with me!

Deflect anger: None of us likes to have people comment on our driving, but I'm saying this because I care about your safety, and I'm concerned with some of the risks you take. I'm also concerned about other folks—particularly older folks—not being able to steer clear of people who drive as fast as you do.

Dismissive: Look, I have unbelievable reflexes. I can steer clear of any problem out there.

Put the onus elsewhere: If everyone out there had your reflexes, there might be no need for concern, but at the speeds you travel you run the risk of hitting someone who's just not as quick or alert as you are.

Sees only the legal angle: The way I figure it, if a cop wants to give me a ticket, I'll pay it. No big deal.

Expand the issue: You're right, a ticket may be no big deal. But what concerns me is your safety, and the safety of other drivers. Speeding increases the risk and severity of accidents, and that *is* a big deal.

Derisive: Well, well. Since when did you become the little safety patrol officer for the family?

Assert yourself: Let me be blunt, Jack. I take this seriously because last year alone over 4,000 people were killed in automobile accidents in our state alone, and I don't want to see you either become a statistic or make someone else one.

Denies responsibility: Look, I drive fast, but I'm on top of things. As far as I'm concerned, everyone needs to be paying attention out there.

Thinks you're alarmist: C'mon. You're making way too much of this. I've never had an accident, and I'm not about to have one now.

Doesn't believe you: No way. Where're you coming up with numbers like that?!?

Agree, in part, but shift responsibility: You're absolutely right; as everyone needs to be paying attention. There are more cars on the roads today than ever before. They're bigger, heavier, and more powerful. And speed limits are up across the country. I think about people like Mom and Dad, and other older drivers we know, and while they're good drivers, I'm not sure they're equipped to steer clear of someone driving as fast as you. They have a right to be out there, but you and I have a responsibility to watch out for them.

Documentation: I've been thinking about this for a while now, as much because of my own driving habits as anyone else's. So I got in touch with the National Highway Safety Administration and got hold of year-by-year statistics about crashes and fatalities. It woke me up to the fact that *I* have to be more careful out there, and it prompted this conversation as well.

Refuses to change: I'm sorry, pal, but I'm gonna drive the way I always have.

Sobered: Okay, okay. I believe you. If it'll make you feel better, I'll slow down, all right?

Close: I'm sorry to hear that, for your own safety's sake. I guess we won't be driving together anymore.

Close; accept even a grudging consent: Even if you do it only to humor me, I'll be eternally grateful. I want to keep you around a while.

Facetious: So what do you want me to do, drive like an old lady from now on, ten miles an hour on the highway?

Close; go along with it: You do that and I won't ride with you! We'll never get anywhere on time! Nah, just the usual stuff; speed limits, seat belts, no drinking and driving, that sort of thing. You're a smart man, I know you can drive smart. Even if it's not as much fun.

adaptations

This script can be adapted to ask a sibling to engage more safely in any number of risk-laden activities such as building a campfire or even horseplay with children. It can also be adapted for use with spouse.

key points

- Your only concern is for safety.
- Drivers have to be responsible not only for themselves but for other drivers and their own passengers as well.
- You can drive prudently without driving prudishly.
- Unfortunately, you can let the facts—accidents and fatalities—speak for themselves.

Bringing Up a Niece's or Nephew's Bad Behavior 4

strategy

I am hard pressed to come up with a topic that can strain your relationship with your sibling more quickly than this one. Even the most well adjusted among us can be fiercely protective of our kids and their behavior, and loath to hear criticism of them from anybody other than our spouses. Still, if a little one is acting out and you feel it's your duty to say something, there are ways to soften the blow. To begin with, avoid a holier-than-thou posture; let your sister or brother know that your kids are no angels, and that you'd even welcome a sibling's critique of them. Also, distinguish between bad behavior and bad kids. Identify the offending behavior while at the same time assuring your sibling that you think he or she is raising a basically good kid. And finally, don't have this conversation come across as a referendum on your sibling's parenting. Remind him that he's a good parent, and part of good parenting involves steering the kids back on course when they wander off.

tactics

- **Attitude:** Be extremely deferential toward your sibling. Don't be afraid to emphasize how difficult it is for you to bring this up; he may respect you for it.

- **Preparation:** Speak with a child guidance expert about the behavior you've observed. Get a sense from them as to whether it's age-appropriate, and whether it in fact *should* be addressed.

- **Timing:** Have this conversation shortly after your families have been together. Also, have this conversation just between siblings; no in-laws should be involved.

- **Behavior:** Treat this as though it's not a big deal, but also not something you can ignore. Be casual about it, but let your sibling know it is nevertheless something that concerns you.

4. Bringing Up a Niece's or Nephew's Bad Behavior

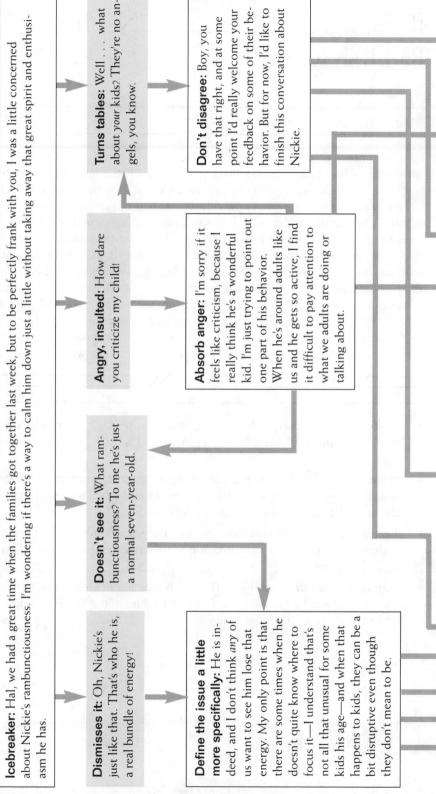

Icebreaker: Hal, we had a great time when the families got together last week, but to be perfectly frank with you, I was a little concerned about Nickie's rambunctiousness. I'm wondering if there's a way to calm him down just a little without taking away that great spirit and enthusiasm he has.

Turns tables: Well . . . what about *your* kids? They're no angels, you know.

Don't disagree: Boy, you have that right, and at some point I'd really welcome your feedback on some of their behavior. But for now, I'd like to finish this conversation about Nickie.

Angry, insulted: How dare you criticize my child!

Absorb anger: I'm sorry if it feels like criticism, because I really think he's a wonderful kid. I'm just trying to point out one part of his behavior. When he's around adults like us and he gets so active, I find it difficult to pay attention to what we adults are doing or talking about.

Doesn't see it: What rambunctiousness? To me he's just a normal seven-year-old.

Dismisses it: Oh, Nickie's just like that. That's who he is, a real bundle of energy!

Define the issue a little more specifically: He is indeed, and I don't think *any* of us want to see him lose that energy. My only point is that there are some times when he doesn't quite know where to focus it—I understand that's not all that unusual for some kids his age—and when that happens to kids, they can be a bit disruptive even though they don't mean to be.

Frustrated: So what do you expect us to do, lock him up?

Make a suggestion: Of course not. But if you're interested in helping him control himself a little better, perhaps you could have a conversation with his teacher or his pediatrician. I suspect they both might have some suggestions.

Irrational response: Look, then maybe we just shouldn't get together.

Reject his rejection: That's the last thing I want to see happen, Hal, which is precisely why I'm bringing this up. I know we can work something out.

Defiance, hostility: Look, why don't you just ignore him if he bothers you. After all, you're the adult.

Be reasonable, and ask him to be reasonable: Hal, it's not easy to ignore Nickie when he's trying so hard to get our attention. You *know* how persistent he can be.

Acknowledges problem; won't do anything: Look, he's always been an active kid; we all know that. And we know it can be disruptive sometimes, but we don't want to discourage him from feeling free to express himself.

Glad he acknowledges a problem: I'm glad you feel that way, because I don't think you have to stifle him at all. All he needs, I think, is to learn when he can be so "expressive" and when he needs to control himself a little more. It's just a matter of learning what behavior is okay in what settings.

Continued on page 144.

4. Bringing Up a Niece's or Nephew's Bad Behavior *(Continued)*

Disagrees with your thinking: I . . . I don't know that you can teach a seven-year-old that kind of control.

Begins to be reasonable: He *is* a stubborn one. But I never thought it bothered anyone.

Still hostile, but less so: So what do you suggest, only getting together when we can get a sitter?

Gives it some credence: Well, I suppose we could run this by his doctor. She may have some thoughts on it.

Empathy: Actually, we've gone through our share of behavior stuff with our kids too, and we found there are some good tricks that can help them learn how to behave in different situations. Our pediatrician was a big help to us with some great resources. Maybe you want to run this by Nickie's doctor.

Soften the blow: I can only speak for myself and how it makes me feel; I suspect it might bother some of us and not others. But you guys are *such* good parents, I think it's the kind of thing you'll be able to get a handle on.

Reinforce, close: I think that's a good idea. And let me know what she has to say. Maybe I can apply her ideas to my own kids!

adaptations

This script can be adapted to suggest psychological counseling for a sibling's child.

key points

- You're not accusing the kid of setting fire to the sofa or pulling wings off houseflies; you're merely pointing out a specific behavior that you find disruptive, inappropriate, unnecessary, and correctable.
- One of the reasons you're bringing this up is that you have full faith and confidence in your sibling and his mate as good parents.
- You're all in the same boat; we all need help and ideas raising our kids.
- Don't generalize; don't say, "This is how your child is." Instead, say, "This is how *I* experience your child."

Bringing Up a Brother- or Sister-in-Law's Bad Behavior 5

strategy

Your approach to this lifescript is somewhat different than in the preceding script, in which you brought up the bad behavior of a sibling's child. Here you take no risk of offending your sister or brother by critiquing their parenting skills, always a touchy subject. Instead, you're zeroing in on one piece of your in-law's behavior that bothers you. With this in mind, you want to be careful to isolate the offending behavior, make the point that it might not bother other people but it does you, and try to enlist your sibling's help in discerning how to handle it. Essentially, you have three options: You can stop spending time with the offending in-law (a drastic measure you would only resort to if the behavior is so offensive that you can't tolerate being in the same room with him and he won't agree to change), intercede directly with him (tell him how he makes you feel), or get your sibling to intercede on your behalf. Ideally, you and your sibling will be able to collaborate and decide which of the last two options would work best for you.

tactics

- **Attitude:** You don't want to appear overly emotional about this; you want your sibling to hear your concern delivered in a cool and somewhat detached voice. That way, you don't sound as if you're speaking from the pique of the moment.

- **Preparation:** If you're married, speak with your own spouse about the behavior you find offensive; see if she has the same reaction. Her support will encourage you to address the problem head on.

- **Timing:** Have this conversation soon after you have all been out together socially, but when it will be some time before you're all together again. This allows the problem, once addressed, to die down in people's minds.

- **Behavior:** You're not indicting your in-law. You're not accusing him of doing anything wrong. You simply want to convey the idea that a part of his behavior rubs you the wrong way. With this in mind, be emphatic that you're not condemning your sibling's spouse, but be equally emphatic that you are bothered by his behavior.

5. Bringing up a Brother- or Sister-in-Law's Bad Behavior

Icebreaker: Jane, I understand this could really put a strain on our relationship, but I need to say this. I take offense at some of the jokes Stan tells us, and I wish he wouldn't do it.

Impetuous reaction: Well! Then maybe we shouldn't get together as couples anymore, if he bothers you so much!

Clarify your complaint: I'm sorry if I made it sound like I don't like Stan, because I certainly do. And I love the evenings we have together. It's just this one part of his behavior that makes me uncomfortable, that's all.

Doesn't share your unease: What's so offensive about Stan's jokes?!? I guess I just don't see the problem.

Make it clear that it's your problem, not hers: I suspect a lot of people don't see a problem with Stan's humor, and maybe I'm peculiar in that way. I'm not saying there's anything wrong with it, I'm only trying to tell you how it affects *me*. Jokes that might not bother others do upset me.

Rejects your feelings: Oh, get over it! Don't be such a baby, for goodness' sake.

Assert your feelings: I've tried to overlook it, Jane, but I can't help but be bothered by it.

Makes light of it: Well, you know Stan. He just loves that sort of stuff, and well, I guess I just accept that side of him.

Keep the focus on you: I understand that not everyone would be offended by this; all I'm pointing out is how they affect *me*. They make me feel uncomfortable.

Irrational response: So you want my husband to stop being funny because you don't like it, is that it?

Rational response: What I'm asking is that you help me figure out what to do about this. Should I talk to Stan? Would you be willing to let him know how I feel? What do you think?

Defensive of spouse: I'm not going to ask Stan to stop telling his jokes; he loves it too much. I'm sorry if it bothers you.

Shift responsibility to in-law: I'm not asking you to do that. But perhaps you can simply let him know how I feel. Perhaps he'll decide to tone things down a little in my presence.

Volunteers to intercede: Well, let me talk to him. I can handle it better than you can.

Defiant, sarcastic: So what are you asking? That I censor my husband?

Ask their advice: Of course not. But now that you know how I feel about some of his humor, maybe you have some idea as to what we can do.

Defers to you: Look, this is between the two of you, not me. If it bothers you, then you talk to him about it. Leave me out.

Protect the relationship: If that's what you consider the best way to address this *and* preserve the relationship the four of us have, then I'll go ahead and do it.

Close: I really appreciate your helping me out with this, Jane. Like I say, I love the time we spend together as couples, and I think this will make me feel a whole lot better.

adaptations

This script can be adapted to discuss offending behavior with a friend, a spouse, or distant relative.

key points

- You are bothered by a particular behavior; you're not rejecting your in-law outright.
- You're not asking that he change his behavior per se; you just don't want him exhibiting the offending behavior in your presence.
- Ideally, you and your sibling can work to achieve agreement on how to handle the situation.
- If all else fails, you may need to be willing to segregate the relationship. That is, if you and your in-law can't come to an accommodation, you may need to see your sibling apart from her spouse.

Confronting a Sibling's Actions That 6 Undermine Your Parental Authority

strategy

Every child needs consistency in order to feel secure. They need to know what the rules of the house are, what's expected of them, what's permissible, and what's forbidden. They shouldn't have to guess. For this reason, child psychologists encourage parents to be of one mind in establishing the rules of the family, and to make it clear that these are the rules the child is expected to obey under any and all circumstances. When your sibling—an alternate authority figure in your child's eyes—introduces rules or boundaries that conflict with yours, the child is at a loss as to what to do. Ideally, your sibling would first consult you to get a sense of what boundaries she needs to enforce, but you can also avoid being undermined by allowing a certain amount of flexibility provided you, your sibling, and your child have discussed it ahead of time so your child can understand that special circumstances are allowing him to play by a different set of adult guidelines. In speaking to your sister about this, the main point you want to stress is that no one family's rules are better than any other's—you're not accusing her of bad parenting simply because hers are different than yours—but that your child knows there is a certain code of behavior expected of him, and it's important that he not be confused by a competing code.

tactics

- **Attitude**: You're grateful your sibling has an active role in your child's life, and you think she's an excellent parent.

- **Preparation**: Consult your pediatrician or a child psychologist so you are prepared to cite the thinking of an expert—if necessary—to bolster your argument.

- **Timing**: Strike while the iron's hot. Engage this conversation soon after your sibling has exhibited the undermining behavior.

- **Behavior**: You're not complaining or finding fault. You're merely asking that your sibling abide by your thinking when it comes to taking care of your child—regardless of whether she agrees with you or not. There is no reason why this should be anything less than a calm and amiable conversation.

6. Confronting a Sibling's Actions That Undermine Your Parental Authority

Icebreaker: Alice, I have an awful lot of respect for your parenting skills, and I welcome any wisdom you might have about how I can handle my own kids. But in some ways our approach to parenthood is different. I need to ask you to be more careful when you're with my children, because they can wind up getting mixed messages from the two of us. Last week, for instance, you let my son skip dinner before he went out with your son, and that's something we don't allow in our home.

Takes it personally: So you don't like *my* parenting? Is that what you're trying to tell me?

Clarify the issue: Not at all; I think all parents handle things in ways we feel are best suited to our kids. I'm simply asking that our rules are enforced with our kids, and I would expect you to do the same of us when we're looking after yours.

Insulted: Well, if that's the thanks I get for looking after your kids, maybe I just shouldn't bother anymore!

Deflect anger: I'm sure it sounds like ingratitude on my part, and I certainly don't mean to come across that way. I really enjoy the fact that we can look after each other's kids, and I hope we continue to do it while they grow up. I think it's important to both of us.

Questions your parenting: Did you ever think it might be good for your kids if you relaxed the rules a little? That's all I was doing, and they didn't seem to suffer from it.

You're happy to discuss parenting skills another time: You know, you may indeed be right, and I'd welcome your thoughts on that. But my point *here* is that as long as our kids do have rules to follow, we need to know they're enforced consistently.

It's no big deal: It's only one little meal, what's the big deal? I'm sure they've got plenty to eat when they went out.

Stress the principle: I'm sure they did too. But one of the rules we have in our house is that the kids need to eat their dinner before they go out. That way we know they've had a decent meal, and it's important to us that we monitor that. We don't want the kids coming to think it's unimportant to us.

Territorial: Well, I'll tell you what I think. *I* think that as long as they're under my care, they should be allowed to play by our house rules. It's only fair to my kids.

Doesn't understand the issue: What's the big deal? Why is this so important to you?

See some merit in this: You know, Alice, that may be a great idea in certain circumstances, provided I have a chance to talk things over with my kids beforehand. For instance, I think I would've been okay with your sending them out without supper if I'd have had the chance to discuss it with them first, and let them know this is a special exception. And you could've backed me up on it, too.

Explain need for consistency: We feel that our kids are better about obeying rules when they repeat them over and over and apply them consistently. If they get mixed signals about what we expect of them—if, for instance, Bob tells them to come right home after school and I tell them it's okay to stop off at the candy store or a friend's house—they won't know whose directions to follow. If they get the same message from both of us, even if they disagree with it, they know to follow it.

Accepts your reasoning: In other words, you don't have a problem with your kids following different rules at our house, as long as you've agreed to it and explained to your kids that this was a special exception?

Understands the principle: In other words, it's less the rules themselves than it is their being applied steadily?

Close: That's exactly right. We want to be flexible with the kids, but we also want to have a very clear understanding of what we expect of them and allow from them.

adaptations

This conversation can be adapted to ask your child's friend's parent not to undermine your authority. It can also be adapted to ask your child's teacher to do the same.

key points

- Children need to receive consistent messages regarding what they should and should not do.
- You respect your sibling's parenting style and skill; you regard yours as *different*, not *better*.
- You're flexible. You're willing to change the rules, provided you have an opportunity to discuss them with your child beforehand.

Confronting a Sibling's Inappropriate 7
Treatment of Your Spouse

A marriage is a sometimes uneasy melding together of two sets of family rules and values into one. What's familiar and comfortable to you may be quite unsettling to your spouse, and vice versa. In order for the marriage to work, it has to begin to formulate its own set of rules, its own determination of acceptable and unacceptable behavior, and this means compromise. So what happens when your sibling, or in the case of this script, your brother, in playing by the old family rules, engages in a behavior that you're quite familiar with but that your spouse (in this case, wife) finds unsettling? The answer is that it's time to educate your brother, to bring him up to speed on how things work in the family that you and your wife have created, not the one that created you. In the interest of preserving both the sibling relationship and the marriage partnership, your brother has to hear three things. First, you're playing by a new set of rules, and you're asking him to play by them as well. Second, this is *not* a major issue; by having this conversation, you're preventing it from becoming one. And third, if push comes to shove and—in his most unreasonable moment—you have to decide between him and your spouse, you will make it clear that your primary allegiance is to her. As with other scripts, you don't want to accuse your sibling of doing anything *wrong*, per se. You simply want to point out that his behavior has consequences he may not have anticipated.

- **Attitude:** This is a serious topic, and you want your sibling to hear it as such. You are not asking him if he would consider changing; you're impressing upon him the fact that he must.

- **Preparation:** Talk it over with your spouse first. Make sure the two of you are of one mind, and make it clear to her that this is something you freely choose to do, not something you feel forced into doing.

- **Timing:** Have this conversation in a quiet time with your sibling, preferably shortly after an incident when he has exhibited the offending behavior. Treat it as a heart-to-heart.

- **Behavior:** You are not punitive, but you are also not willing to compromise. Your focus in on getting this resolved to your satisfaction and then putting it behind you.

7. Confronting a Sibling's Inappropriate Treatment of Your Spouse

Icebreaker: John, I have something I think we really need to talk about. I'm sure you don't intend any harm, but I want you to know that when you make fun of Sally, when you kid her about not being terribly bright, we both take offense at it. I want to ask you to stop.

Overreacts: Omigosh! I'm so sorry. I didn't know it hurt her. I feel terrible. I don't know if she'll even want to see me again.

Put some perspective on it: I certainly appreciate your sensitivity, John, and I'm glad you're willing to back off. But you needn't be so hard on yourself; Sally understands that you mean no harm by it, and the last thing either of us want is for you to feel unwelcome in our lives.

Embarrassed, wants to avoid the entire situation: I gotta tell you, I'm kind of embarrassed; I never knew I was hurting her. I don't know if I can look at her without feeling bad about this.

Disparaging of women: Jeez, women! Why do they have to be so sensitive?

Don't ally yourself with his way of thinking: John, I suspect we all have certain areas that are sensitive to us, that we don't like to be teased about. I know I do. This just happens to be one of hers, so it needs to stop.

Rekindles family history: Oh, c'mon! You and I have always kidded around like that. People expect it from us.

Doesn't think it's bothersome behavior: What's the big deal? I mean, I kid *my* wife that way. Heck, *you* kid my wife. And she doesn't get upset.

Focus on your spouse's feelings: You're right in that it's not a big deal to you and me, or to your wife. I guess it's not one of *our* sensitive subjects. But it is for Sally, so it needs to stop.

Make a distinction: You're right; that's how you and I have always kidded around, especially with one another. We grew up that way, and we're used to it. But it's not how Sally grew up, and it's not what *she's* used to. To her it's hurtful.

Refuses to relate to the situation: Look, I'm sorry, but I still don't get it. You can kid with me all you want, make fun of me any way you want. It's just not gonna bother me. So I just can't understand Sally's being so sensitive.

Unreasonable, dogmatic: Look, this is who I am, and I'm not gonna make apologies for it. What am I supposed to do, keep my mouth shut around her, or just sit there and compliment her on how *smart* she is?

Time to move on: John, please understand that Sally and I don't mean to create an uncomfortable situation; we're simply trying to avoid one. Sally really enjoys being with you, and we're both eager to put this whole thing to rest. In fact, we knew you'd understand, so we were hoping you'd come over for dinner next week.

Softens: Well, I suppose that's the only way to get over it. But please don't bring it up again, okay?

People are different: Y'know, I've always admired your ability to take a good ribbing, but you can't expect others to be as resilient as you are. That's why I'm calling this to your attention.

Still doesn't respect the scope of the situation: It sure seems like a tempest in a teapot to me. Why don't you have a talk with her, instead of me?

Take your stand: John, in matters like this I'll always look out for my wife. This has to be your move, not hers.

Affirming individuality: You're right again, John. Your style of humor *is* a big piece of who you are. And Sally's sensitivity to being kidded about her intelligence is a big piece of who *she* is. But when those two personality traits collide, something's gotta give, and what I'm saying is that for us to enjoy one another's company, you're going to have to find other ways to kid around with her.

Begrudgingly accepts your request without agreeing with you: Well, I don't buy it. But if it'll make you two happy, I'll tone it down. But don't think I'm gonna lay off teasing *you*, you'll always be fair game!

Close: I really appreciate your willingness to cut us some slack on this, John. I think your kindness is an even bigger part of your personality than your humor.

adaptations

This script can be adapted to confront a sibling about inappropriate treatment of his own spouse.

key points

- This is something that both you *and* your spouse want to change.
- This is not something you see as intentionally malicious or hurtful. It stems from a lack of understanding that you're attempting to correct.
- You want very much to preserve your relationship with your sibling as well as the relationship between your sibling and your spouse, but if there's no concession made, you will stand, uncompromisingly, by your spouse.
- Your sibling may need to understand the difference between the "rules of engagement" you shared when you were growing up and the ones you and your spouse have committed to.

Stopping a Sibling's Comments about Your Weight

8

strategy

If this is a hot-button topic among siblings, there's a good chance it's indicative of a broader pattern of criticism and ridicule. Most siblings who are generally supportive of one another are loath to criticize a brother or sister because of the weight he or she is carrying. What this means is that the offending party has to come to understand that this is one area that needs to be kept off-limits. There's too much hurt that can be inflicted, and the barbs and comments only serve as fuel for the fire; people who eat more than they should and are made to feel poorly for it in turn eat to assuage their low self-esteem. With this in mind, the focus here has to be on educating the sibling who's throwing the verbal darts. You operate from the assumption that the one thing the two of you have in common is that you'd both like to see you at a healthy weight, and from there you point out to your sibling that the only way to achieve that goal is through support and encouragement.

tactics

- **Attitude**: You want to come across as strong-willed and determined. You're not begging for mercy, you're educating the ignorant. Take control of this conversation.

- **Preparation**: Either speak with a nutritionist or read some literature that explains the dynamics behind weight problems. Equip yourself to quote the experts, if necessary.

- **Timing**: This is a good conversation to have in your home when you are alone with your sibling and the two of you have just finished a healthy meal that you prepared.

- **Behavior**: Be patient with your sibling's skepticism and defensiveness; it's difficult for her to understand the workings of a condition that she doesn't share.

8. Stopping a Sibling's Comments about Your Weight

Icebreaker: I know you don't mean to be hurtful, but I need to tell you that your comments about me being overweight really bother me, and I want you to stop.

Misguided love: I know they hurt, and that's why I make them. I'm hoping to shame you into doing something about it.

Defensive; makes light of it (no pun intended): Oh, come on, we've always gotten on each other's case about stuff. It's what brothers and sisters do!

Aggressively blunt: Well, if you must know, I find your weight disgusting. I'm really ashamed of you.

Doesn't know what else to do: Well, you don't expect me to just accept it, do you? You really need to lose weight, and that's all there is to it!

Calmly educate: Well, in a weird way, then, I appreciate your concern. But what you need to know is that a lot of people who are overweight—myself included—respond much better to encouragement than to ridicule. When you make hurtful comments, it just makes me feel worse about myself, which makes me want to eat more. It may sound screwy, but that's how it works.

This is special: I've always enjoyed our give-and-take too, but what you need to know is that this one particular area of my life is unlike anything else, and if I'm going to try to maintain a healthy weight I need support, especially from you.

Her position is understandable but misbegotten: I certainly can understand why you'd feel that way, and it may come as a surprise to you, but like many people who are overweight, I'm not happy with it either. I'm working very hard to get it under control, but your comments only undermine my efforts. What I need in order to lose weight is to know that I have your encouragement and support.

More education: I don't just accept my weight, and I'm not necessarily asking you to either, but weight gain and loss is a lot trickier than just eating less. Doctors and nutritionists will tell you how much our eating habits are tied in to issues like how happy or unhappy we are, what's going on in our lives, whether we've experienced a sense of loss. There are a whole bunch of things that factor into whether or not we really feel like we have the power to eat less.

Misguided interest: But how am I supposed to help you without browbeating you about it?

It doesn't compute: When I don't want my kids to do something, I scold them, and they don't do it. So what makes this so much different?

Wants to strike a deal: Tell you what. You lose weight, I'll congratulate you. You keep it on, I'll keep letting you know how ashamed I am.

Simplistic thinking: Sounds like a bunch of psychobabble to me. I don't buy it.

Propose a reasonable set of options: Let me give you two options, either of which would help achieve the goal you and I both want me to achieve. Either encourage me to lose weight, or say nothing at all, because if I'm going to do this it can be with you but it can't be *despite* you. Now, you don't know what it feels like to be me, so you're going to have to trust me on this.

Draw an analogy: Listen very carefully to what I'm about to say, because there's a lot more at stake than simply "how I look." Eating can be an addiction, just like smoking cigarettes or drinking liquor. But one part of the solution for the smoker or drinker is to stop the destructive behavior entirely. There's no such thing as smoking or drinking in moderation because it will retrigger their addiction. I think you know this. With eating, you can't just stop. You have to eat in moderation, which makes it all the more difficult. This is what I'm up against, and the only way to overcome it is by believing that I can, not hearing that I can't.

Skeptical: I don't know that I agree with you, but if it'll make you feel better, you tell me you're really trying to control this and I'll keep my mouth shut.

Can't relate to it: I really can't relate to what you're saying because I've never been addicted to anything. But if this is how you see it, who am I to argue?

Close: It would be easier for me if you could understand this the way I do, but even if you can't, I sure welcome your willingness to respect my need to not be criticized or kidded about this.

adaptations

This script can be adapted for someone who is ridiculed for being under-weight, or for someone whose weight gain is related to an existing condition, such as a malfunctioning thyroid. It can also be adapted for conversation with a parent.

key points

- You give your sibling the benefit of the doubt by telling her you're sure she meant no harm.

- She needs to see weight gain as a physical and psychological problem, not a moral lapse.

- You work from the assumption that she doesn't understand the connection between weight and self-esteem.

- By encouraging you, she can play a pivotal role in your working yourself to a healthy weight.

Bringing Up a Sibling's Bad Hygiene 9

strategy

Well, here's a conversation you're probably not overly eager to have. It's awfully difficult to broach this topic without dusting up a mix of embarrassment and anger, so you're best off not trying to prevent either feeling from surfacing. Instead, anticipate them and be prepared to soothe them. The premise here is not that your sibling's hygiene is terribly bad, but that the honesty and respect you have for one another compels you to bring this to their attention; you would expect them to do the same if the smelly shoe was on the other foot. Stress that this is not a big problem, but you want to prevent it from becoming one. Tell them you've discussed your own hygiene with your physician (many doctors will tell you that hygiene needs change as we age). And by all means, don't look for them to cry "uncle." If they absolutely refuse to discuss it, let it go. And even if they are willing to hear you out, you can be sure they'll want this conversation to end as quickly as possible, so be prepared to give them a graceful exit. The thing you want to do here is plant the information in their mind; they'll then tend to it in private.

tactics

- **Attitude**: You're very nonchalant about this. Although it's a personal issue, you want to treat it somewhat clinically. You're detached and matter-of-fact.

- **Preparation**: Speak to a doctor and see if you can't get her to give you a clinical explanation of your sibling's problem.

- **Timing**: If possible, have this conversation at a time when your sibling won't be seeing many people for a few days, as it can leave him feeling fairly self-conscious. Obviously, you want to hold this conversation in an extremely private setting.

- **Behavior**: *Don't* be tenacious. Give him the information and let him do with it as he will.

9. Bringing Up a Sibling's Bad Hygiene

Icebreaker: Jack, I have a fairly touchy topic to discuss with you, and I only bring it up because I've always appreciated the honesty of our relationship. I suspect you may not be aware of it, but I think you might want to give some consideration to bathing just a little more often than you're used to.

Overstates the case: Really? You mean, like, people *notice?*

Lighten things up: Look, people aren't keeling over in the streets, if that's what you mean. No, actually I don't think too many people notice anything at all, but I can detect it because we spend so much time together, and as I understand it, it *could* become a big deal *if* we don't attend to it.

Anger: You don't know what you're talking about. I'm clean, I'm healthy, I take good care of myself! Why don't you just lay off!

Absorb anger: I'd be angry too if someone who cared about me brought something this personal to my attention, but it's precisely because you take good care of yourself and because I admire that in you that I thought you'd want to know this.

Disbelief: You . . . you're joking, right?

Gently press the point: Well, actually, no. It's not a big deal, but I thought you might appreciate me bringing it to your attention so that it doesn't become one.

Humiliations: My gosh, this is incredibly embarrassing! No one's ever said anything to me about this. I . . . I don't know what to say!

Empathy (with a little white lie, if necessary): It's not a big deal, really. I found myself in the same position, and I spoke with my doctor about it. He explained to me how our bodies change over time, that this is quite normal, and that we're often not able to detect a problem like this in ourselves.

Rejects you: Y'know, I don't want to hear this. I think you're nuts.

Wants clarification: Well, what exactly is the problem?

Interested in what doctors say: What do you mean, our bodies change over time?

Don't push it: I understand why you'd feel that way, Jack. I give you a lot of credit for just hearing me out. I didn't really believe it when my doctor pointed out the same problem in me. I just felt it might be helpful to you if I called it to your attention, that's all.

Be straight and unadorned: Your body is just beginning to give off an odor. It's really just barely detectable, but I think it's the kind of thing that can become more pronounced over time.

Provide some information; make this more of a clinical topic than a personal one: It's pretty interesting, actually. You know how young kids don't need deodorant, and only later in life they have to use it? It's just another piece of the aging process.

Awkward, wants to end conversation: Well, okay, um, thanks for the advice. Can we talk about something else now?

Looking for companionship: And you're telling me you've experienced this, too?

Reinforce: Yeah, and I suspect a whole lot more people than just the two of us, as well.

Agree, close by changing topic: Sounds good. So what's going on at work these days?

adaptations

This script can be adapted to bring up a sibling's need to pay closer attention to breath odor, or to discussions about inappropriate attire.

key points

- You're only saying this because you're pretty sure no one else will.
- It's not a big problem, but you could see it becoming one.
- You're not looking for him to promise to do anything; you're just giving him information.
- You can't broach this topic in any way that will avoid uncomfortable feelings for both of you.

Expressing Fears about a Sibling's Health 10

strategy

You're not going to express fears over a sibling's health if all her symptoms don't warrant it, so the assumption here is that she's showing signs that something serious *might* be wrong with her, and she's not having a doctor look at her. She's frightened, so she enters into a state of denial, of wishful thinking: "I'm getting worse, not better, but I won't have anything seriously wrong with me unless a doctor tells me so. Therefore, I'll ignore my symptoms and hope they magically disappear." When somebody is in this form of denial, you have to do three things. First, recognize that there *may* be some truth to what she says; she *may* be just fine. Second, give voice to what she is refusing to say herself; this could be something that demands attention. And third, be visibly concerned but not panicky; let her know you'll see this through with her and that you have full faith and confidence that seeing her doctor is the best course to follow.

tactics

- **Attitude**: You want to take this head-on. Be straight with her, but at the same time convey calm. Treat this as a serious problem for which the two of you will find a solution.

- **Preparation**: If possible, research your sibling's symptoms, either by looking them up in a family medical manual or by consulting your own physician.

- **Timing**: You want to have this conversation at your earliest opportunity. But avoid weekends, when doctors can't be called for an appointment, and by all means avoid later afternoons and evenings, when problems seem magnified. Finally, do this at the outset of a day when you will be spending a good bit of uninterrupted time with your sibling.

- **Behavior**: Refuse to weaken or relent if she shows persistent indifference or hostility. Don't convey a sense of fear in your voice, but speak in reasoned, modulated tones.

10. Expressing Fears about a Sibling's Health

Icebreaker: Ellen, I have to tell you that I'm concerned about that cough of yours. You've had it for several weeks now, and it's not clearing up. What have your doctors told you?

Lies to you: The doctor says I'm fine. So don't you worry.

Challenge them: It may have been some time since you've seen her. I don't know anything about medicine, but I certainly know you don't look and sound like you do when you're perfectly healthy. She needs to take another look at you.

Rebuts you: She doesn't need to see me again. I'm all right.

Anger: Why doesn't everybody just leave me alone and mind their own business?!?

Absorb anger: I know it must seem like we're just meddling, but looking after one another is part of what we do as a family. I know if the shoe was on the other foot, you'd be dragging me to a doctor so fast my head would spin!

Insists on handling it herself: Look, it's my life, so let *me* handle it. Okay?

Denigrates doctor: Ah, what do they know, anyway? I don't trust them—I'm okay.

Acknowledge her feelings, but bring her back to reality: I know doctors aren't perfect, but you've always trusted yours. You owe it to yourself and to us to see what she has to say about this, even if she tells us it's nothing but a bad cold.

Offers a deal—halfheartedly: Look, I'll tell you what I'll do. I'll give it another week, and if I still have the cough, I'll call her, okay?

Tries to slough you off: Don't worry, it's nothing. Just a little bug . . . I'm fine.

Persist: If you were fine, you wouldn't be coughing. I know you must be uncomfortable—and maybe a little nervous—about talking about it. I would be too. But whatever's wrong isn't going to get better unless you let a doctor help you.

Still trying to dodge you: It's just a really, really bad cold. Now stop worrying about me!

Be firm: Listen to me, Ellen. This may be nothing more than a stubborn cold that just doesn't want to quit. I suspect there's a good chance that's exactly what your doctor will tell you. But we don't know that, and if it's anything that needs attention, the sooner you get it, the better off you'll be. You need for her to tell us what we're dealing with here.

Firm up the offer: I will come and see you one week from today. If you still have the cough, you'll call the doctor and make an appointment. Then I'll clear my schedule so I can go with you.

Growing frustration with you: Why won't you just let this thing go?!

Stiffen your resolve: You're right. I'm not going to let this go, because I'm concerned, and because I know you are too. Whatever you're dealing with here, you're not going to go through it alone. And if it is something that requires attention, the sooner we get on it, the easier and more effective the treatment will be.

The truth comes out: To be perfectly honest with you, this thing scares me, and I don't want to hear what the doctor has to say.

Empathy, support: Let *me* be honest with *you*. It concerns me, too. That's why we have to know what we're dealing with. If it's nothing, then we'll all be relieved. And if it is serious, there'll be any number of options open to us for dealing with it, but only because we've gotten on top of it right away.

Wears down, gives in: All right, all right. If it'll make you happy, we'll go and see my doctor.

Close: Even if you're just doing it to calm my fears, I want you to know I appreciate it. You'll make the call, I'll go with you, and together we'll see exactly what we're dealing with and how your doctor plans to get you back to health again.

adaptations

This script can be adapted to express fear to a sibling about the health of her own son or daughter.

key points

- Don't let her live in denial over this, but don't shatter it either. Agree with her that this may be nothing to concern yourselves with, but emphasize that you both need to hear that from the doctor.
- Reinforce your willingness to see her through this; don't ever let her feel alone in it.
- The more her resistance persists, the more strident and unvarnished your words should become. Be as blunt as you have to be.
- If she expresses a willingness to see a doctor, even if it's just to appease you, be clear and get agreement about when the appointment will be made.

Discussing Division of a Parent's Estate with a Sibling

11

strategy

Dividing a parent's estate can be a source of comfort and warmth or suspicion and jealousy. If you anticipate problems dividing your parent's personal effects equally, take the lead by telling your sibling that this is something you must do, that you should agree on a plan for how to do it, that you're open to his thoughts on how to proceed, and that you have some ideas of your own you'd like to share. And, if in the course of the discussion it's clear there's one item your sibling is itching to get hold of, whether for emotional or material reasons, relieve his anxiety by telling him that yes, of course he can have it, but you still need to agree on an overall plan of action.

tactics

- **Attitude**: You are stressing evenhandedness, regardless of whether or not all siblings felt they were treated evenly by the parent when she was alive. You're genuinely interested in whether or not your sibling has a plan for proceeding.

- **Preparation**: Speak with your parent's religious leader—if they had one—to get an idea of what sort of emotional issues might get stirred up when you go to divide the property.

- **Timing**: It's often good to wait a while after someone has died, so that raw emotions can subside and reason can take over. If, however, you sense that a sibling is beginning to lay claim to certain pieces of property, it's time to have a family meeting.

- **Behavior**: You want to proceed rationally and calmly through what could be an emotionally vexing process. Be the voice of reason.

11. Discussing Division of a Parent's Estate with a Sibling

Icebreaker: Martin, as you know, Mom stipulated in her will that we divide her personal possessions between ourselves as we see fit, and I'm wondering if you have any ideas as to how you'd like to proceed with that.

Puts in a claim: Well, I can tell you right off the bat I want that grandfather clock of hers.

Feels uncomfortable: Gee, it feels kind of ghoulish picking through her things like that.

Doesn't know what to do: I've never done anything like this. I haven't a clue as to how to do it.

Indifferent: I don't really care how we do it, let's just get it over with.

Slow things down a little: I'm more than happy to let you have Mom's clock, Marty, but what I'm talking about now is just some sort of system for determining who will get what.

Reassure: I know what you mean. All of this stuff reminds us of Mom, and it can feel strange taking it into our own homes to enjoy. But she very much wanted us to have these things, rather than see them turned over to some stranger. I think it made her feel good to know we would take care of them, so why don't we figure out how we want to do that?

Make suggestions: Well, we could each make a list of the things we'd really like to keep for ourselves. We could then compare the lists. Anything that doesn't show up on both of them belongs to that person, and anything we both want, we can then discuss. Or we can each choose one item at a time. What are your thoughts?

Fixed on what they want: As long as I get the clock, that's all I want. And the piano. Otherwise, I don't really care.

Press the point: Right now, why don't we just agree to two things? We'll agree on a system for dividing Mom's possessions, *and* we'll make it fair for both of us. With that in mind, how do you want to proceed?

Agrees, but reluctantly: Well, I'm still not comfortable with it, but I guess this is what she wants. Okay, how do *you* suggest we proceed?

Chooses an option: Okay, let's take it one at a time and see where that gets us. But I'd like to go first.

Close: That's fine with me. You take whatever you'd like, and then I will do the same.

adaptations

This discussion could take place with a parent who is still alive, provided they are eager and willing to do so.

key points

- All you want is a fair way to proceed.
- If one particular item means a great deal to a sibling, let him have it. If there are two or three, tell him that those decisions can best be worked out after you've agreed on a plan of action.
- Don't let him shy away from doing this because he's uncomfortable. Feel free to wait a while, but remind him that this is something that needs to be taken care of.

Discussing Division of a Parent's 12
Financial Obligations with a Sibling

It's often difficult for us to acknowledge that our parents—who always took care of *us*—would ever turn the tables and need us to take care of them. We see it all around with older folks, and we may have even seen our parents care for our grandparents, but it's still hard for us to face that day in our own lives. And when we do, it's often made more difficult by the fact that looking after them might entail more than running errands, paying visits, or making phone calls; that it might also include helping with their bills. We might be in no hurry to part with that money, might have financial constraints of our own, and might wonder if other siblings aren't in a better position to help out than we are. We also might wonder how expensive this can get, and whether we're committing ourselves to a financial black hole that will drain us of our savings and security. The way we combat this is by taking the numbers head-on, looking at the parent's assets, income, and expenses, and projecting what is expected to happen to those numbers in the ensuing months. Having done that, siblings can then analyze their own financial situation as a group, noting where money can come from to close any gaps in the parent's budget and, if necessary, where *in all three budgets* (both siblings and the parent) cuts and alterations can be made. The idea here is to eliminate resentment and anxiety by ensuring that the load is shared equitably and the amount of assistance needed is equal to the amount you're able to collectively offer.

tactics

- **Attitude**: There's no sugarcoating this: it is a fact of life that must be taken head-on. Acknowledge that it may be a burden, but at least it's a shared one.

- **Preparation**: Draw up a budget for yourself and for your parent and be prepared to share this with your sibling.

- **Timing**: Have this conversation soon after one or both of you have spent time with your parent. Shortly after a birthday may be a propitious time.

- **Behavior**: Don't plead with your sibling as if you're asking for a favor. Present this as two adults facing an unavoidable—if unpleasant—reality.

12. Discussing Division of a Parent's Financial Obligations with a Sibling

Icebreaker: I think we both know that Dad's no longer in a position to take care of all of his bills. It's time we talk about how much we can each afford to do to help him out.

Anxious: I guess I saw this day coming, but frankly, I'm worried that his illness and expenses could cost us a fortune, and I just don't have that kind of money.

Estrangement: You know he and I haven't exactly seen eye to eye over the past few years. I guess I don't feel much like helping him out right now.

Feels they've already met their responsibilities: Actually, what with all the errands I've run for him and all the visits I've made, I feel like I've done enough for him already. I think it's someone else's turn.

Puts onus on you: Well, you have a lot more money than I do. I think you can handle it.

Cries poverty: Well, I'd like to, but I really don't have any money to spare.

Ease their fears: I can appreciate your concern; I'm concerned too. I think we can avoid putting ourselves in a hole financially if we sit down with our budgets and his and figure out just how much we can afford to contribute.

You appreciate how difficult your parent can be: I understand that. He can be very difficult, and I know things have been strained between the two you lately. But I suspect you'd like them to improve, and I have to believe he'll be grateful that you're helping him out.

Acknowledge their generosity: You have done a lot for him, and I know how grateful he is. But right now we're the only ones in a position to help him out so I'm afraid this responsibility is going to fall on our shoulders.

Show understanding: I certainly understand that money may be tight right now; we're both going to have to make some sacrifices, and if I have more cash at my disposal than you, I'm willing to chip in a little more for Dad. But we need to sit down with our budgets and his, and see what we can work out.

Wants to protect himself: Well, okay, but I want to set some limits of what I'll contribute right off the bat.

Feels especially put-upon: But why am I always the one helping him out?

Has his doubts: Well, he'd *better* be!

Still anxious: But . . . but what if we *can't* pay all the bills?

Offer reassurance: Once we sit down with the budget, I'm sure we'll be able to work out a limit as to what it should cost each of us to help him out.

Offer to shoulder some of the burden: I know it feels that way, because you *have* done so much for him. And I want you to know that if it looks as though I'm in a better position to help him out financially than you are, I'll be happy to do so.

Acknowledge his magnanimity: This is really very kind of you, *especially* with all the two of you have been through. I'll bet it helps a lot.

Offer some perspective: We don't need to think in terms of *whether* or not we'll be able to meet these bills but rather, between the three of us, *how* we'll meet them.

Cautious, but willing to go forward: Well, okay, I guess. But how do you want to start taking a look at this thing? I mean, I don't have a budget drawn up for myself, and I have no idea what *his* looks like.

Close: I've gone ahead and gathered information about his assets, his income, and his expenses. And I have some figures for myself as well. Why don't I give you copies of these, and you can use them as a blueprint to help put your own financial situation in print? We can get together next Saturday and begin looking at the big picture.

adaptations

This script can be adapted for use in discussing helping out with the financial obligations of a sibling who has special needs.

key points

- This can't be avoided; your parent is simply in no position to pay all of his own bills anymore.
- You're not worried about *whether* you and your sibling can work this out; you're merely determined to figure out *how*.
- You want to remind your sibling that your parent *does* have assets and income that can be figured into the equation.
- You want to divide the burden equitably; a sibling who's in a better position to help out should do so accordingly.

part 3

Life*scripts*

for talking to children

Informing a Young Child That Your Marriage Is Ending

strategy

There are a few things you need to keep in mind when you're engaging your young child in this difficult conversation. First, as the chart indicates, children receiving this information can explode in a burst of different emotions and concerns, often ricocheting back and forth between each other and following no logical progression. This is because the news is so momentous that they find it difficult to know how to process the information. Related to this is the fact that you'll need to pay particular attention to fashioning your responses not only to what they're saying but to what they're feeling. Although they have a wide range of questions, what they're primarily doing is expressing the fear, sadness, and anger that comes when a young person's life is summarily disrupted and a once-secure future is thrown into doubt. Do what you can to calm those fears, acknowledge that sadness and anger, and reassure, reassure, reassure the child that he is still loved and always will be. Finally, remember that it is going to take time for your child to fully assimilate what is happening. New patterns have to be established, new anchors dropped, old insecurities have to gradually fade and disappear. Set modest goals for this conversation: Use it to deliver the news, inform the child that things will in fact be different now, and assure him that you will both continue to parent and love him.

tactics

- **Attitude**: If you hold anger toward your spouse, don't show it here. Show the sadness that you feel over what is happening but also reinforce the fact that this is a decision the two of you have made and will stand by.

- **Preparation**: Speak with your spouse and decide between the two of you who is going to break the news. The other should be prepared to spend time with the child soon thereafter. Over the long haul, you may want to consult a child psychologist or read some literature regarding the short- and long-term effects of divorce on children.

- **Timing**: If possible, have this conversation at a time when the child will be able to spend a day or two with each of you, to begin to absorb what is happening, and then return to school, to begin to come to terms with the changes that are occurring.

1. Informing a Young Child That Your Marriage Is Ending

Icebreaker: I have some very sad news to tell you, son. Daddy and I have decided that we have to end our marriage, which makes us both very unhappy. You and I will continue to live here, but Daddy is going to live in an apartment very near to us so he and you can see each other every week. We both love you very much, and we wish we didn't have to do this, but I'm afraid we do.

Fear: Don't you love me anymore? Is Daddy still going to be my Dad? Are you going to leave too someday?

Sadness, tears: But I don't want you to break up! I want to keep being a family!

Anger: But this isn't fair! You're my parents, and you gotta stay together and take care of me!

Confusion: Will Daddy come live with us again? How often will I see him? Am I going to get a new Daddy? Am I going to have to live somewhere else, too? Don't you love each other anymore?

Begin to reassure him: We both love you more than anything else in the world, and we promise that we always will. You'll always be our son, and we'll always be there to look after you and care for you and help you whenever you need us.

Sad for you, too: It's real sad for us too, son. And we wish we didn't have to do this, but I'm afraid we do. But understand that we'll always be your parents, and you'll always be our son.

Absorb anger: You're right, you're absolutely right. This *isn't* fair. I know your Dad and I have let you down, and I'm awfully sorry about that. I wish we didn't have to do this. But even though we're going to live in separate homes, we'll both keep taking care of you.

Begin to explain: Your Dad and I don't have mean feelings for one another, but the hard thing is that I'm afraid we don't love each other enough to stay married. But we'll both always love you. You'll always be our son, and even though your daddy won't be living with us, the three of us will make good and sure that you get as much time with him as possible.

More confusion and uncertainty: But why can't you just stay together and take care of me?

Uncertainty about specific issues: But what about stuff like my birthday? And Christmas? And parents' night at school? Who's coming to parents' night?

Wants more immediate information: When is Daddy leaving? Am I going with him?

Reinforce his place in the family: Son, your dad and I both wish we could've gotten along better with one another so we didn't have to do this, but unfortunately we simply can't. We have to do this. We won't all live together, but we'll still take care of you just like we always have.

You will work that out: You'll be able to spend time with both of us to celebrate things like Christmas and your birthday, and you'll still get lots of presents. And if you want both of us to go to parents' night, or school plays or pageants, we'll both be there, I promise. You'll always have both of us as your parents.

Provide a schedule: Daddy's moving into his new apartment the day after to-morrow, which is Wednesday. On Friday, you'll go visit him and spend the weekend there. You'll have your very own bed-room, and the two of you will want to set it up. You may also want to bring some of your toys and stuffed animals over there for the weekend. On Monday, Daddy will bring you to school, and I'll pick you up and bring you back home here.

Still insecure: Are you sure you'll both still love me?

Begins to see the future: But it won't be the same, will it?

Close: Things will be different, and it will take us all a while to get used to them, but we will. And your dad and I will always love you. Now, your dad and I thought it would be a good idea if the two of you had a chance to talk about this, so you'll be spending tomorrow afternoon to-gether, just the two of you. You might want to start thinking if there's someplace special you'd like to go with him.

- **Behavior**: Give the child wide berth to vent his feelings, and receive them all with patience and understanding. Also, try to read his body language; offer to hold him if he'd like, but keep your distance if that's what he indicates.

adaptations

This script can be adapted to inform an older child that your marriage is ending, or to inform children that you and your spouse are going to enter into a trial separation.

key points

- For all the change that is about to ensue, the one thing that isn't changing is your or your spouse's love for the child, and your commitment to look after and protect him.
- Avoid recrimination and blame; don't ever force the child to stake out his allegiance.
- Don't expect the child to come away from this conversation resolved with what is happening.
- Have the next move planned out, preferably one that begins to introduce the child to the changes that will be occurring (such as going out to purchase furniture of his choosing for his new bedroom).

Telling a Child about a Relative's Serious Illness   2

strategy

There are a number of variations on this difficult theme; in some instances you're telling your teenage son about his great-grandfather's heart failure, in others you might be telling your six-year-old that a favorite aunt—perhaps your age—is unexpectedly sick with a debilitating illness. In some instances the illness will be terminal, in others the outcome is less certain. Regardless, though, in most cases you will find four recurring themes to be aware of: Giving the child a sense that there is something *she* can do to help their relative; assuring them the relative is being made as comfortable as possible; *not* giving them any false hope; and assuring them that their lives and their immediate family are still secure—that *you* are not ill nor planning to be anytime soon. The example I have chosen for this script is one of the more difficult but more common ones; telling a young child that Grandpa is very ill and may not live.

tactics

- **Attitude**: Be straight with your words but gentle with your tone; your children deserve to hear the truth, and to hear it as compassionately as you can present it.

- **Preparation**: First, get as clear an understanding of the severity of the relative's condition as you can possibly gather from him and the medical staff attending him. And second, ask him how they would feel about a visit from your child.

- **Timing**: Have this conversation early enough in the illness that the child does not have to "suspect" there is something wrong without being told. Also, have it on a weekend, when the child has the opportunity to make something (a card, a picture, a poem, etc.) for the ill relative.

- **Behavior**: Be patient to answer all questions. Encourage your child to ask more questions as the illness plays itself out. When speaking to her, touch her, perhaps keeping your hand on her arm. This is assuring to them.

2. Telling a Child about a Relative's Serious Illness

Icebreaker: Mary, your grandpa has become very ill, and while we don't know what's going to happen, we're going to do everything we can to try and help him get better.

Wants to play a productive role: Can I help too?

Solicit her help: You certainly can. Grandpa's spending a lot of time in bed, so he would love it if you would draw him some pictures for his room. You can also write him one of your poems, and we'd all like it if you would come with us to visit him. You really brighten up his days.

Takes it head on: Is he gonna die?

You don't know, but you won't skirt the question: He might die from this illness, but we don't know yet. What we do know is that it's very serious, and that right now he's resting comfortably; he's not in any pain.

Puts faith in you that everything will be all right: So you're gonna make him better, right?

Don't make promises you can't keep: I don't know yet if he's going to get better. But I do know we're going to make him comfortable and get him the best care he can have.

Seeks a point of reference: Is it like when I got the chicken pox?

Be frank, but not brutal: No, it's good bit more serious than that. He may come out of this okay, but there's a chance he may not.

Can't yet face the truth: But I don't want him to die! I want Grandpa to live forever!

Wants to get closer: Maybe Grandpa can move in with us, and we can make him better!

Expresses fear: I'm scared. I'm scared Grandpa's gonna die, and then I'm never gonna get to play with him again!

Inject some reality into the situation: Where he is now, in a hospital, is the best place for him to be, because he can get the care he needs from doctors and nurses. But your Dad and I are in touch with him every day, and now you're going to be helping him out too.

Join with her wishes: You know what? I wish he could live forever too. It makes me really sad that people we love have to get old and die, it really does. It hurts.

Join with their fears: I'm scared too, but we have to be strong right now and do everything in our power to make him comfortable and make sure he gets the care he needs. I'm really counting on you to do your part.

Begins to claim some control over the situation: I'm gonna go draw Grandpa a big sunny picture for his room, right now!

Fears closer to home: Mom, are you gonna die?

Assuage fears: Mary, I'm not planning on dying for a long, long, long time; not until you're all grown up, have kids of your own, and I get really, really old!

Tentative acceptance: Well . . . okay. I wanna go make grandpa a great big get-well card.

Close: He'll love that, Mary. Grandpa's very eager to hear from you, and we'll be taking you over to visit him very soon.

adaptations

This script can be adapted to tell an older child about a relative's illness or about the illness of a close family friend.

key points

- Make sure your child feels a part of the process of looking after the relative.
- Reinforce her personal sense of security.
- Assure her that everything possible is being done for the ailing relative.
- Feel free to share your own fears and anxieties with her, in moderation.

Telling a Child about a Relative's Death

3

strategy

This conversation is never easy to hold with a child, and certain variables will make it more or less difficult. The younger the child, the more difficult it can be to convey death to him. Also, the younger the relative who has died, the more difficult it is for a child to grasp that death is *largely* but not exclusively reserved for the very old; if my uncle dies, he'll wonder, how do I know my mom and dad won't? In addition, the nature of the death will influence how a child accepts this, because when a relative has been ill for some time, kids can begin to experience "anticipatory grief," but when the death is sudden, their whole world can feel uprooted in an instant. They lose their balance and bearing, and will rely even more heavily on their parents to see them through this strange and troubling time. With this in mind, don't be in too much of a hurry for your child to "accept" the death; be prepared just to plant the information in the child's mind and let him "catch up to it." Also, don't try to contrive answers to a lot of their questions; the questions are often simply expressions of rage, hurt, and confusion, and you do well to minimize what you say and maximize the love, comfort, and assurance you shower on your child. Finally, while the script shows a conversational progression, be prepared for your child to bounce around from one topic to another, one feeling to another, often returning several times to one. Above all else, keep reminding him that you are there for him, that you're not going anywhere, and that you will always be looking out for him. The example we cite is one of a young relative dying suddenly, and a parent breaking the sad news to a young child.

tactics

- **Attitude:** Look your child straight in the eye when you speak to him. Speak slowly, and try to maintain some body contact (holding hands, stroking his arm) while you speak. Once you deliver the icebreaker, give him plenty of room to react.

- **Preparation:** It's difficult to prepare for this, but if the relative has been ill, your best preparation comes in keeping the child apprised of the relative's worsening condition.

- **Timing:** Your best bet is to tell the child in the morning, at a time when he has no responsibilities, and when you and your spouse can spend the entire day with him.

3. Telling a Child about a Relative's Death

Icebreaker: Matthew, I'm afraid I have some very sad news to tell you. I just got off the phone with Aunt Ellie, who told me that Uncle Bert died suddenly and quietly in his sleep last night.

Disbelief: No way! We were just with Uncle Bert last weekend! He and I played checkers. He was fine!

Empathize: I know! I'm just as shocked as you are! It's awfully hard to believe, isn't it?

Tries to measure the loss: Does this mean I'm never, ever going to see Uncle Bert again? Never play checkers with him again?

Weighs the personal nature of the loss: But . . . but, Uncle Bert was my favorite! He can't die!

Blind anger: But that's not fair! It's not fair! He's a young guy, just like Daddy!

Don't try to dissuade: You're so right. It's *not* fair. This is just one of those really terrible, unfair things that sometimes happens to families. I'm really angry about it too.

Generalized fears: Is anyone else going to die?

Tears: (It's entirely possible that your child will say nothing, but break down in tears.)

Identify and uphold the personal nature of the child's loss: Oh, I know he was, Matthew. And y'know, I think you always had a real special place in Uncle Bert's heart, too. He really loved you.

Broader concern: What's going to happen to Aunt Ellie? Is she going to be okay?

Reach out (Extend your arms in an offer of embrace): Oh, I know how you feel; I feel the same way. Isn't it just awful?

Challenges you: I thought you said people die after they get really old.

This is rare and unexpected, but it does happen: You're right, that's what happens to most of us, and it's what will probably happen to Daddy and me years and years from now. But *sometimes*, someone will die at a younger age, like Uncle Bert did.

Begin to introduce some assurance into the child's life: Aunt Ellie has a lot of people who love her, like us. And we'll all look after her and make sure she's okay. I know it's going to mean a lot to her to know that you're thinking about her.

Highly unlikely: Well, that's awfully unlikely, Matthew. Uncle Bert was just real unlucky. This is why Daddy and I take such good care of ourselves, so we can do everything in our power to make sure we live a long, long time.

Be straight with them: Yes, Matthew, you're exactly right. You and Uncle Bert enjoyed some wonderful times together, and you'll have to remember them because you won't be seeing him again.

Curious about what happens next: Is Uncle Bert going to be buried in a hole?

Explain what will happen: There will be a service for Uncle Bert, where we'll say goodbye to him, and after that, his body will be buried in a cemetery. And later on, we'll put a gravestone there so we have a place to go when we want to and think of him.

Continued on page 192.

Resists the reality: But I don't want my Uncle Bert to be dead!

Empathize, and reinforce the reality: I don't either. I really loved him. It's going to be hard not having him around anymore, isn't it?

Anger at God: I know I'm not supposed to, but I *hate* God right now!

Support their feelings: You go right ahead and be as angry at God as you want to. You can even tell him so, if you want to.

3. Telling a Child about a Relative's Death (*Continued*)

Seeks permission: I can do that? I can tell God how angry I am at him?

Grant permission: Of course you can. Whenever you want.

Wonders about his own opportunity to grieve: Will I get to say good-bye?

Provide encouragement: Of course you will. I think it'll make you feel better, and I think it would mean a great deal to Aunt Ellie.

Reality begins to sink in: I'm sure gonna miss him.

Close: Yeah, me too. Maybe over the next few days you and I can write down some of our favorite Uncle Bert stories and give them to Aunt Ellie. I know it would make her feel better, and I bet Uncle Bert would want us to do just that.

- **Behavior**: Don't try to contradict or dissuade whatever emotions he might express, even if they contradict your own. Listen patiently, address his questions, and constantly buttress the fact that he is safe and that his immediate family is not in jeopardy.

adaptations

This script can be adapted to inform a child of the death of a close family friend.

key points

- Don't be afraid to show your own feelings; your vulnerability affirms your humanity in your child's eyes. It also gives him permission to feel whatever it is he's feeling.

- Gently reinforce the fact that this is a permanent change; that the relative is not coming back.

- If possible, try to impress upon the child that the death was not a violent or painful one.

- Ask the child if there is something he might want to do for the relative's surviving spouse, sibling, etc. This can prevent your child from feeling utterly powerless and vulnerable and at the same time infuse him with a sense of responsibility appropriate to his age.

Telling a Child about Her Own Serious Illness

4

strategy

Here is a chapter I hope nobody has to read, but if you do, keep in mind that there are three vital resources your child has to draw upon in this difficult time: her own grit and determination, the wisdom and compassion of her doctors, and the relentless support of her family. By doing this the child understands that while she may be up against something quite serious, she's not without help or hope. In addition, you want to walk a fine balance here with what you present to your child in the first conversation. You don't want to minimize the seriousness of the illness (she needs to know you're being straight with them, or she won't trust you later on down the road), nor do you want to give her more information than she can handle (which will leave her feeling overwhelmed and despairing). What she needs to know is that she's fighting something serious, that you don't yet know the limits of the illness, and that everyone who cares about her is going to have a role in her treatment and convalescence. Though circumstances can obviously vary widely, I've chosen to present a serious—but not necessarily fatal—illness to a young child who is old enough to talk rationally about it.

tactics

- **Attitude:** Be as calm as you can possibly be; you want to show the child that you are in control of yourself, so that the ensuing discussion can get to the business of what you're going to do about this, not simply how awful you feel about it.

- **Preparation:** Speak with the doctor first. Get a clear sense of what is involved with this illness. See if there is any family-friendly literature you can share with your child. Also, find out if anybody your child knows, or any celebrity she might be familiar with, has survived this illness (organizations like the American Cancer Society or the Leukemia Foundation can be helpful in this regard). Finally, ask the doctor if there are any recovering patients who would be willing—at a later date—to share their experiences with your child.

- **Timing:** Have this conversation as soon after the diagnosis as possible. Have it on a Saturday or other time when the child is not going to have to go right to school or otherwise meet any obligations.

4. Telling a Child about Her Own Serious Illness

Icebreaker: Rhonda, I spoke with your doctor today. She got your tests back, and you're fighting a pretty tough disease called leukemia. I'd like to tell you a little bit about what it means to have leukemia and how we're going to try and treat it.

Forthright: Is it going to kill me? Am I going to die?

Curiosity, naiveté: What does leukemia mean? Is it like a really bad cold?

Fear: All I know is that it hurts, and it scares me!

Free-floating fear: Are you gonna take care of me? Is the doctor gonna take care of me? When am I gonna get better?

Be straight: Listen very closely to what I have to say. Leukemia *is* a very serious illness, and we don't know yet exactly what kind you have, or *how* serious yours is. But you need to understand that your doctors are going to do everything in their power to make you better. I promise you that.

Educate: It's a bigger deal than a really bad cold. It goes into you and tries to weaken your blood. So the doctors are going to use their medicine to try and get the bad blood cells out of you. Your doctor gave me a booklet you and I will read that tells us a little more about what leukemia is and how they're going to treat you.

Acknowledge the fear: I know you're frightened, honey. There's something in your body that isn't doing what it's supposed to do, and that would scare any of us. But you're a real fighter. And I'm here, and I'll be with you for all of your care and treatment.

Offer comfort and assurance: The doctors are going to use everything they've ever, ever learned to try to make you all better. We don't know exactly what's going to happen yet, but I promise you I'm going to be with you every single time you see the doctor. You're not going to go through anything alone.

Preemptive fear: But what if I have the really horrible, worst kind? It *can* kill me, can't it?

Wonders what the procedure will be: What's going to happen now? Am I going to see a new doctor? Is treatment going to hurt?

Anger and fear: I don't want this stupid disease! Why does this have to happen to me?!? (Might show hysterics.)

Looking for reassurance: But when am I going to feel better? How long is it going to take before I'm better?

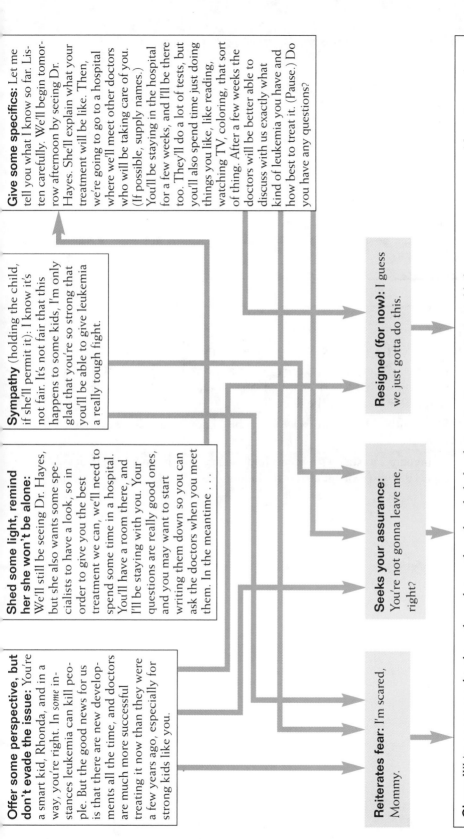

Offer some perspective, but don't evade the issue: You're a smart kid, Rhonda, and in a way, you're right. In *some* instances leukemia can kill people. But the good news for us is that there are new developments all the time, and doctors are much more successful treating it now than they were a few years ago, especially for strong kids like you.

Shed some light, remind her she won't be alone: We'll still be seeing Dr. Hayes, but she also wants some specialists to have a look, so in order to give you the best treatment we can, we'll need to spend some time in a hospital. You'll have a room there, and I'll be staying with you. Your questions are really good ones, and you may want to start writing them down so you can ask the doctors when you meet them. In the meantime . . .

Sympathy (holding the child, if she'll permit it): I know it's not fair. It's not fair that this happens to some kids, I'm only glad that you're so strong that you'll be able to give leukemia a really tough fight.

Give some specifics: Let me tell you what I know so far. Listen carefully. We'll begin tomorrow afternoon by seeing Dr. Hayes. She'll explain what your treatment will be like. Then, we're going to go to a hospital where we'll meet other doctors who will be taking care of you. (If possible, supply names.) You'll be staying in the hospital for a few weeks, and I'll be there too. They'll do a lot of tests, but you'll also spend time just doing things you like, like reading, watching TV, coloring, that sort of thing. After a few weeks the doctors will be better able to discuss with us exactly what kind of leukemia you have and how best to treat it. (Pause.) Do you have any questions?

Reiterates fear: I'm scared, Mommy.

Seeks your assurance: You're not gonna leave me, right?

Resigned (for now): I guess we just gotta do this.

Close: We're gonna see this thing through together; the whole family is going to support you and help you any way we can. Now, since we're seeing the doctor tomorrow, is there anything special you'd like to do today? We'll do whatever you want.

- **Behavior**: Turn on every facet of parental love and understanding you have at your disposal. Hold your child, let her get mad, let her punch, let her break down, let her ask any question she wants. Let her know that at this moment, your entire world is turned over to her for whatever she might need.

adaptations

At the risk of sounding as if I am minimizing an extremely important issue, this script _can_ be adapted to tell a child of the terminal illness of a favorite pet.

key points

- Don't minimize the seriousness of what she's up against.
- Reinforce the resources she has at her disposal.
- If she asks questions that can't yet be answered, let her know that this is information that will be clarified later. You might ask her if she wants to start making a list for the doctors.
- Show faith in the doctors; let your child know you believe in their abilities.
- Be prepared to stay with your child twenty-four hours a day, if possible, especially when hospitalization is required.

Discussing Potentially Damaging Relationships   5

strategy

This is a conversation you want to have with your child in his early teens, when he's old enough to understand that some relationships can get him into real trouble but that those relationships can nevertheless be extremely seductive. The most popular kid in the seventh grade may be the one who stole the principal's hubcaps. Your best bet, though, is to have this talk *before* any danger signs appear; before your son or daughter starts showing up with kids of dubious merit. The reason you want to jump the gun on this is because the real purpose of the conversation is to let your child know that although he's growing up, you will still wield the authority to monitor and regulate the friendships he chooses. And although you're likely to get a heavy dose of resistance from him, take some solace in knowing that deep down he still wants you to protect him from the dangers of his own world. So when a troublemaker offers him his first cigarette, if it's tough for him to say he doesn't want to smoke it, you at least give him an out by allowing him to tell the kid, "Look, if my folks get wind of this, I'll be grounded for a month, so I better not."

tactics

- **Attitude**: You are in charge, but you don't want to seem imperious. You want to make it clear that you will play as active a role in your child's choice of friends as you have to, but by the same token you want to see him exhibit the maturity necessary to make his own wise choices.

- **Preparation**: Discreetly sound out your child's teacher as to which children to watch out for, and ask the teacher to alert you should your own child start to exhibit any subtle but troublesome behavioral traits.

- **Timing**: This is a good conversation to have at the outset of a school year, especially if the child is entering a new school. Just prior to seventh grade is a logical juncture, because it signals the onset of adolescence and a move from primary to secondary school.

- **Behavior**: Speak with the child in his room. Let him feel comfortable. Don't raise your voice, threaten, or preach. Simply let him know that, for his own benefit, you will be keeping an eye on the kinds of relationships he seems to be drifting into.

5. Discussing Potentially Damaging Relationships

Icebreaker: John, it strikes me that some of the boys in your class are really good kids, but others look as though they might not be the best ones to be hanging around with. I think we need to be in general agreement regarding what kind of kids you're going to spend your free time with.

Insolent: They're *my* friends. Why should you care?

Defiant: You can't tell me who I can be friends with and who I can't. That's my business.

Believes he has it under control: Don't sweat it; I know who to hang out with and who to steer clear of.

Defensive/angry: Are you saying you don't trust me? Like I don't know who I should hang out with?

Establish control (I): You're right when they say they're your friends. But let me tell you why it matters to us. It matters because we need to know you're spending your time with kids who make for good friendships, not bad ones.

Establish control (II): It is your business. And it's ours as well. It would be irresponsible of us to let you spend time with a kid we think is going to make for a bad relationship, and we won't let that happen to you.

Feel him out: I think you're a really bright kid. Tell me some of the things you want to steer clear of in choosing your friends.

Deflect the anger: It's the bad kids I don't trust, because if *they* want to get into trouble, they usually know how to get others to go along with them.

Wants to pull rank: *Mom! Dad!* (extreme exasperation). I'm not a kid anymore. I'm thirteen years old. I can make my own decisions.

Wants to assure you: I'm gonna stay away from the kids who drink, or use drugs, or stuff like that.

Grant him limited authority: There are some decisions, like what you're going to wear to class or how late you'll sleep in on weekends, that you *can* come to on your own. There are also some, like whether you can stay home from school for a day, or what chores you're expected to do, that we're responsible for making. Others, like who you're going to be friends with or how late you'll stay out on a Friday night, we'll make together.

Offering some parental guidance: I like your thinking, but let me tell you my concerns, and why we're going to insist you stay away from certain kids altogether. Some kids will tell you that in order to be their friends you'll have to do what they do, or think the way they think. They may seem like good enough kids, but they'll want to pressure you to do things you might not want to do. Maybe it's spraying graffiti on the school, or stealing a candy bar. I don't want you to find yourself stuck in a situation like that, but if you do, I want you to feel as though you can back out of it by saying your parents won't let you participate in whatever's going on.

Rebellious: This is *so* unfair! All the kids get to pick who they want to hang out with, and their parents don't interfere.

Relenting: Geez, you're not gonna let this thing go, are you?

Offers assurances: Don't worry, I'll be cool. I'm not looking to get into any trouble.

Continued on page 202.

5. Discussing Potentially Damaging Relationships *(Continued)*

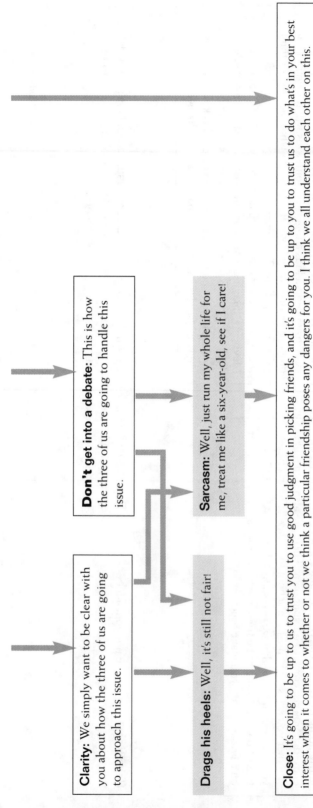

Clarity: We simply want to be clear with you about how the three of us are going to approach this issue.

Don't get into a debate: This is how the three of us are going to handle this issue.

Drags his heels: Well, it's still not fair!

Sarcasm: Well, just run my whole life for me, treat me like a six-year-old, see if I care!

Close: It's going to be up to us to trust you to use good judgment in picking friends, and it's going to be up to you to trust us to do what's in your best interest when it comes to whether or not we think a particular friendship poses any dangers for you. I think we all understand each other on this.

adaptations

This script can be adapted for use by a parent whose child is starting out in a new school district (possibly because the family has recently moved) and has not yet developed any friendships. It can also be adapted for use by parents whose children seem to be making friends with kids who they feel can be dangerous.

key points

- You want your child's choice of friends to be a cooperative one; one in which he makes the right choice based on his own common sense and the guidelines you have instilled in him.
- If need be, you will leave open the option of not allowing your child to associate with certain other kids.
- You're not looking for agreement on this, only obedience.

Discussing a Child's Trouble with Schoolwork

6

If your otherwise able child is suddenly having trouble with schoolwork, there are three things you can do to be sure she will resist all efforts of intervention on your part. You can preach to them about how hard she has to work, you can punish her for getting failing grades, or you can jump to conclusions as to why she's gone into this mysterious tailspin. If you do nothing more than avoid these pitfalls, you're already well on your way to getting her turned around. When she's having trouble in school, what she needs to hear from you is that you're on her side, you're open to listening to her problems without judgment, and you're ready to help her solve them. Now, assuming this is your first conversation with her about the schoolwork, be prepared to help her devise a plan for getting herself straightened out, but at the same time be equally prepared to hear that the roots of her difficulties are not necessarily academic.

- **Attitude**: You want to show concern but not anger. You also want to make it clear that this is a trend that must be turned around.

- **Preparation**: Speak with her teacher first, in confidence, if you'd like. Get a sense of what else might be going on in your child's life that you might not be aware of, and ask for tips on how to attack the problem.

- **Timing**: Have this conversation on a Friday afternoon so the child can relax over the weekend, knowing you're going to be working with her to rectify things.

- **Behavior**: Have the conversation in her room. Make it relaxed and amiable. Demonstrate a willingness to listen at least as pronounced as your willingness to speak.

6. Discussing a Child's Trouble with Schoolwork

Icebreaker: Alice, you seem to be having a rough time with your schoolwork lately. I think we need to talk about what sort of problems you're having. Then we can put our heads together and figure out how to get things back on track.

Dismissive: Look, the truth is, there's no real problem here. I'll be all right. Just leave me alone, okay? Don't bother me; I'll work it out.

Assert yourself: Your grades have slipped pretty considerably in the past month, but what has me even more concerned is the fact that you're putting less effort into your schoolwork. We—you, us, maybe even your teacher and guidance counselor—are going to figure out what the root of the problem is and then devise a plan for getting you back on track, and I want you to begin to give some thoughts as to what that plan should look like.

Self-denigration: The *problem* is that I'm stupid. I just don't "get" school anymore. I'm probably going to flunk everything!

Identifies the problem area, exhibits frustration: It's algebra! I go around and around and around with it, all the other kids get it, and I just can't figure it out to save my soul!

Empathize: When I was your age, it was chemistry. I was sure I was the only kid in my class who couldn't figure out the chart of the elements. The fact is, though, *every* student comes up against a subject that's tough for them, and for you it's algebra. But I have absolutely no doubt we can get you through this.

Begin to isolate the problem: We all know you're a smart kid, you've done well in the past, and you'll get things straightened out now. You know, the problem might not even be the schoolwork itself. A lot of times if there's something else bothering us, say, like a friendship breaking up or a disagreement with someone, it's difficult to concentrate on our work. Happens to me, in fact. I want us to work together to figure out exactly where the problem lies and how to go after it, but I also want to leave open the option of discussing it with your teacher

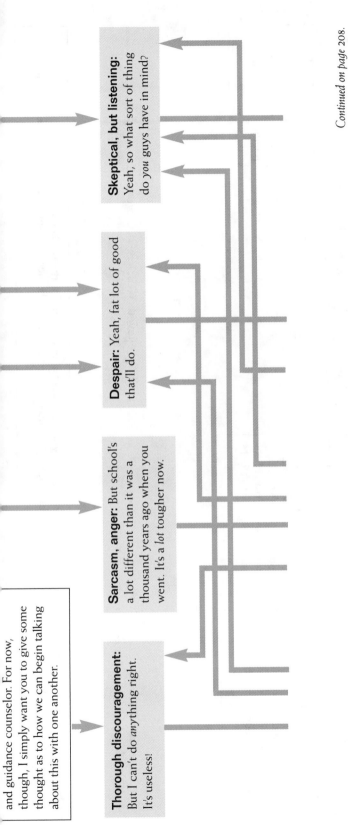

and guidance counselor. For now, though, I simply want you to give some thought as to how we can begin talking about this with one another.

Thorough discouragement: But I can't do *anything* right. It's useless!

Sarcasm, anger: But school's a lot different than it was a thousand years ago when you went. It's a lot tougher now.

Despair: Yeah, fat lot of good that'll do.

Skeptical, but listening: Yeah, so what sort of thing do *you* guys have in mind?

Continued on page 208.

6. Discussing a Child's Trouble with Schoolwork *(Continued)*

Offer a deal: You might be right, though I doubt it. So before we reach that conclusion, here's what we're going to do: We're going to get together with your teacher and your guidance counselor, devise a plan that makes sense to all of us—including you—to get you back on track, give it a couple of weeks, and then we'll get together again and see what kind of progress you're making. I'm going to call your teacher first thing Monday morning.

Deflect anger: You may be right about that, but the one thing that isn't different is that most students hit bumps in the road just like the one you're hitting right now, and they get over it by working with their teachers and parents to figure out what the problem is and how to solve it. That's what we're going to do. We'll meet with your teacher next week and come up with a plan of action that makes sense to all of us—including you.

Assert yourself and avoid her self-pity: I don't know what will come out of it, but I do know you're a whole lot happier when you're doing the kind of work you're capable of than you are now, and that's why we're going to get after this thing.

Give ideas, but include her: I don't know exactly what the plan will look like because I want you to have input into it as well, but next week we'll talk about it, maybe schedule a meeting with your teacher or counselor, and work something out. I believe you can be pulling yourself through this thing in a couple of weeks, and I'm willing to do whatever I can to help you.

Mildly relieved: Well, I guess it's worth a try.

Still (outwardly) discouraged: Well, I'll do it if you're gonna make me, but don't get your hopes up.

Close: What I want you to do now is get your homework done so you can forget about all this for the weekend and just enjoy yourself. Then, first thing next week, you and I will talk about what might be going on, how to correct it, and whether we want to include your teacher and counselor in our discussion.

adaptations

This script can be adapted for use with a child who appears to be putting too much pressure on herself to simply "get good grades."

key points

- There is a reason for your child's trouble, but you don't yet know what it is, so don't guess.
- She really wants you to help her, but may be afraid or ashamed to ask.
- You want to include her in the design of the game plan for correcting the problem.
- You are not *suggesting* to her that a plan be devised; you're *informing* her.

Talking to a Child about Birth Control

7

strategy

In this script I make certain assumptions without which the entire dialogue would be fruitless. We assume you and your child have had some conversations about sexual activity and responsibility, that you would have reason to believe your child may be sexually active, and that you are generally accepting of this. Having said this, there are three things you hope to accomplish with this talk: You want to impress upon your child the need to have informed advice about choosing a birth control method, you want her to be prepared ahead of time, and you want her to understand that your primary concern is for her safety, health, and well-being, all of which can be compromised by choosing a method that is not suited to her. In the case you are about to read, I'm choosing a conversation between a mother and a daughter in which the method of choice is the pill. I do this because the pill is safe, effective, and easy to use, but has hidden risks that require the steady monitoring of a qualified physician.

tactics

- **Attitude:** You are quite matter-of-fact about this. You don't see this as a moral issue but as an issue of personal responsibility. There is no question in your mind that if you and your child have tacitly consented to her being sexually active, she must make a reasoned choice about birth control.

- **Preparation:** Do some reading so you are informed about the choices, risks, and advantages of all your child's options (including both abstinence and "withdrawal"). Be prepared to argue for and against their merits.

- **Timing:** If possible, have this conversation when you think your child is starting to get involved with someone with whom she *may* have a serious, intimate relationship.

- **Behavior:** You want to let her feel free to share her thoughts, either with you or with someone else, such as her doctor or a guidance counselor. But you also want her to understand that you will not tolerate a lazy approach to this topic. You're relaxed and comfortable talking with her, but if need be you will be stern.

7. Talking to a Child about Birth Control

Icebreaker: You and I have had some very useful conversations about what "responsible sex" is all about, and I think it's smart to talk now about the importance of safe and effective birth control.

Uncomfortable topic: Um, actually, I'd rather not talk about this, if it's all the same to you.

You understand: I understand how this could be a difficult topic for you to discuss with me. You do, however, need to talk it over with *someone* who can be sure you're using the best method. Unless you can think of who you'd like that to be, what I'll do is arrange for you to speak confidentially with my gynecologist.

Already using a form of birth control: Don't worry, I'm already protecting myself.

Specifics: I'm really relieved to hear that, but I need to know you're using the best method for you. How, exactly, *are* you protecting yourself?

Knows everything there is to know: Not to worry, I know everything I have to.

Suspicious of ulterior motive: Are you trying to figure out if I'm having sex or not? Is that what this is about?

Ask for the information: That's good to hear. But I still need to know what *you* think is the safest and most effective method of birth control for you, if or when you have need for it.

Allay fears: I can understand why this might sound like I'm "sneaking up on you," but the truth is, whether you're having sex now or not, at *some* point you're going to have to know about this. So I need to know you're making the most informed decisions you can possibly make.

Counter proposal: I'll talk to my G.P. (general practitioner) the next time I see her, if that'll

Has sought out her own "expert" advice: I've talked to a couple of friends, I think I know

May not have thought about it: I honestly don't know what I'd use, to tell you the truth.

Speaks "with authority": If you must know, I happen to think the pill is the best form. It's easy,

Somewhat forthcoming: Well, for your information, I'm *not* having sex. But if I were, I'd take

make you happy.

what I'd use.

and it doesn't get in the way.

the pill. It's easy, and it doesn't get in the way.

Not quite good enough: I'll make a deal with you. If you don't want to discuss this with me, you can either schedule an appointment today with your G.P. *or* you can call your gynecologist and talk to her. Which would you prefer?

Needs to speak to an expert: You need to see if your friends' recommendations are the most suitable *for you.* You and I can talk about your options, or you can speak to your gynecologist. What would you prefer?

The need to plan ahead: I can certainly understand that. But I think you realize this is a decision you have to come to well before you're in a position of needing to use something. Do you want to talk about your options, and their various pros and cons?

Support, but question: I'm glad to know you've thought this out. What has your doctor said about possible side effects from the pill, or what to do when you temporarily have to stop taking it?

Digs heels in: I'm telling you, I don't *need* to talk to anyone else about this!

Will speak with a professional: All right, I'll talk to my gynecologist.

Agrees to talk: Yeah, I suppose we could talk about it.

Gives assurances: Yeah, we covered all that. I know what I'm doing.

Close; hold your ground, veil your threat: It's too dangerous and too easy for someone to make the wrong decision because they don't have all the information they need, so in order to continue to enjoy the freedoms we allow you, you're going to have to accept this responsibility. And if you don't want to talk with me about this, either you will call your gynecologist this afternoon to arrange an appointment or I will.

Close; reaffirm their thinking: You're really showing a lot of responsibility. Clearly you realize how important it is to avoid risk by making smart choices. And if you *do* have any questions about birth control, I hope you'll feel free to bring them to me if you wish.

adaptations

This script can be adapted for use between a father and son. It can also be used by a parent who has extremely strong feelings for or against a particular form of birth control.

key points

- This is not about whether or not your child is engaged in sexual activity.
- What you want is for her to be confident that she is using a method that is both effective and well suited to her, and that she convinces you that her confidence is well founded.
- If need be, you will exercise parental power to see to it that she takes this responsibility seriously.

Discussing a Child's Inappropriate Clothing or Appearance **8**

This is a topic most likely to arise in early adolescence, at an age when your child is needing to establish some distance between himself and his family, and is particularly eager to gain the approval of his peers. In other words, it is a time of real transition; he's not old enough to do whatever he wants, regardless of his parents wishes and expectations, but he is old enough to begin to experience the privilege and responsibility of his own decision making. If you push too hard against his assertion of independence, he's likely to resent you and find a way to make you pay later. On the other hand, if you give him carte blanche to dress and present himself as he wishes, you not only run the risk of letting him establish habits you might consider unseemly or even detrimental, but you also risk letting him believe you're relinquishing control over him altogether. What you want to do, then, is strike a balance that respects this special stage in life while at the same time asserting that you are the parents, he is a member of the family, and you are still the final arbiters over what will and will not be permitted.

- **Attitude**: Don't be punitive or judgmental. Don't say there's anything inherently "wrong" with the way he appears, but that you don't approve of it in your family. You're sympathetic to his needs to express his individuality, but you still insist on monitoring the extremes to which he will be allowed to take it.

- **Preparation**: Consult the child's teacher. Get a sense of what kids are wearing to school, what seems to be acceptable, and what different kinds of clothes represent. (Does a certain outfit or color scheme represent affiliation with a gang, for instance? Or are there ensembles for which your child would be unmercifully ridiculed?)

- **Timing**: This is a good conversation to have on the eve of a school vacation, so you and your child can alter his wardrobe, hairstyle, etc., with time for them to make a psychological adjustment to it before returning to school. The onset of summer vacation is good for this reason too.

- **Behavior**: You are not asking for him to change; you are informing him that he has to. On the other hand, you want him to understand that he has significant input into what the final product will look like.

8. Discussing a Child's Inappropriate Clothing or Appearance

Icebreaker: James, I'm afraid we're not altogether happy with some of the clothes you've been wearing lately, so we need to talk about making some changes.

Defiance: You can't tell me what to wear; I'll wear what I want to wear!

Conformity: But all the other kids dress like this! What do you want me to do, stand out like a sore thumb?

Appeal to justice: But that's not fair! You guys get to wear whatever you want, why shouldn't I?

Generalizes: You're always trying to tell me what to do. What don't you just leave me alone once in a while?

Assert yourself: I know you want to make these decisions for yourself without our interference, but one of the more miserable parts of growing up is having to do what your parents tell you to do even when you disagree with them. That means we have to reach agreement on things like the clothes you wear, the style of your hair, and how you present yourself in public.

Sympathize, to a point: I know a lot of kids dress in a way that we won't let you dress, and I suspect that may make you feel like you "stick out" in your crowd. I hope the friends you choose are big enough to not let that get in the way of your friendships.

Who said this is a democracy?: You're right, we decide how we need to present ourselves. That's a right all adults are expected to exercise, as you will when you grow up. For now, what we want to do is find a style of clothes and appearance that we'll approve of *and* you'll be happy with.

Stay on the point: If you'd like us to, we *can* tell you exactly what to wear, but what we want to do now is come to an agreement with you on how you present yourself in public.

Digs in his heels: You can't make me! This is what I wanna wear, and you can't make me change! I won't do it.

Laments: But they'll laugh me out of the gang. They'll think I'm a geek or something.

Fearful: But what if we can't? What if you won't let me wear any of the clothes I want? What if all the clothes you pick out are really nerdy?

Doesn't want to become a parent clone: You're just gonna make me dress like you do!

Stay in charge by presenting options: Okay, here's the deal. The way I see it, we have three choices. We can find clothes that both you and we are comfortable with. Or you can simply wear the clothes that we pick out. Or you can take on the privilege of wearing whatever you want by giving up other privileges, like TV time, or sleepovers at your friends' houses. Feel free to be angry at us, and I can understand why you would be, but those are your alternatives.

Offer some assurances: You're right, people do judge us based on the clothes we wear. So let's be sure we stay away from clothes people might think are "geeky." We'll also stay away from clothes that others might think are disrespectful, or that might be worn by someone looking to get into trouble.

Let him assert his individuality (and his youth): Let's agree that whatever clothes we look to buy for you, we don't choose ones that make you look like us unless you want to.

Still complaining: This is so unfair!

Wants further assurances: You better mean that!

Still anxious: But what if I don't like anything you like? Then what?

Close: This is what we're going to do: We will go to the store tomorrow, and I assure you I will be fair and reasonable. I expect the same attitude from you, because the more reasonable you are, the more slack I'm likely to cut you in terms of what I'll let you buy.

adaptations

This script can be adapted for use by parents wishing to discuss such things as body ornamentation, tattoos, body piercing, hair dyeing, etc. with their child.

key points

- You must recognize and respect his need to assert his individuality as a person apart from the family.
- You understand that this doesn't sit well with him, but you want to work with him to find a solution.
- You *will* resort to threats, if absolutely necessary.

Asking a Child about Potential Shoplifting

9

strategy

This is a critical issue that can also be used as a valuable opportunity. The assumption in this script is that by all appearances your child has broken the law and, if he's like most kids, will then try to lie his way out of it—not because he's inherently deceitful but because he's incredibly scared. You want to do two things: Impart to him the seriousness of the issue, *and* avoid rushes to judgment. Let him know this will not go overlooked, but also let him know that you'll grant him room to explain to you what motivated him to use such incredibly poor judgment. You won't use these as excuses, but by the two of you understanding what compelled him to do this, you will be in a better position to fashion a response that both punishes him for what he's done and lessens the likelihood of his doing it again. Finally, even if he deceives you out of fear, don't forfeit the opportunity to stress that you are as disappointed in his dishonesty as you are in his thievery.

tactics

- **Attitude**: You are stern but not hysterical. Remain evenly modulated, and give him ample space to talk. If there is an awkward silence in the room, wait and let him fill it.

- **Preparation**: If you have the time, speak to the desk sergeant at your local police precinct and find out if there is a special youth outreach officer who can give you additional tips on how to approach this with your son. They often have a keen understanding of the youth in your community, what drives them to misbehave, and what sanctions work well when they do. Also, of course, gather a much information as possible on the crime itself so you have some sense of just how implicated your child might be.

- **Timing**: You need to strike quickly, bringing this to your child's attention shortly after you've been informed.

- **Behavior**: Have yourselves sitting across from one another so that his attention won't wander. Maintain eye contact every time you open your mouth. Speak slowly.

9. Asking a Child about Potential Shoplifting

Icebreaker: Carl, I received a phone call today from the head of security at McTeague's record store, telling me that you and a couple of other kids may have been shoplifting there this morning. They're investigating it now. Do you know anything about this?

Offers an excuse: The truth is, I put some CDs in my pocket that I meant to pay for on the way out, but I forgot they were there. Honest!

You're not buying it: Why would you put them in your pocket, why would you forget to pay for them, and why would you not go back and do so after you discovered your mistake?

Stays with his excuse: I dunno, I guess I just left my brain at home or something.

Tries to recast it: Oh we were just goofing around, we were gonna return the tapes tomorrow and let Mr. McTeague know it was just a joke.

Press the seriousness of the issue: It doesn't appear as a joke to the store owner. He's looking at it as kids stealing his merchandise from him, and he may want to prosecute. This is quite serious.

Looks for an out: We'll go and talk to Mr. McTeague tomorrow, explain the whole thing. I'm sorry he feels that way.

Tries to pass the buck: Y'know, the kids I was with may have done something I don't know about. But I didn't do anything.

Challenge him to expand on this: What makes you think other kids may have been involved in something?

Tries to pass the buck: There were kids in the store the same time I was; maybe they did something stupid like stealing some CDs or something. I don't know.

Panics, stonewalls: I don't know what you're talking about. I don't think I was even *in* McTeague's this morning.

Give him an out: Think real hard now, because they tell me they can see you on the store's videotape. Is it possible you were in there, maybe briefly, and forgot?

Takes your offer: Y'know, come to think of it, we might've dropped in there for a minute or two. But I didn't steal anything.

He has to take responsibility: In other words, for whatever reason, you walked out of the store without paying for the CDs, and then tried to hide the truth from me. Now you'll have to make amends. How do you suggest you do that?

Amend his plan: I think it's a good idea for you to talk to him, but you and I will go together, without your friends. You'll explain that you did do this, you'll apologize, and you'll ask him if there's any way you can make it up to him. Whatever he chooses to do at that point will be up to him. After that, *we'll* talk about why this happened and what needs to be done to make certain this doesn't happen again.

Provide a rationale for the accusation: So you're saying the evidence—the store's videotape, the security guard—will show you to be in the clear?

Ask for his thoughts: What do you suppose this complaint is about?

Confession, of sorts: I dunno, maybe we were messing around a little bit. We didn't mean any harm though.

Fearful: What's going to happen then?

Close: There are two things that happened here that disturb me deeply: your stealing and your lying. This is very serious, and I'm concerned enough about you that before I decide what to do, I'm going to talk to some experts about how best to keep this from happening in the future.

adaptations

This script can be adapted for use if a schoolteacher has accused your child of being a part of a group who bullies other children.

key points

- You're not initially accusing him, but you're telling him he's been accused, and must answer for himself.
- Leaven your anger with patience; only that way can you use this as a learning opportunity for your child.
- Let him have a say in how he thinks he should rectify the situation, but ultimately decide for yourself how to handle it.
- After the initial crisis passes, give serious thought to employing a family counselor to help sort out the underlying issues and devise a strategy for preventing this from happening in the future.

Criticizing One Child's Treatment of Another 10

Siblings present us with one of the most predictable and exquisite examples of a love-hate relationship we'll ever find. Fiercely protective of each other, they're also sworn enemies. They'll play and laugh and eat and work together, bathe and hear bedtime stories as toddlers together, and sow the seeds of a relationship that will last a lifetime. They'll also squabble, sabotage, and haunt each others' waking day. If you see this in your family, congratulations, they're normal. But sometimes a line is crossed; bickering becomes incessant, barbs are tossed that *really* hurt, one child bullies another, perhaps fists are even tossed. When your kids' typical skirmishes begin to escalate in tone or frequency, it's time to intervene. Begin with the one who is presenting the most offensive behavior, but keep in mind that arguments between siblings are dances, almost always done in tandem. What you want to do is threefold: Let the child know that the behavior has to stop, let him know you're willing to listen to his complaint about his sibling, and let him know they'll both be given a full opportunity to air their gripes for the purpose of bringing the problem to a resolution. In other words, first stop the offending behavior, then dig into its root causes.

tactics

- **Attitude:** Be firm in your insistence that you will not tolerate the mistreatment you're witnessing. At the same time, show openness to the child's point of view.

- **Preparation:** Discreetly ask parents of your child's friends if they've seen any change in their kids' behaviors. Get a sense of whether the mistreatment is directed only at a sibling, or if there is a wider pattern of misbehavior going on.

- **Timing:** Have this conversation soon after the offending behavior manifests itself, but at a time when heads are cool and problems can be discussed rationally.

- **Behavior:** No finger-pointing, no accusations. Show patience and tolerance. Let the child know that the solution to this problem is negotiable, but your expectation of their behavior is not.

10. Criticizing One Child's Treatment of Another

Icebreaker: Peter, we need to talk about something. I'm not happy with the way you've been treating your sister lately, and it needs to change.

Passes the buck: But she's always hanging around when my friends come over, she won't leave us alone, and she won't stay out of my room. She's really bugging me.

Generalized persecution complex: You're always getting on my case because I'm older! Why don't you criticize her once in a while?

Tries to minimize the problem: Aw, I treat her all right. I know I treat her better than a lot of kids my age treat their younger brothers and sisters. She's just a crybaby.

Use this as a starting point: I figured there might be things she's doing that bother you. Do you think it would help you if we talked them over with the two of you?

Be specific: Right now I'm talking to you about something specific. I don't like the way you're treating your sister. That's what I'm concerned with right now.

Define your discontent: Let me be specific about what I see that bothers me. I've seen you make fun of her in front of your friends, and yell at her when she's asked you for a ride. I've also seen you belittle her at the dinner table. These are the things that aren't okay.

Conversation stopper: Fine, if you don't like the way I'm treating her, I'll just stay away from her for good, and you tell her to stay away from me, okay?

Wants details: What do I do that's so bad?

Sarcasm: Okay, fine. From now on, anytime she wants to hang around with my friends and bother us she can, and I won't do anything about it.

Stubborn and uncommunicative: There's nothing to talk about. She's my sister, she's a pest, and I'm stuck with her. Case closed.

Protect other child, offer conditions: That's not going to happen because you and your sister both have rights in this family. If what you're interested in is having her stay away when your friends are here, and if you have other disagreements with her, they can be worked out. We can discuss this as a family and reach an agreement we can all live with.

Insist on working it out: Listen carefully to what I have to say. You and your friends have a right to your time together, and you have a right to a life without your little sister interfering in it. We can work that out. But if that's what you really want, it will mean talking it over as a family, setting up some new rules for how the two of you are to behave toward one another, and making sure you both stick to them.

Doubtful: Well, I don't see what good that'll do. She'll just keep bugging me.

Willingness to negotiate: Well, I'll talk about it if she will, but you gotta tell her to stop pestering me!

Close: Here's what's going to happen: This Saturday we'll get together as a family, listen to what both of you have to say, listen to what we expect from both of you. We promise they'll be fair. In the meantime, I will tell her to stay away when your friends are here and stay out of your room, and you will stop picking on her or making fun of her. I expect that's clear enough.

adaptations

This script can be adapted for use when your child is mistreating another child at school or play.

key points

- Chances are this behavior is not going to go away any time soon unless you intervene.
- Let the child know there is probably culpability on the part of both parties.
- If appropriate, remind the child that more patience and tolerance is expected of older children.
- Remind him that if he has a problem with a sibling, it's always best to bring it to a parent for adjudication.

Telling a Child to Clean Up Her Room

11

In this script, there are two tactics that will spell sure defeat for you. First, don't present it as a request. There is not a child on this earth who will gladly suffer you on this one. And second, don't expect your child to be anything but irritated with you. You don't win her vote for parent of the year with this. Still, you want to be sensitive to how she's hearing what you're saying. Her room is the private domain she's chiseled out of a home she otherwise has to share with others, and the older she gets, the more she treasures that personal space. When you tell her to alter it, she can feel invaded, as though there is *nothing* she has jurisdiction over. For this reason, you have to be both clear and convincing as to why you're telling her to do this. It's not enough for you to want her room to look as neat as yours, or to "teach her discipline or orderliness." Instead, you have to show how her private actions in her private space have consequences for the rest of the family.

- **Attitude:** You're quite resolved about this. The room must be attended to. But you're also eminently reasonable and want the child to understand your reasoning.

- **Preparation:** Make sure the rest of the house is fairly orderly before you bring this up. It bolsters your case.

- **Timing:** Wait until the room is sufficiently messy that it's beginning to interfere with the child's life. Things are misplaced. Homework can't be found. A slice of last month's pizza has sprouted a colony of something or other on a plate under the bed.

- **Behavior:** Have this conversation in the child's room but don't be condemnatory or impatient. Stay even-tempered, relaxed, patient, and persistent.

11. Telling a Child to Clean Up Her Room

Icebreaker: Karen, you'll need to keep your room cleaner and more organized from now on. The mess makes it hard for you to find things you need, and the dirty clothes you leave lying around can spread germs to all of us.

Claims "turf": But it's *my* room, and *my* stuff. Why can't I keep it the way I want?

Offers half a loaf: Look, I'll just keep the door closed so you don't have to see it, okay?

Generalized anger: You're always telling me what to do! I'm not a baby anymore!

False promise (you've heard it before): Oh, I'll clean it tomorrow. Or some-thing.

Be reasonable, and be specific: Let me be clear about the problem. When things are strewn everywhere and you can't find your homework or your sneak-ers or your hairbrush, I wind up having to look for them with you, and that slows all of us down. And if there are dirty clothes left around, we all run the risk of getting sick. It *is* your stuff, but the way you treat it is starting to affect all of us, which is why you have to take better care of your things.

Deflect anger: You're angry because I'm asking you to do something you don't want to do. But if I were to treat you like a baby, I'd go in and straighten it up my-self. You're a responsible girl now, though, which is why I'm counting on you to do this yourself.

Push for an exact time: Unless you have something important to do, I want you to take care of it now. If there is something you have to do, let me know what it is, and before you do it we'll agree on a time for you to take care of the room, either later today or first thing tomorrow.

Tries to draw others into it: Why don't you ask the others (other children) to clean up *their* rooms?

Begrudging okay: Jeez, all right, if you're gonna keep bugging me about it I guess I have no choice.

Still resistant: I just don't see what the big deal is anyway.

Has an excuse: Well, I *do* have some things to do. I need to make a bunch of phone calls. I'll do my room another time.

Arrange a time: Fair enough. Let's arrange a time.

Adolescent vagueness: Um, I'll get to it this weekend. Sometime.

Stay to the point: What matters right now is my concern about your room and your need to address it. I expect you to take care of this now so that we don't have these problems again in the future. Any questions?

Close: Here's what you'll do, then. Tomorrow morning you'll get up and have breakfast. After that, you'll take care of the room. When it looks to me like you've taken care of the problems we've talked about, you'll be free and clear to do whatever you want with the rest of your weekend.

adaptations

This script can be adapted for use with a child who leaves her belongings in a den, study, playroom, backyard, or other shared space in the family.

key points

- This isn't just a matter of "cosmetics." The room has to be straightened up in order to be functional.
- Agree upon a time—preferably in the next twenty-four hours—and make sure it's adhered to.
- Avoid tangents; don't get into an argument about how put upon the child feels or whether or not you're as hard on the other kids in the family.
- Be ready to offer plenty of praise and reinforcement when it's done.

Telling a Child He Is Grounded   **12**

Three things are particularly helpful to a parent who's doling out punishment. First, make good on your threats; before a child violates an established rule, let him know what the punishment will be and then follow through on it. Second, make sure the punishment is proportionate to the "crime"; you don't want to take away his car privileges for a month simply because he forgot to make his bed this morning. And third, make the punishment fit the offense. By this, I mean if a child spends money on something he wasn't supposed to, suspend his allowance. If she sneaked candy into her room after hours, take away desserts for a week. If he fails to come home on time, or goes somewhere he isn't supposed to go, ground him. In other words, don't make punishment arbitrary; make sure the child understands the connection between what he's done wrong and what you're taking away from him. In the script that follows, the assumption is that a young adolescent boy was due home from a party at 11:00 P.M. and, without phoning, didn't come home until well past midnight.

tactics

- **Attitude**: Your voice isn't raised; you're thoughtful and patient. You want the child to understand why you're imposing this punishment at this time.

- **Preparation**: Spouses should discuss the terms of punishment beforehand, and even if there are disagreements, once you've chosen what it will be, you must present a united front.

- **Timing**: This should be dealt with almost immediately. If the offense occurs at night, be prepared to announce your punishment the next morning.

- **Behavior**: Show an enormous amount of resolve in the face of what might be a withering attack on your sense of fairness and reasonableness. No matter what the child says to try to wear you down (flattery, bribes, tantrums), keep coming back to the fact that your mind is made up and the punishment stands.

12. Telling a Child He Is Grounded

Icebreaker: We've discussed your punishment, Steve, and we've decided the most appropriate thing to do is ground you for two weeks. That means you can go to school and to practice, but then you must come straight home and stay here. It also means you'll be home for the next two weekends. You may have friends come over here on Saturday and Sunday if you wish.

Blind anger: You guys are so unfair! What are you trying to do, ruin my life?! Why are you doing this?

Sees it as too strict: Oh, c'mon, other guys missed curfew, and their parents aren't grounding them!

Wants to negotiate with you: No, no! Anything but grounded! Cut off my allowance or take away TV or something, but please don't ground me.

Acknowledge anger: Look, we didn't expect you to be thrilled with this, just as we weren't thrilled with your coming home so late last night. So if you want to be angry with us, that's okay. But the punishment will stand, and your best bet is to accept that, put in the two weeks, and be done with it.

Acknowledge that it is strict: It is a strict punishment, but the reason for that is that we need to impress upon you the seriousness of what you did. Our hope is that in the future this will make you better about getting home on time.

Explain your rationale: Maybe it will help if you understand our reasoning. As you grow older, we give you more privileges, all of which carry more responsibility. When you fail to live up to that responsibility, we suspend that privilege long enough for you to come to terms with how important it is.

Self-pity: Man, this really stinks! I swear I'm the only guy I know who's ever been grounded. Thanks a bunch!

Bargains with you (I): How about "time off for good behavior"? I could help with the dishes, maybe do some extra yard work.

Bargains with you (II): Okay, but there's this really big dance next Saturday night that *everyone's* going to. Can't I go to that and then get an extra day stuck on at the end?

Hold your ground: You're a smart kid, so I think you'll learn your lesson this time. The last thing in the world I want is to have to do this again, especially because next time we'd have to be even stricter. My hunch is you'll make this your first and last grounding.

Begins to resign himself: These are going to be the longest two weeks of my life.

Close: Here's the deal: This punishment starts today. Two weeks from today, if there haven't been any problems, you're free to go out and resume your same privileges, same curfew, same rules. This is harsh, but it's also fair.

adaptations

This script can be adapted for use any time a strict punishment is warranted, provided the content of the punishment is tailored to coincide with the offense the child has committed.

key points

- You aren't coming at this rashly. You've given it a good deal of thought.
- Both parents are in agreement on the punishment.
- It's helpful for the child to understand why you've chosen this form of punishment.
- You don't deny that it's strict, but you have no intention of wavering.

Turning Down a Child's Request   **13**

If you want to get out of this conversation alive, keep two things in mind. First, no matter how reasonable you'll be, your child is going to loathe, detest, and resent you for it. And second, she's entitled to an accounting of your thinking. You're depriving her of something that—I assume—she feels entitled to and desirous of. Give her the logic behind your thinking, and her anger and disappointment will still boil over but will, in time, dissipate. The example I cite here is of a girl, say, in mid-adolescence, who has come home from school on a Friday afternoon and asked to attend a rock concert at the local auditorium that night. The plans are vague, and the parents are wary.

tactics

- **Attitude**: Let her know there is no joy in turning her down. Express your own disappointment. And let her rant if that is her wont.

- **Preparation**: Here again, parents have to be in agreement on the decision and present a united front. Also, be prepared to explain the logic of your thinking in excruciating detail to your child. She probably won't buy it at the moment, but later on down the road she'll appreciate your thoughtfulness and fairness.

- **Timing**: The child is waiting expectantly for you to grant her her wish, so you owe it to her to announce your decision as soon as you've committed to it.

- **Behavior**: You give her plenty of room to vent, bargain, and plea, all the while standing by your decision not to allow her request.

13. Turning Down a Child's Request

Icebreaker: Alison, I'm afraid we can't let you go to the concert tonight because there are too many uncertainties surrounding your plans.

Pathetic begging (you may get a few rounds of this one, too): Oh, but I'll promise to be good, and I promise I'll come right home after the last number. Please? *Pleeeeeze?*

Let her know her entreaties won't work: We can't. We trust you to make smart decisions on your own, but tonight you may be in a dangerous situation that you have no control over, and we're not going to risk that.

Wants clarification: Like what? What are you so uncertain about?

Clarify: That's a fair question. The last time there was a rock concert at the auditorium, fights broke out, and we don't know anything about security provisions tonight. We also don't know a number of the kids you planned to go with, and we don't know anything about the girl who's supposed to be driving you. These are not insignificant issues. Next time, call this to our attention earlier.

Anger (you actually may get a few rounds of this): I can't stand you! You never let me do anything! Ever!

Abscrb anger: Look, to tell you the truth, I don't expect you to feel anything but boiling anger toward us right now. I know this isn't a popular decision on our part, and I'm sorry it couldn't work out this time.

Will feel left out: Oh, but all the other kids are going, why can't I?

Stay with your argument: As I said, we have too many questions—particularly about logistics and safety issues—that you can't answer right now. We have to say no this time.

Risks dropping a peg in the social order: I'm gonna be the only girl who doesn't get to go tonight, and everyone's gonna think I'm a jerk. Thanks a lot!

Accuses you of bad faith: You just don't trust me, that's all! You don't trust your own daughter.

Surrender, camouflaged as unvarnished hostility: Well, thank you both very much for ruining my life! I'll be in my room, unless you think *it's* too dangerous.

Close: Listen to me very carefully. The next time something like this comes up, you need to realize what *we* need to know in order to give you permission to go. So be ready. And give us a little more notice than two hours. Because that's how *we will* be able to permit you to go to anything like this.

adaptations

This script can be adapted for use in telling a child she must wait—possibly indefinitely—for something she's asked for.

key points

- You want her to hear your thinking so she understands that you feel it's in her best interest that you turn down this request.
- Be prepared for an overflow of emotions. The child may say nasty things she doesn't mean. Don't rise to the bait. To the best of your ability, let them pass.
- Let them know the circumstances under which you *would* grant her request in the future.

Criticizing a Child's Work on Chores

14

strategy

If a child is slacking off in doing his chores, keep in mind that he's probably either bored of them, resentful of them, or both. The trick in getting him to do a better job is to acknowledge that this may well be the case, and his attitude is understandable, but he has to do them just the same. So stroke his ego a little; tell him the family counts on him to do his work. Let him know that the chores you give him are a sign that he is growing up and shouldering more responsibility. And by all means *don't* give him the "You don't begin to know how much harder I had it when I was your age" speech. That will only deepen the resentment. Finally, reassure him that you trust in his ability to do a good job, that you have confidence in him and respect for him. Sometimes that alone is enough to compel him to put more effort into it.

tactics

- **Attitude**: Criticize without being critical. Show concern for the fact that the work isn't getting done right, and inquire as to whether the child is having a problem with it that you can help with.

- **Preparation**: When you notice the work slipping, give him a few chances to rectify it on his own. After two or three poor performances, you're ready to discuss it.

- **Timing**: Have this conversation on a Friday evening so that you're prepared to work with the child the following day to get him back on track.

- **Behavior**: Make this a private conversation with the child; no other siblings within earshot. Show sympathy by nodding knowingly to the complaints he offers, feed that sympathy back to him, but explain to him that you nevertheless expect him to maintain a certain standard in his work.

14. Criticizing a Child's Work on Chores

Icebreaker: Peter, I'm a little disappointed in the job you've been doing on the lawn lately; we really count on you to take good care of it for us, and I know you're capable of doing a better job if you put more care into it.

Whining, argumentative: Why do I get stuck with all the hard chores around here? How come no one else has to cut the grass?

Feels self-defeated: Heck, I can't do anything right. I can't cut the grass without screwing it up! I'm sorry.

Legitimate problem: I know I've slipped up, but now that I have baseball practice I don't have the same amount of time I used to have, so I have to rush through it.

Deflect anger: Yeah, I know what you mean. I never liked the chores I had to do when I was a kid either. And I especially hated doing the lawn, so I understand how you feel. But we all have chores, and you're the only one in the family I really trust to do this right.

Be supportive: I know chores can be a real drag sometimes, but let me tell you something. I've seen you work, and when you really put your mind to it, I don't know anyone who can do a better job with that lawn than you can. The family really needs you to do this work for us, son.

Show consideration: I see what you're saying. Your schedule's a lot tighter now. You still need to take care of the lawn, and we still need you to do a good job on it, so maybe we have to take a look at that schedule and see where we might be able to pry up a little more time. Can I help you with *that?*

Generalized complaints: It's just such a big job. It takes so much time. And it gets boring. Can't someone else do it for a while?

Resistant: I don't know that I have any more hours in my week. Can't I just let it slide for a little while?

Close: Here's what we'll do. This Saturday, when we both have plenty of time, we'll get out into the yard. You'll do the lawn, and I'll take care of other chores around the house. If you hit any snags or have any problems while you're mowing, let me know, and I'll help you out. Then afterward, we'll sit down and make out a schedule for you so you have enough time to do everything you have to do and want to do.

adaptations

This script can be adapted to introduce a new and particularly onerous job—say, scrubbing out the trash cans or cleaning up after Rover—to your child.

key points

- You need him to do this job. It's not a form of punishment; it's his unique contribution to the family.
- You're willing to help him figure out a way to do the job better.
- You have assigned this task to him because you have faith in him.
- There's no getting around the fact that some jobs are simply tedious and have to be endured.

Bringing Up a Child's Bad Hygiene **15**

strategy

There are two things you can count on *not* getting from this conversation: admission, and agreement. This is an extremely sensitive topic for your child, and the last thing in the world he wants is to have to acknowledge not only that his hygiene could stand some improvement, but that it's *noticeable.* You know how easily your child gets embarrassed; believe that if you mishandle this one, he'll remain red-faced and humiliated for the better part of his adolescent years. How to avoid this? A couple of ways. First, disguise your concern in the form of a new product—say, a soap especially designed for teenage skin—that you'd like him to try and that you wish existed when you were his age. Also, as you engage the topic, don't talk about his hygiene per se, but that of kids in his age range, including his friends. And finally, when you've said your piece, assume the message has been heard and heeded, if not acknowledged. Then, for heaven's sake change the topic!

tactics

- **Attitude**: Be extremely casual and nonchalant about this. Bring it up almost as an afterthought.

- **Preparation**: Consult your child's doctor or a dermatologist to see what specific product might be useful for the child to try—even if all he needs is more frequent baths.

- **Timing**: This conversation should be conducted in private by the parent of the child's sex. Hold the conversation shortly before the child will be going out to some social function where he'll need to prepare himself anyway.

- **Behavior**: You are a teacher here, giving an informal, almost off-the-cuff lecture about how our bodies change as they develop. This is a good conversation to have when you're driving the car and the child is your passenger; you can convey informality by the mere fact that you're doing something else besides talking to him, you have his ear, and when you've made your point, you can quickly jump to something else.

15. Bringing Up a Child's Bad Hygiene

Icebreaker: I picked something up at the store today that I'd like you to try tonight. It's a special soap, designed specifically for kids your age. I'm anxious to know what you think of it. I really wish they had something like this when I was your age.

Indifferent, dismissive: Huh, oh, whatever.

Gently press your point: Have you or your friends ever heard of this product before, or products like it?

Embarrassed: Gee, this is a pretty embarrassing subject. Can we please not talk about it?

Empathize: Yeah, I feel a little funny talking about a personal topic like how to keep my body clean. So let's not make a big deal of it. Changing our bathing habits is just something that goes along with how our bodies change, that's all.

Defensive: Are you saying that I smell, or that I'm dirty?

Explain yourself: No, not at all. I guess what I'm saying is that as we get older, we have to take care of our body differently. You're at a very active age right now, and your body is also going through a lot of changes. So this is a time when you and your friends have to pay more attention to things like washing and bathing.

Questions the efficacy of the product: What if I don't like this stuff?

Defensive: What's wrong with the soap I use now?

Oblivious: Uh, no. I mean, it's not the kind of thing we talk about, y'know what I mean?

Patience: Yeah, I suppose that makes sense. Still, seeing as how you're now at an age when your body's changing so you have to do things like bathe more often, I'll be curious to see if you think this soap works well for you.

Agrees, if only to shut you up: Yeah, well, give it here. I'll try it. Let's just drop it then, okay?

Reiterate your case: The soap we use now is mild enough for little children, so it doesn't have the strength to be effective for someone of your age and level of activity.

Open to options: Well, I think the idea behind it is a good one, because all kids your age need to be paying closer attention to your hygiene, bathing more, that sort of thing. So if you don't like this, we can do one of two things. We can look for another product, or we can ask your doctor if she has any ideas.

Skeptical: Well, I have my doubts, but I'll give it a try if that's what you want.

Close: I know stuff like proper hygiene is pretty boring to think about, so I'm glad you're willing to do this tonight. I'll be interested to see how it holds up after a day of activity.

adaptations

This conversation can be adapted for use with a child who needs to take better care of his clothes.

key points

- Generalize; this is not something unique to your child but common in his age group.
- If he seems embarrassed, acknowledge that it's a touchy subject for you, too.
- Don't push your point.

Bringing Up a Child's Bad Manners 16

strategy

This is one script you don't "negotiate" with your child. How she behaves among her friends—assuming no one is getting hurt—is pretty much her business. But when her behavior in other social settings (including within the family itself) is boorish or out of line, it's time to impose your authority by telling her what you expect of her, and why you expect it, hoping that she understands, but insisting upon it even if she doesn't. You press this point for two reasons. One, the "rules of engagement" with adults or family members are different than with her friends, so what's acceptable in one circle is taboo in another. And two, this is training for when she begins to come of age and assume the mantle of responsibility that comes with adulthood. Good behavior in difficult settings is the social equivalent of broccoli at dinner: you don't expect them to like it, or even accept why it's good for them in the long haul. You simply expect them to do as you tell them.

tactics

- **Attitude**: If you have to raise this issue, it means it's already been a problem in the past. Be matter-of-fact with them; instruct them as to how they will behave and leave no room for counterargument on their part.

- **Preparation**: When the opportunity presents itself, observe other children of the same age to validate your assumption that your child's behavior is *not* simply age-appropriate.

- **Timing**: Have this conversation shortly before the child will be placed in a social setting where the risk of bad manners exists, and where you will have an opportunity to observe her.

- **Behavior**: Use a tone of voice that conveys authority; don't ever sound as if you are *asking* for something from the child.

247

16. Bringing Up a Child's Bad Manners

Icebreaker: Mary, before we go to this party tonight, I need to tell you that I'm counting on you to behave the way I know you can in adult company. I know it's not easy, I understand that. But I still expect you to speak with people when they try to have a conversation with you, and show some interest in what they have to say. Do you understand why?

Defiant: Those people treat me like I'm a baby! "Oh, look how cute!" "My, my, hasn't she grown!" Ugh!

Whiny: Oh, *why* do I have to go to these things? I never have a good time.

Sullen: I'm just gonna sit by myself anyway. I don't want to talk to any grown-up.

Sympathize but press your point: I can understand how some older people might get on your nerves. Maybe we can even have a good laugh about it on the way home. But we expect you to humor them, be polite to them, answer their questions, and make some effort to talk to them. This is just one of those "growing up" things you need to do. Do you have any questions?

Explain obligation: I understand that you don't enjoy this sort of thing, and I gotta tell you, I didn't like it too much when I was your age either, though there *will* be children your age there as well, so you can spend most of your time with them. But the reason you're going is because these are members of our family, and even though you don't understand it now, they need to see you. Especially the older ones. It means a great deal to them. So you have to do this. Do you understand?

Give orders: Here's what I expect you to do: I expect you to talk to anyone who talks to you, and I expect you to treat them with courtesy. And here's *why* I expect this of you: First of all, poor behavior hurts people's feelings the same way you feel hurt when someone mistreats you. And second, as you get older you're going to have more and more exposure to grown-ups, so now is the time we expect you to behave properly around them. Do you have any questions?

Capitulates, but isn't happy about it: All right, I'll behave. But I won't like it.

Doesn't understand the consequences of her actions: Why should these people care about me or how I act?

Explain action/consequence: I think as we get older we expect a certain amount of respect from younger folk. I also think you're old enough to begin to appreciate the fact that people can be hurt or offended by behavior that they think is rude. I don't want you to have that effect on anybody, so you'll behave the way you know to behave.

Agrees, if begrudgingly: Well, all right. I'll keep my act together.

Self-pity bordering on indolence: Yeah, just one. Why do I even have to go to this thing?

Your expectations and your sense of family reciprocity: Maybe it's a little like one of us taking you to soccer practice; there are some things you do as a favor to the family, and this is one of them.

Close: It'll be a pleasure for me to see you behaving well tonight, and I'll look forward to the ride home so you can tell us how it felt for you.

adaptations

Although the script example is of a child in a social setting, this script can be adapted for use with a child whose bad manners manifest themselves either in the classroom or at home.

key points

- Whether she likes it or not, this is a part of growing up that she's simply going to have to come to terms with.
- Remind her that all family members have a responsibility to one another, and you consider this a responsibility she has to you.
- Show empathy to a reasonable extent, but when you do, remind the child that she nevertheless must do as you are instructing her.

Talking with Your Child about Sex 17

Let's begin by acknowledging that we don't simply "sit down and talk to our child about sex" as though one isolated conversation is going to answer every question she doesn't want to ask you in the first place. Your child's understanding of sex begins to be formulated very early in life and matures as she does. Input includes how children see parents interact, how their parents interact with them, what they see on television and in magazines, what jokes they hear, what their friends and siblings tell them about it, and, more subtly, how they come to regard and respect themselves, their bodies, and their ability to make wise decisions. That said, what we can do is watch for a time when they seem to be beginning the dating dance, acknowledge that this is a difficult subject to discuss, acknowledge too that the most important thing about sexual exploration is that they don't do anything out of a sense of pressure or expectation, and remind them that there are adults—yourself included—who are willing to listen and talk, without judgment, about what they're going through.

tactics

- **Attitude**: You're cautious because this is difficult for both of you, but you're not apologetic about raising the topic.

- **Preparation**: Speak to your child's teacher and try to get a sense of whether he or she feels your child is beginning to show an interest in this topic and is ready for such a conversation.

- **Timing**: Have this conversation when you can be assured of total privacy. Have it toward the end of the day so the child isn't preoccupied with other thoughts or responsibilities. Also, if possible, the parent of the same sex should conduct this conversation.

- **Behavior**: Try to create as relaxed an atmosphere as humanly possible. Sit on the floor of the child's room if that seems like a natural place for such a conversation. If she shows hostility or hesitancy toward what you have to say, plod on but assure her you respect her privacy.

17. Talking with Your Child about Sex

Icebreaker: I know this may be an embarrassing topic for both of us, but now that you and Todd are dating, I want us to talk a little bit about kids getting sexually involved with one another. It's not easy to discuss, but I know it will make me feel better, and I suspect it might make you feel better as well.

Cautiously open: Um, what *kind* of stuff did you want to talk about?

Peremptorily shuts down: What I do is *my* business! No one else's!

Nervous and hesitant: It *is* embarrassing! Jeez (with the typical adolescent roll of the eyes).

Wants to disengage: Uh, can we please talk about something else?

You're open, but you offer one particular slant: First of all, you should know that I'm always open to discussing *anything* that might be on your mind. But I also thought it might be good to talk about how to know whether or not you're comfortable with making your own choices when it comes to any sort of sexual involvement.

Protect her privacy: You're absolutely right, and you don't *have* to discuss what you do. That's not what I'm really concerned about, anyway.

You're in agreement: Y'know, *I've* always hated it too when important topics that *bad* to be discussed were tricky to talk about! So maybe we can avoid the really embarrassing stuff.

Vague: I dunno. I'm okay I guess. Things are cool.

Slightly hostile: Well, what is it you want to know?

Fatalistic: Well, I guess I can't stop you from talking about it if you want to, now, can I?

Accept this as an "invitation": I appreciate that you're at least willing to hear me out, because this is such an important topic in your life at this age.

Reassured: I'm glad you feel as though things are okay. My concern, really, isn't so much what kind of sexual activity you choose to engage in—because there's nothing I can do about that—as it is you feel comfortable with it. That you're making your own free choice, that you have the courage to say no if that's what you want to say, and that you're not simply reacting to pressures you might feel from other people.

Reduce it to simplest terms: You know what I want to know? I want to know that for all the pressures you might feel from other people, anything you choose to do is what you *freely* choose. That you don't do anything you're uncomfortable with. That you don't do something just because other kids say they do, or because Todd or any other boy you might one day date pressures you.

Dismissive of your concern: Don't worry. It's cool.

Self-confidence, either genuine or feigned: Of course I do whatever I want. No one's gonna tell me what to do. Why should they?

Close; show faith and concern: I just know it can be really hard to do what you believe in when others around you want to influence you to do something else. I know that it's really tempting for some to want to get involved in sex without even taking the other person's feelings or needs into consideration, and I really respect you for handling yourself so intelligently.

adaptations

This conversation can be adapted for use with a younger child who is not yet exhibiting any real interest in the opposite sex but who asks about sex.

key points

- You're not asking for any specific information about your child's activities.
- You have modest expectations for what this conversation will accomplish.
- You want to remind your child of the importance of only doing whatever she feels comfortable with, in an atmosphere of respect, affection, and reciprocal agreement.

Trying to Stop a Child's Foolish Action   18

Seeing as how a young child can always be ordered not to do something, this is a script for the parents of an older adolescent, with whom they're apt to be in a considerably weaker bargaining position. What you really want to do here is avoid telling the child what you think he's doing is foolish, and instead set the groundwork for him to come to that conclusion himself. To do this, you want to acknowledge the legitimacy of whatever passion has arisen in him that has driven him to want to take this action, and from there begin to ask questions about how well he's thought this thing through. You're not saying, "Don't do this!" but rather, "If this is what you think you want to do, look at it closely enough to see if there are any flaws or gaps in your thinking." The example we use here is of a college student, on the verge of his senior year, who has decided to give up school and move to Hawaii.

tactics

- **Attitude**: You are exceedingly respectful of his desire to do what he wants to do, and you simply want to provide an analytical component to what is now a half-cocked idea.

- **Preparation**: Take time to explore the actions the child is contemplating. Be aware of its appeal as well as its pitfalls. Be prepared to offer an alternative approach to the same action (i.e., finish college first, then go to Hawaii, with enough money to return home if you need to).

- **Timing**: Don't react negatively right off the bat; wait until the idea has sunk in awhile. But by the same token, don't let too much time go by without voicing your concerns, or your child will assume he has your blessing. Intervene in time for him to revise his plans.

- **Behavior**: You share his excitement for what he wants to do, and you empathize with his desire to change his life as it's currently situated. You listen attentively and react slowly.

18. Trying to Stop a Child's Foolish Action

Icebreaker: Mark, I think your desire to move to Hawaii could have some real merit to it, but I also think it's wise for us to talk about some of the specifics of your plan. I want to be assured that you're approaching this properly.

Dreamer: Look, you should see the pictures; it's beautiful there. I can't wait to get there. Once I arrive, I figure I'll get a job, find a place to crash, play it by ear. I'll be okay.

Resistance: Y'know, you can't stop me. I'm old enough to do this on my own.

Half-baked confidence: I've been dreaming about this for a long, long time. Don't worry, I've got it all figured out.

Generalized defensiveness, anger: I knew it! You hate the idea, don't you? You think I'm a flake, and you just want me to stay in school and be a good boy, don't you?

Express concern: You're right, it *is* beautiful, and a lot more attractive than your college campus. But you don't want to be there a few months and have to turn around and leave all that beauty because the rents are too high or the wages are too low or the good jobs go to the residents, or something unexpected like that.

Restate your intentions: I certainly understand that, and I don't want to stop you if this is what you want and if you've thought it through thoroughly. Even though you're an adult, though, it's my obligation as a parent whose son is planning an enormous move to see it that you've thought of everything and that you're doing this properly. It's like telling someone, I don't want

Looking for details: Good, I'm glad to hear that. In fact, that's what prompted me to ask about this in the first place. I'm very eager to hear exactly how you have this figured out.

Absorb anger: What I want is to know that before making such a big change in your life you've examined every angle. If your desire is to get to Hawaii, the question you need to ask is, How do I best do that?

He's running on pure emotion: But it's *so cool* there! And I'm so sick of school! Dad, I really, really want to do this, and I know I can make it work!

you not to build your house, I just want to make sure your plans make sense and the house will stand up.

Asks, somewhat impatiently, what your concerns are: All right, all right. So what do you want to know about my plans?

You can relate: I can sure understand how beautiful it looks to you, and how tiresome school can get. On the other hand, really wanting something and being able to swing it are two different things, so my question isn't whether you want to make it work, but how you plan to make it work.

Get into your specifics: Well, for starters, what will it cost for you to live there and be able to do everything you *want* to do in such a paradise? How will you go about getting a job that will pay you enough to do that? For that matter, what do you know about things like the cost of living, the availability of jobs, the cost of housing, the cost of health insurance, those sorts of everyday things? Also, with one year left in your college education, how and when would you plan to finish that off?

Sketches out a vague plan: Well, I have a little money saved up that I can at least get started with. And there's a kid at school whose uncle owns a restaurant and who tells me he can get me a job there.

Don't discourage him, but do probe him: That sounds like a good start, but I think you need to ask some follow-up questions too. For instance, what does it cost to live there? And is this job guaranteed? And if so, what exactly is it, and does it pay enough for you to live the way you want? Also, in the long run, you need to figure out how and when you will finish your education.

Continued on page 258.

18. Trying to Stop a Child's Foolish Action (*Continued*)

Agrees to come up with answers for you: Look, I'll tell you what I'll do. I'll look into all that stuff and I'll get all your questions answered. But I'm gonna make this trip happen!

Painfully vague: I dunno, I guess I just figured I'd work all that out when I got there.

Close: Let's figure out together how best to make this happen for you, if it is in fact what you really want. I'll make a deal with you. I'll write down all of my questions, you do your research and come up with answers for them, and we'll proceed from there. You may decide you can do this now, or that it might be wiser to wait a year so that you can finish school first. But whatever you arrive at, *if* you've satisfied my concerns, then I'll do what I can to help you pull it off. I'll give you a list tomorrow, and let's plan to talk a week from Saturday.

adaptations

This script can be adapted for use with an adult child who is contemplating a foolish action.

key points

- Acknowledge that the action may have some real merit to it.
- Emphasize that you're not necessarily trying to stop the action as much as help the child think it through a little more thoroughly.
- You're willing to help him think it through.
- If nothing else, agree to keep talking about the idea before he acts upon it.

Talking with Your Child about Drugs

19

strategy

As is the case with talking with your children about sex, this is not a topic to be resolved or exhausted in a single conversation. One would hope that talk of the hazards of drug use would begin to infuse itself into several informal conversations well before the time a child is likely to be confronted with the choice of trying drugs, and would continue throughout adolescence. Nonetheless, one place to focus in is when the child is in the seventh grade, twelve to thirteen years old, because experts note that this is the time that the vast majority of kids get their first exposure to marijuana. If a natural opportunity for discussing drugs arises (a documentary on television, report of a local teen arrested for possession, a classroom discussion, etc.), seize it. Otherwise, use an occasion such as an upcoming party or dance to raise the subject (as we have done here). Then, having done so, stress how difficult some people find it to be in a place where other kids are using drugs and they're not. Acknowledge the pressure kids can feel when they want to say no but they don't want to suffer rejection. Help him devise a safe plan to protect himself. Also, remember that you don't have as much control over his life as you once did; haranguing or threatening him about drugs isn't going to be helpful. In fact, it may spur rebelliousness in your child. Instead, you have to rely on his ability to discern right from wrong and to act on what he believes is right. And finally, whenever you're talking about drugs, sound believable. Don't try to scare him into thinking that casual use of a drug like marijuana will do him serious harm, because when he doesn't see evidence of that in classmates who use the drug, you'll have lost your credibility.

tactics

- **Attitude**: You're concerned that your child knows what he will do when confronted with the opportunity to use an illicit drug. You also have faith in him to look out for himself.

- **Preparation**: Talk to your student's teacher and find out if she sees any evidence of drug use among any of the students. Also, if your child is planning to attend a party, quietly call some of the other parents to see if they know of any potential drug use among the kids who might be attending. Finally, read some of the copious literature available on how to talk to your kids about drugs; your doctor's office or a local hospital would be able to furnish you with materials.

19. Talking with Your Child about Drugs

Icebreaker: Tom, I heard from Rick's mom that there might be some kids at the party you're going to tonight who smoke pot. How do you intend to handle it if they're smoking there tonight?

Tries to shrug it off: I dunno. No big deal. I'll be all right.

Shield of privacy: I don't have to tell you everything, do I? Just trust me, I'll take care of myself.

Anger: Look, I don't do drugs, okay? Isn't that what this is about?

Denies there may be a problem: Oh, come on! My friends don't do drugs. Nothing's gonna happen!

Affirm your faith, voice your concerns: I have a lot of faith in you; I don't think you'd get mixed up in drugs. But I also know that when drugs are made available at a party there can be a lot of pressure to try them, even if you don't really want to.

Deflect anger: I don't mean to sound like I'm accusing you of anything. But because you don't do drugs, my concern is how you're going to handle it if other kids—maybe kids you know and like—offer you some. There can be a lot of pressure to try it.

Interject a little reality: I wouldn't be surprised to know that none of your friends do drugs, but I also wouldn't be surprised if you and your friends find yourselves in situations where drugs are being used and offered around. If that happens tonight, I want to know that you'll know how to handle yourself.

Hadn't thought about it: Well, I don't really know what I'd do. I don't wanna come off as a geek, but I don't want to do drugs, either.

Offer some strategies: There are a few things you might want to keep in mind. You might want to talk it over with some of your friends before you go, and decide among yourselves that you'll stick together. You also may want to bring our cell phone with you and, if you get uncomfortable, give us a call. We can even pick you up on a corner away from the party so no one notices. What do you think?

Wants assurance of anonymity: If I call, you wouldn't make a big deal of it or anything, would you?

Continued on page 264.

Has things under control: If I don't like what's going on, I can always just leave the room. That's all.

Has a plan: I'll be fine. If anyone smokes pot, I'll just stay away from them, and I'll stick with my own friends.

No pressure: Nobody pressures anybody into anything. People just do what they want.

Relate your own experience: I think it's terrific that you feel as though you'll have things under control. I just remember the first few times I saw people smoking pot; it seemed as though everyone was getting high, having a great time, and I was the only one staying straight. I'm glad I did, but it was pretty uncomfortable being the odd one out.

Incredulous: Your friends smoked pot when you were my age?!?

Wonders about you: So . . . did *you* ever try it?

19. Talking with Your Child about Drugs (*Continued*)

You tried it and admit to it: I did a lot of stupid things when I was a kid. I never tried pot when I was your age, but I did try it when I was older.

You never used drugs (or won't admit to it): No, but I can't deny it was tempting now and then, just to see what it would feel like. But now I'm glad I didn't give in.

Put it in context: No one I hung around with when I was your age did any other drugs. When I was older I knew some kids who tried it, but not many. Do you know anyone who's used it?

Reinforce the choice: I think you're really smart to do that. You and your friends know what you're doing, and I admire that. It certainly makes it easier for us to trust you.

Give assurance: If you want to leave the party, you tell me how you want to do that, and I can meet you wherever you want.

Can he try it?: So what about when I get older? Can I try it?

You recognize it's ultimately his choice: I never want you to try drugs, but I also recognize I don't have as much control over what you do as I did when you were younger. You're going to make your own choices. As far as drugs go, I hope you're smart enough to realize there are some real dangers in using them, and I also hope you're smart enough to realize you can talk to me any time about that.

Doesn't see a problem now: I think things are fine; besides, I don't think anything will be going on tonight that I can't handle.

Close: I have a lot of faith in your ability to make smart choices, and I don't ever imagine you doing anything to shake my faith in you.

- **Timing**: Key this conversation to an upcoming event where drugs might or might not be in evidence; ask your child how he plans to handle things if confronted with drug use.

- **Behavior**: You aren't moralizing or preaching to your child; your behavior is that of a parent who trusts her child but is also concerned about difficult situations he might be placed in. Try to maintain a "conversation of equals."

adaptations

This script can be adapted to discuss alcohol consumption with a child.

key points

- You can no longer control your child's environment. At best you can talk with him about how *he* can best control it.

- Don't be afraid to draw from your own experience as a learning tool.

- Put yourself at your child's disposal if he wants to extricate himself from a situation where drugs are in evidence but doesn't want to lose face.

- Express confidence and faith in your child.

part 4

Life*scripts*

for talking to adult children

Requesting That an Adult Child Move out of Your House

strategy

The success of this script is predicated on three assumptions: First, you should have had some family discussions already about when this move might take place. If you've done this, there is an implicit assumption that the child *will* move out. Second, you want to be polite, but you also want to make it clear that this is something you expect to happen, whether he wants it to or not. And third, you want to let him know that you're doing this for him, but you're doing it for you, too; you want your own lives now. With this in mind, cut the knot without severing the relationship: reinforce the idea that you will help with the transition (but put clear boundaries on the extent of your assistance), and that you will all still have a relationship after the child has settled into a new place. You may even want to tentatively schedule your first get-together there and then.

tactics

- **Attitude**: You are, in a word, parental. You see this as the natural exten-sion of your child's maturation process, and you are telling him that he must take this step.

- **Preparation**: If money is a potential problem, scout out apartment prices in your town and draft a rough budget so he can be assured he'll be able to stay afloat.

- **Timing**: Have this discussion early in the month and set a date at the end of the month (or, if you want to give him more time, the end of *next* month) for the move to be executed.

- **Behavior**: You want to communicate your love to your child while at the same time letting him know that you actually *want* this to happen. Don't communicate pity, sorrow, guilt, or regret.

1. Requesting That an Adult Child Move out of Your House

Icebreaker: Harold, we believe it's time for you to move into a place of your own, and we want to help you find one. I think we can get you in somewhere close by the end of this month.

Fearful: Gee, to be perfectly honest with you, I don't know that I'm ready. Even the *thought* of a move kind of scares me.

Dismissive: Yeah, well, I'll start looking in the next few days or something, so don't worry about it.

Wants to sell you some guilt: What, you don't love me anymore? You don't want me around?

Bargains with you: Look, I'll do more of the work around here. And I'll be real, real quiet. I'll even pay you some rent if you want, okay?

Nudge the bird out of the nest: I know it can be scary, and that's why we'll help you make the transition; we'll help you find a place, and, if need be, we'll loan you some money to get started. You need to live your own life, and so do we. And we're prepared to make it a *little* easier to do.

Dose of reality: You need to start looking tomorrow, because we expect you to have it wrapped up by month's end. If you have trouble looking, we can just choose a place *for* you, but I suspect you'll want to choose your own place.

Don't buy it: It isn't a matter of not wanting you around—that's why we're hoping you'll get a place not too far from here—but a matter of you needing to live on your own now. We're not writing you out of our lives, we're simply helping you take your next step as an adult. It's time for you to be out on your own, and time for us to be on *our* own again as well.

There's nothing to negotiate: This is not a question of how the three of us can live together, Harold. We have no complaints with you. But you're now old enough and responsible enough to live on your own, so it's time you did so.

Still frightened: But I don't know how. I can't cook, I can't clean, I've never had to pay rent before. I don't know that I'll make it.

Wants assurance that there's still a place for him in your lives: Well, can I still come home for supper now and then?

Wants a safety net: But if I can't do this, I can come back here, right?

Offer assistance: Let me tell you the extent of the assistance we can offer you: We'll help you design a monthly budget for yourself. And you'll get some simple cookbooks. Whatever questions come up along the way, you should feel free to call us, and we'll help you figure out how to solve them yourself.

Offer an exchange: Why don't we schedule a dinner here the first week you're in your new place, and a dinner at your apartment the following month?

Offer assurances to help him, but not to take him back: It won't do any of us any good to have you move back here, because that will only put us all at square one again. *But* we'll be here to help you gain your independence, so come to us with any questions, and if we can help you answer them, we will.

Resignation, if not enthusiasm: Well, I suppose I better get started, then.

Close: We really think you're going to find this to be a great experience. I know it was for me when I first went out on my own.

adaptations

This script can be adapted for use when a young married couple is living with one of their sets of parents.

key points

- You've talked about this before, so it should come as no surprise.
- This is a natural extension of the maturing process.
- You are available to your child after the move, but only to help him discover and reinforce his own sense of independence.

Questioning an Adult Child's Pending Second Marriage

2

strategy

Your son's been married and divorced and has now succumbed to the classic rebound. A new love enters the picture, and before the ink is dried on the divorce decree from marriage number one, he's ready to head down the aisle a second time. This of course is by no means uncommon; in the weeks and months following divorce, a person can feel lonely, adrift, angry at their ex, and maybe even a little competitive with her. The recently single say things like they want to "get back on their feet again," "put the past behind" them, or "start over." What they lose sight of, however, is that divorce takes a long time to recover from—up to three years, according to some experts—and although they may find passing happiness with a new partner, that by no means ensures that they're thinking clearly enough to make a commitment as serious as marriage. When you see this happening, you want to gently pull them back to reality, knowing full well that the real world won't hold nearly as much fascination and pleasure for them as the fantasy world they're occupying now. With this in mind, you want to encourage them not to call off the wedding but to defer it until they've both had time to give it the thought and time it deserves.

tactics

- **Attitude**: You're concerned for your child, and you're not afraid to show it. You're not setting off any alarms, but you do want to urge him—strenuously—to think more clearly.

- **Preparation**: Read some literature about divorce and second marriages. Speak with a marriage therapist and ask her to confirm your thinking— that it's wise for your child to wait.

- **Timing**: Have this conversation soon after his intentions are made known to you. Have it in private with your child.

- **Behavior**: Although your child is an adult, you can still act "parentally" toward him. Don't be afraid to tell him you think he's making a mistake. Offer to help him learn a little more about the emotional nuances of divorce.

2. Questioning an Adult Child's Pending Second Marriage

Icebreaker: I'm awfully glad you and Sharon are so fond of each other, Jack, but seeing as how your first marriage ended just a short time ago, if the two of you really want to give this relationship the best chance of succeeding, I think you may want to consider waiting a while before you actually get married.

Head in the clouds: But we're crazy about each other! I just *know* this one's going to be great!

Sings her praises: But how can you say that? You've met Sharon. Isn't she just great?

Anger: Hey, my personal life is nobody's business. If you're not going to accept us, well, that's your problem.

Won't repeat past mistake: Don't you worry about me! I won't make the same mistake I did the first time.

Bring him back to earth: I think you share every couple's optimism, which is fine. But you owe it to Sharon to take some time before plunging into a second marriage. I think when anyone goes through a divorce, there are wounds that have to heal first, and sometimes we're not even aware of those wounds.

Temper your praise: I believe she is, yes. What the two of you need to find out, though, is whether you'll be great to-*gether*, and I think you need some time to let your divorce sink in before you'll be fully ready to make another commitment of this magnitude.

Absorb anger: I can see how this might feel as though I'm throwing cold water on your happiness, and I hope you know I'll always accept you. All I'm trying to point out is that it's in both of your best interests to wait a while so you can gain some distance and perspective from your first marriage.

Remind him how he felt the first time: No, I'm sure you won't. But I do remember that you went into your first marriage certain it would last, only to find you weren't emotionally prepared for it. I guess what I'm saying now is that I think you need to get some distance from your first marriage in order to better prepare yourself emotionally for a second one.

Believes his first marriage is behind him: Well, thanks, but I know I'm over Elizabeth. I don't even think about her anymore.

Stubborn: Well, we know we're meant to be together. We're sure. That's all that matters.

Condescending: Who made you the expert on marriage and divorce?

Cite experts: You're right, I'm not an expert. That's why, when you told me how serious you and Sharon had become, I decided to do a little reading on the subject. What I'm telling you is only advice I've gleaned from marriage counselors and other authors on the subject of remarriage.

Finally shows some interest: Well, why do they say it takes so long? I mean, Sharon and I really, really love each other.

Digs his heels in: That doesn't mean they know everything. I'll bet there are plenty of second marriages that work, even if they happen soon after the first.

Close: There's a good deal more to marriage than there is to courting or dating. Old habits sometimes repeat themselves. Feelings we didn't even realize we had come slowly to the surface. A couple has to negotiate an awful lot of differences before they can make their marriage work. You two will do what you want, and I can't stop you. But I will offer to send you to a professional premarital counselor who will work with you to explore all of these issues. It can only help to strengthen the relationship you're building. You two talk it over.

adaptations

This script can be adapted for use with an adolescent son or daughter who is moving with some rapidity from one "serious" relationship to the next.

key points

- You think quite highly of both your child and his prospective mate.
- Your child owes it to his mate to give this ample time and consideration.
- Postponing a wedding isn't a sign of doubt in the future; it's a commitment to a more certain future.

Turning Down an Adult Child's Request for Child Care Help

3

strategy

The real danger here comes when new parents allow themselves to assume that the doting grandparents will stop their lives on a dime and eagerly commit themselves to endless hours of on-demand child care. The truth is, grandparents do adore their grandkids, but the extent to which they're willing to look after the little darlings might only be a measure of their own availability, not their love. They do, after all, have lives of their own. When a child approaches you to ask you to look after the little one and you just aren't in a position to say yes (either because you can't or because you simply don't want to; both are perfectly legitimate reasons), be ready to argue logic against passion. Your child is likely to play one if not two guilt cards ("Gee, we're *really* stuck!" or "Your own *grand*child! How could you possibly turn your back on her?"), and you have to be prepared to answer by telling her three things: First, you love this child unconditionally; second, that doesn't mean the child's parents should assume your availability to care for her; and third, child care is one of a multitude of puzzles parents must work out for themselves. You're willing to advise them if they wish, but *you're advising on how they can solve their problem, not how you can solve it for them.*

tactics

- **Attitude**: You're sympathetic to your child's predicament, but you also see this as one of the burdens of parenthood.

- **Preparation**: Prepare for this discussion in two ways. First, be clear in your own mind as to your reasons for not being able to provide the child care. Discuss it with your spouse if you think that will be helpful. And second, try to identify other young parents who may have faced this dilemma a year or so ago, and find out how they handled it.

- **Timing**: Chances are you'll want to deliver this information as soon as possible, so as to give your child a chance to make alternative arrangements.

- **Behavior**: You're putting yourself at your child's disposal in whatever way you feel you *can* be of assistance, so you want to convey a willingness to help out on your terms.

3. Turning Down an Adult Child's Request for Child Care Help

Icebreaker: Shelly, I really love my grandchild, but I'm afraid I can't help out with child care because the amount of time you need coverage is a good bit more than what I have available. I certainly appreciate your need for steady, consistent help, but I'm afraid you may have to hire someone.

Angry: Well, that's just great to hear! And I thought I could count on you to help out with your own flesh and blood!

Deflect anger: I can understand you being angry at this situation; you made an assumption that you didn't check out, and now you're feeling stuck without coverage for when you go back to work. Perhaps we can talk about the options that *are* open to you.

Plays a guilt card: But this is your *grand*daughter!

Don't rise to the bait: She's pretty special, all right. That's why, seeing as how I won't be looking after her every day, I really want you to be sure she gets the right person to do so.

Didn't think it through: But I guess I just assumed you'd help out.

Never assume: If you had asked me ahead of time, I would have told you that I wasn't available to you, and you could have thought about alternative plans. It's a little late now, but maybe you and Bob and I can put our heads together and come up with another option for you.

Gets dramatic: I don't want some stranger watching your grandchild!

Don't make her problem your problem: Well, let's take a look at the situation. You and Bob both have to go to work. I'm not available. And you don't want to hire someone. What do you see as your other options at this point?

Overreacts and shuts you out: Just forget it, okay? I don't *want* your help. We'll figure something out.

Disdain: Well, I suppose I'm just gonna have to hire someone. Boy, I sure wasn't counting on this.

Reinforce this: I guess you'll want to start talking to other couples who've had success hiring people and ask them for their ideas.

Despair: Oh, I just don't know what I'm going to do now!

Help them strategize: There is at least one thing that comes to my mind. Ultimately, of course, it's your responsibility. But you may want to begin by speaking to other parents who have been in this position and ask how they handled it.

Starts to come around: (Sigh.) I guess we're not the first family to be in this predicament. But it would've been nice if it could have worked out with you taking care of her.

Close: Let me say just one thing that is important for you to hear. This is a hard time in any family's life. You go through a lot of adjustments and they're not always easy. I will do whatever I can for my grandchildren, and I hope that in the future you'll see clear to ask what you want of me. Because if I *can* provide it, I will.

adaptations

This script can be adapted for use by a grandparent who is asked to help out with a grandchild's college savings fund, camp tuition, or other significant expenditure.

key points

- This matter should have been discussed long before it became a pressing issue.
- You understand completely why your child would be upset with you, but at the same time you are resolved to keep this problem in her lap.
- You won't let this be a referendum on your love for your grandchild.
- You do want to play an active role in the grandchild's life, in a way that is acceptable to both you and the child's parents.

Criticizing an Adult Child's Driving **4**

In this lifescript you are relying less on your power than your influence; you can't make your child drive smarter, but you can hope that whatever you have to say will be taken to heart and, at the very least, given some consideration. Use this script to point out to your child that his actions have consequences; that his driving is not a solitary exercise, but involves every other motorist, pedestrian, police officer, and guardrail on the road. Encourage him to think not only in terms of his own safety but of the safety of others who might not be able to avoid his aggressive or dangerous antics. And use what little real power you have by informing him you won't be riding with him if he doesn't change his habits. Even if he calls you on this, the emotional pressure he'll feel for having literally driven you away like this will be too great a burden for him to bear.

tactics

- **Attitude**: Be firm in your conviction but not punitive in your voice. Emphasize the seriousness of the topic but discuss it rationally and calmly.

- **Preparation**: Gather a few statistics on traffic accidents and fatalities, not to beat him over the head with but to toss in to underscore the fact that the child's actions bear consequences.

- **Timing**: Have this conversation immediately after you've ridden with your child, but do so in private, where no one can interrupt you.

- **Behavior**: Take him aside to have this conversation. Go behind closed doors. This underscores the severity you ascribe to the issue. Sit down and have him sit as well, across from you. This shows that it's a discussion, not a confrontation.

4. Criticizing an Adult Child's Driving

Icebreaker: Jack, I need to tell you that while I know you're going to drive any way you want to, I was extremely uncomfortable with the speed you were going and the unnecessary risks you were taking just now. You're going to have to drive more safely if I'm going to be in a car with you, and I certainly hope you'll slow down whether I'm with you or not.

Gets defensive: I drive fine! I haven't had an accident, and I don't intend to! And I know what I'm doing out there, okay?

A different perspective: I want you to understand what your driving looks like from where your passenger sits. Although you may feel perfectly comfortable behind the wheel, I see a lot of unnecessary risks to yourself and to others, and you need to think of that when you drive.

Shrugs it off: My driving's no big deal. The cops expect you to drive a little over the speed limit anyway.

You're not buying it: I'm not the least bit concerned with you getting a ticket, Jack. What is a big deal is your speeding, your unwillingness to wear a seat belt, your cutting other drivers off, and your weaving through traffic.

Belligerent: Look, with all due respect, I'm not a kid anymore. You need to let me handle things my own way, okay?

Acknowledge the limits of your authority: You're absolutely right, I can't *tell* you what to do. But I do have a right—and an obligation—to tell you what I feel, especially when I think you're posing a risk to yourself and to others.

Makes light of it: Aw, c'mon, Mom . . . just a little hot-rodding. You don't expect me to drive like Grandma, do you? Tell you what, you can wear a crash helmet next time.

Press your point: I'm quite serious about this, Jack. All I want is for you to drive intelligently, and it's what I'll expect when I'm your passenger.

He's not alone: Look, everyone I know drives a little fast every now and then. It's not like I'm driving any faster than most of my friends. We all do it; it's common.

The "everybody does it" approach doesn't cut it with you: I suspect that's why there were over 42,000 traffic deaths last year, mostly from speeding, and why it's the leading cause of death for people your age. Like I said, I can't make you do anything, but I can ask you to think about this before someone gets hurt.

Sobers him up: I didn't realize it was that bad.

Offers half a loaf: All right, I'll tell you what. As long as you're a passenger in the car, I'll drive more slowly, okay?

Insolent: Fine, then don't drive with me. I don't care.

Begins to get at the problem: I'll agree to that, but it only solves half the problem. My deeper concern is for your safety and for the safety of people around you when you're out on the road. If nothing else, I want you to tell me you'll give this some thought.

Tentative agreement: All right, I'll think about it, okay?

Stubborn pride: Yeah, yeah, sure, sure. Can we just drop this now?

Close: I have no doubts about your skills as a driver, son. But things happen out there that we can't always see coming, and every driver needs to be alert to that.

adaptations

This script can be adapted for use by a parent who doesn't want their child riding on or purchasing a motorcycle.

key points

- Your primary concern is for his safety, your safety, and the safety of others.
- You can cite specific examples of his recklessness (i.e., speeding, weaving, etc.).
- You absolutely refuse to drive with him unless he changes his habits.
- You recognize and acknowledge that this decision is ultimately his to make.

Turning Down an Adult Child's Request for a Loan

5

strategy

In order to successfully execute this script, you need to come to the table with three things: empty hands, an explanation as to why they are empty, and an alternative plan for your child's financial bind. The assumption here is that you're turning the child down not because you can't afford to make the loan (if indeed you couldn't, there wouldn't be a need for a script; one can't get cookies out of an empty jar), but because you don't want to. Maybe you want the money for a lavish vacation. Or to shower on your grandchildren. Maybe you don't think your child will be sufficiently grateful, or the reason he wants the money isn't sufficiently compelling. Whatever the reason, though, you're better off in the long run if you make your case to the child, and do so articulately, convincingly, and honestly. And finally, direct him to other stones he might turn over either to find the money he wants or to find ways to live without it.

tactics

- **Attitude**: You're not being punitive in denying this loan, but you are being strict with your money. Don't be apologetic, but at the same time express sympathy for the child's plight ("I'm sorry you're in this bind, but I don't regret not making this loan to you").

- **Preparation**: Prepare a cogent argument as to why you're refusing this request. And explore alternative means of financing.

- **Timing**: Take your time in making the decision, then present it as quickly as possible. If the child doesn't hear from you forthwith, he'll probably assume you're going to green-light the loan.

- **Behavior**: If practical, go to his home to break the news. Sit in a quiet place and explain your position slowly and deliberately.

5. Turning Down an Adult Child's Request for a Loan

Icebreaker: Alex, we've given an awful lot of thought to this, and as much as we'd like to see you get that new addition on your house, I'm afraid we're not going to loan you the money to build it. I hope you work things out some other way.

Slightly incredulous: But, but I thought you two were doing all right financially. I thought you had enough to be able to float me this loan.

Begs: But we really, really need this room. And I promise I'll be good for the loan. You'll get your money on the first of the month, every month. I guarantee it. *Please?*

Guilt trip: You mean you're just turning your back on me, just like that? You'd deprive my family of this room we need?

Let him down, gently: I understand how much you and your family would like to have this addition to your house, but when we look at your finances, the numbers simply don't add up. After you wrote that check to us, and another one to the mortgage company, you wouldn't have enough left over to meet the rest of the family's needs.

Feels cornered: But what are we gonna do? We really had our hearts set on that addition!

Rephrase: What we're saying is that your finances are such that you simply can't to afford to live the way you'd like to live, even with a friendly loan from us. Like everyone else, you need to live within your means, and we don't feel you'll be able to do that if you carry this debt to us.

Desperation: I hate to ask you this, but could you see your way clear to make it a gift—maybe even just a portion of it?

Explain your reasoning: Son, to be perfectly honest with you, it's not a matter of our finances, it's a matter of yours. We've taken a good hard look at these numbers, and we think you're going in over your head. You've had trouble meeting your debts in the past, and this loan would really strap you.

Petulance: Fine! Never mind then! We don't need your money. We'll manage. Somehow.

Brings up a loan you made to your other son: But what about that loan you made to Bob and Stephanie last year?

Explain the difference of circumstance: That's right, we made a loan to Bob and Stephanie. But that was only because we knew their income was sufficient to cover it.

Absorb anger: I can understand your anger, son. It doesn't feel good to be turned down by your own parents. But perhaps we can be of assistance to you in getting your finances in better shape.

Not prudent: Believe me, we considered that. But we decided not to because we thought it more important in the long run that you learn how best to live within your means. And *that* I'd like to help you with.

Disappointment hurts: I know how tough it is to take disappointment like this. But I think I know of a way you might be able to get yourself on better financial footing, so that you may be able to get that room later on.

Starts to weaken: Well, I guess I'm not going to see that money from you. I guess we'll have to get along without the room we need. Thanks anyway.

Curious: Well, what do you have in mind?

Offer some sensible help: We won't be giving you the money but there is a way I think I can help you deal with your finances in the long run, if you're willing to listen.

Close: I think that a good financial adviser can sit down with the two of you and help you look at your whole financial picture—your income, your earning potential, your spending habits—with an eye toward getting you on a better financial track so you'll eventually be able to take care of your family the way you want to. That's something I'm willing to help you pay for. Give it some thought, and let's talk tomorrow about making an appointment.

adaptations

This script can be adapted for use when you think your child would benefit from your unsolicited advice as to how they could better handle their finances. It can also be adapted to turn down a sibling's request for a loan.

key points

- This is your choice; you're not hiding behind a pretense of poverty. Your child has a right to know this.
- You are not rejecting your child or showing the child any less love or concern; don't let him lay that on you.
- You feel no joy in denying this request, but you do feel resolve.
- You still want to help him out financially, but not in this manner.

Confronting a (Young Adult) Child about His Drinking or Drug Problem

6

strategy

Just as when we have to confront a parent or sibling with a drug or drinking problem, the most effective intervention with children (particularly those who are older—late adolescence or early twenties) is to surround them with friends and family members who care about them and who have had their own lives negatively affected by the child. This approach accomplishes three objectives. First, because the evidence is so overwhelming, it prevents the child from denying his problem. Second, because the child is hearing from people he has hurt, he can't make the claim that "this is my problem, and no none else's." And third, because he's being confronted by people who care about him, he begins to realize that the intervention is not a punitive measure but a caring one, and knowing that people care about him despite his affliction will help him realize he's not having to face this situation alone.

tactics

- **Attitude:** Be firm in your convictions and steady in your voice. Let the child know this is not a decision based solely on emotion; there is a great deal of thoughtfulness behind it as well.

- **Preparation:** Gather friends and other family members who will be willing to engage in an intervention. Ask a substance abuse specialist for directions on how to conduct one. And prearrange for a bed at a detox center.

- **Timing:** You want to intervene as soon as you can bring people together. Do it early in the day, hopefully before the child has had an opportunity to drink or use drugs.

- **Behavior:** If possible, have the child seated. Be strict and inflexible in the tone and content of your words.

6. Confronting a (Young Adult) Child about His Drinking or Drug Problem

Icebreaker: Jerry, we're here to tell you that you have a serious drinking problem, that you need professional help, and that we'll do anything in our power to help you get straightened out and stay sober.

Denial: You don't know what you're talking about. You don't even know me.

Anger: How dare you accuse me of drinking! Especially in front of all these people!

Throws it back in your face: What a bunch of hypocrites you are! Where do you think I learned how to drink in the first place? You guys drink whenever you want to, and now you're accusing me of being a drunk?!?

Rationalizes: Look, I have a couple of drinks with my friends, that's all. Why don't you leave me alone already!

Make your case: You come home early with alcohol on your breath. You drink in your room. You miss school. Other people tell us of seeing you drunk around town. You need help, and we're going to see that you get it.

Absorb anger: I'd be mad too, Jerry. But the fact is, everyone is here because they agree with us and they want you to get help.

Focus on the child: All that matters is that you have a problem that you can't control, and you're going to need to get help. That's the only reason we're all here today.

Press your point: The fact is, you drink almost daily, and it's always more than a couple of beers. You may not realize it, but you have a dangerous addiction, you're going to need help, and we're going to help you get it.

Offers to quit: All right, all right. If it'll make you happy, I'll quit drinking. Now leave me alone.

Bargains with you: All right, just leave me alone, and I'll confine myself to one beer a day . . . or one beer every other day. Now let's drop it.

Defiant: You can't *make* me do anything. I can just leave if I want to.

Reality check: The truth is, if you were not to agree to get professional help, we would have the power to sign you in to a detox center, which we'll only do if you force our hand. What we *hope* is that you'll agree to it voluntarily, because that will make the whole procedure of getting straight easier for you.

No room for discussion: *We've* consulted experts on this, Jerry, and here's what they tell us: You can't drink in moderation, and you can't stop drinking on your own. You're going to have to spend some time in a detox center, and then you're going to need constant counseling. On their advice, that's what we're arranging for you, and that's what you're going to do.

Raises logistical issues: But I just can't up and leave. I've got my job, my friends—I need time to prepare.

Resigns himself: Well, I guess you're not gonna let this thing go, are you?

You have that covered: We'll take care of telling anyone who *has* to know that you're not well, and that you'll be back in a short while. There will be no repercussions at your job.

Close: We've made arrangements for you to be admitted to our local hospital to begin treatment. I'll get the car, we'll go over together, and we'll get you squared away.

adaptations

The example here is of an older child with a drinking problem. This script can be adapted for use with a younger child and/or with a child who has a drug habit.

key points

- You aren't asking that the child seek help; you're insisting on it.
- You *do* have the power to have him committed, provided he poses a danger to himself or others.
- You are there to support him and see him through this.
- You're not interested in debating whether or not he has a problem; he does, and you're taking measures to correct it.

part 5

Life*scripts*

for spouses

Telling Your Spouse You've Just Lost Your Job   1

strategy

Even when you lose your job through no fault of your own—downsizing, merger, etc.—it's awfully tough to come home and tell your spouse that the place you've come to rely on for your work identity and your paycheck no longer requires your services. And losing your job because your superiors were unhappy with your work can only add insult to injury and make the news that much harder to deliver. If you find yourself faced with this dilemma, keep in mind that while your spouse might experience a wide range of emotions—anger, embarrassment, fear, frustration—ultimately what she is going to want is assurance that your tilted ship will be righted again, that this is a temporary setback, and that your security as a family is not in peril. With this in mind, you want to do three things when you tell her what has happened. First, leave plenty of room for the venting of those emotions. Second, be prepared to offer assurances that you can weather this storm financially. And third, be ready to offer the beginnings of a game plan that will put you back to work.

tactics

- **Attitude**: Your sadness and anger are mixed with determination and cautious optimism.
- **Preparation**: Meet with your human resources officer, find out what your severance will be, what the company will do for you in terms of outplacement counseling, and what other rights you have as a terminated employee (health insurance coverage, sick pay, etc.).
- **Timing**: You owe it to your spouse to tell her what has happened as soon as you learn of it.
- **Behavior**: Crises often bring families closer together; emphasize that this is not just your problem, but a challenge you're facing together. Encourage teamwork.

1. Telling Your Spouse You've Just Lost Your Job

Icebreaker: Ann, I'm afraid I have some bad news. My boss called me into her office today and told me they weren't happy with my performance and were letting me go.

Panic: Omigosh! What are we going to do? We'll be broke!

Anger: How could you?! How could you be so irresponsible?

Won't accept it: Well, you just have to go down there and fight for it back. Tell them you'll do anything they ask. Just get that job back.

Embarrassment: What am I going to tell people? What will our parents think? No one in my family's ever been fired before.

Appeal for calm: We'll be okay, and let me explain why. We have savings, I'll be receiving a decent severance package, I'll apply for unemployment, and I'll begin looking for a new job first thing Monday morning. I already have some ideas for how and where to look.

Absorb anger: I know you're angry, I'm angry too. I don't think they dealt fairly with me, but I'm also angry that I didn't do a better job. But I can tell you this: This experience is really going to make me more determined to do well in the next job I take.

Reality check: I'm afraid their decision is final; they were quite clear about that. I think what we need to do now is begin looking for a new position, one I can be happier in and one that's better suited to my skills.

You're not alone: I'm sorry this is so embarrassing for you; I'm certainly not proud of it. But it does happen to an awful lot of people—more people now than ever before, as a matter of fact—and I think the healthiest thing we can do is begin planning for my next move.

Anxious about the future: But . . . but how do you know you're even going to *get* another job? Especially after being fired?

Wants a game plan: So what's your plan? How are you going to get going again? And how do you know you'll be able to *keep* the next job?

Close: I've already begun to give this some thought. First, I think we should make a budget that will carry us for the next few months, if necessary. Next week, I'm going to meet with an outplacement agency that specializes in helping people in my position find new work. I'll talk to some of the clients who I got along well with and see if they have any openings. I'll get in touch with some friends as well and see if they know of any positions I'd be suited for. And I'll be in touch with the managers at my old job who did like my work and will be willing to be references for me. It may take some time, but we'll be okay.

adaptations

This script can be adapted for use by people who have been put on probation at work or who have decided to quit their job.

key points

- Accept your measure of responsibility for what has happened.
- Have a game plan for securing your next job.
- Make sure that plan ensures your taking a position for which you have the skills and in which you have the interest.

Suggesting That a Spouse Get Psychological Counseling

2

We often don't want to appear weak, in need, or unable to cope, even to our spouses. So when one of us may be in need of psychological counseling, the other must tread lightly in raising the subject. For this reason, if you think your spouse might react negatively to the idea of seeing a mental health professional, suggest instead a visit to her general practitioner. Also be prepared to do a balancing act. On the one hand, you want to be convincing when you present a case for her needing help. You want to cite a series of behaviors or moods, over an extended period of time, that indicate a persistent problem. But on the other hand, you also don't want to sound alarms, or give your spouse to believe she's "falling apart." What she needs to hear is that she has a problem she can't seem to lick on her own, but help *is* available, and the problem can be corrected. Finally, any form of psychological disorder can be terribly alienating to the person suffering from it. Reassure your spouse that you'll be there for her throughout their treatment and recovery. The example we give in this script is of someone suffering from a general anxiety disorder. For an adaptation of this script with a different disorder, lifescript 16 in part 1, "Suggesting That a Parent Get Psychological Counseling," where the example is of a person suffering from a mild depression.

tactics

- **Attitude:** You are concerned without being alarmist. And you are quite insistent that your spouse take *some* kind of action in this matter.
- **Preparation:** Consult your physician to learn about what your spouse's symptoms might represent.
- **Timing:** Unless she appears to pose a danger to herself or others, give your spouse a week to ten days to return to her normal state of mind.
- **Behavior:** You are above all supportive. Hold your spouse's hand or gently hug her as you talk. Keep eye contact to the extent that she'll permit it. Both be seated in a comfortable and private place in your home, with no threat of interruption.

2. Suggesting That a Spouse Get Psychological Counseling

Icebreaker: Janet, I'm concerned that you're still not eating and sleeping well and still seem to be agitated much of the time. I'm thinking we should pay a visit to a doctor.

Minimizes the problem: I'm just a little stressed out at work, that's all. I'm sure I'll be fine in a day or two. Don't worry about me, okay?

Angry and defensive: I'm all right, now just leave me alone! Why does everybody have to butt into my business all the time! I'll take care of myself!

Loses control, perhaps weeping: Oh, I don't know what's wrong with me! I think I'm losing my grip, and I'm never going to get better. I swear I can't take it anymore.

Provide evidence to the contrary:
That's what I thought too, but I'll tell you why I think differently now: You've never been this agitated over work. A mood like this has never lasted this long in you, or been this intense. And this is not the first time in the past few weeks you've told me you'll come out of this, but you still haven't. I believe we need to speak to somebody about it.

Absorb anger: I know this is extremely sensitive, and if I were in your position, I think I'd be angry too. But I'm raising it because you're not happy, I'm not happy seeing you like this, it's upsetting the kids, it's not getting any better, and I'm concerned it's only going to continue to wear on all of us.

Put some perspective on it, and offer a game plan: We can get a handle on this, and I can help you. First, we'll make an appointment to see your doctor. He may be able to prescribe antianxiety medication to deal with your symptoms. Then he'll refer us to a psychologist, and if you want, we'll go see that person together. In the meantime, if you'd like, we can arrange for you to take some time off from work, and we can talk about whatever responsibilities you have around the house that I might be able to take over for you. This is a problem, but we can manage it.

Refuses help: I'll handle this myself. Leave me alone.

Bargains with you: Just give me a couple of days, until this report is done for work. Then I'll be fine.

Reaches out, skeptically: So what would you have me do, just drop everything and take a vacation?

Set limits: I can't see us waiting very much longer than this. Today's Friday, so let's give it the weekend. Then, if necessary, I'll call your doctor on Monday morning.

You've tried leaving her alone, but it hasn't worked: You're such a strong person that I have let this go for some time now, because I thought you'd just pull yourself through it. But it's been several weeks now, and it's having an effect on all of us, so you and I really need to do something.

Afraid of being alone: Look, you gotta promise me you won't leave me alone, okay?

Submits, without condition: Well, I hate to do this, but all right. If need be, let's make an appointment with the doctor, see what he has to say.

Agrees only to see her doctor: All right, I'll tell you what I'll do. I'll see my doctor about the stress. But that's all I'm going to promise.

Close: I will call your doctor, we will see him together, and you are going to be fine. This is a good move you're making—we'll get things straightened out in no time, and we'll see it through together. I promise.

adaptations

This script can be adapted to suggest that a sibling seek counseling or a spouse see a medical doctor about a persistent physical condition, such as recurring pain, bleeding, headaches, etc.

key points

- You know your spouse is not happy about how she feels.
- You've been observing this behavior for some time.
- It's affecting other members of the family.
- She must understand that you will not abandon her.
- Be prepared to offer a plan for how the two of you can proceed to take care of this problem.

Criticizing a Spouse's Spending Habits 3

There are two ways to approach the dilemma of a spouse's sloppy spending habits. You can be direct, and take the issue head-on, or you can be indirect, and discuss in more general terms the need for the family to do a better job of living within a budget. In this script we offer the indirect approach, and we do so because if it fails you still have the option of taking the matter head-on, whereas if you tried—and failed—being direct, you would be left with little recourse. The idea, then, is to identify the nub of the problem (spending's out of control), cite evidence ("I don't know that we can afford your $200 neckties"), and agree to work out and adhere to a reasonable monthly budget. Then, in order to keep the playing field level, include in that budget a certain amount of discretionary money for each of you so that your spouse has a preestablished dollar amount to spend as he sees fit, which allows him the freedom to spend without breaking the bank. Remember, what you're looking to do is establish new *habits;* a working budget is the surest way to modify your spending behaviors.

- **Attitude**: Your attitude is that the family has a problem, and you want to get your heads together to fix it. You are fairly insistent that you do this, but you're not alarmist or accusatory as to the reason for the problem.

- **Preparation**: Go through old bills and receipts so that you can document patterns of extravagant spending, the kind that your family can't afford.

- **Timing**: Have this conversation at the end of the month, when bills need to be paid. It's the most logical time for you to be assessing your finances.

- **Behavior**: Sit down with your spouse at a table and have papers with you that will document your concerns.

3. Criticizing a Spouse's Spending Habits

Icebreaker: John, I've been looking over our bills for the past few months. We need to talk about how much we're spending and what we're spending it on.

Honest interest: What seems to be the problem?

Blasé about money: Oh, we're fine. The money's there when we need it.

Wants to avoid the topic: Um . . . some other time, okay?

Preemptively defensive: You don't like the way I spend my money, do you? I work hard for it, and I want to enjoy it.

Deflect the defensiveness: You *do* work hard, and you're right, we *should* be able to enjoy our money. What I'm saying is that we can also be careful with it so that we can meet our obligations and still have something left over to spend as we wish.

Still defensive: Well, I only spend money on what I need, so there's nothing I need to be more careful about.

Be specific, and be objective: Well, let me tell you what I see. Over the past several months we've been spending about $300 more than we've been making. I think we need to take a closer look at how we should be spending that money.

Don't delay discussion: We need to discuss this now because our bills need to be paid today, and because we have the time right now.

Vague, empty promise: Well . . . we'll just tighten our belts; I'll be a little more careful about what I spend, and you do the same.

Wants to work it out: Well, what do you suggest we do about it?

Offer specifics: I think we need to write out a monthly budget and stick to it, but in the meantime let me show you some of the things that jumped out at me. You're spending about $175 on lunch each week, and about $500 each month on clothes, and I think we should be able to budget a little less for you on both. I think I can cut back on my phone bill, and perhaps on gasoline consumption for my car. That's at least a start. The main thing, though, is that we discipline ourselves to spend less than we're taking in.

Pin him down: I'm afraid we need to be more specific than that, John. We need to budget ourselves, and we need to change some of our spending habits.

Gently press your point: There are a couple of items it would be useful for you to look at, John. For instance, I think you can get away with less than $175 a week for lunch, or $500 a month for clothes, which is about what you're averaging.

Sees luxuries as necessities: I need those things, those are important, they're all tied in with how I do my work.

Mild bullying: Remember now, I make more than you do. I should be able to spend more.

Close, by offering to negotiate: You know, we may have disagreements about where the cuts should come from, so why don't we begin by determining how much we have to spend, look at our fixed expenses, and then allot a certain amount for each one of us to spend each month as we see fit. If we can't work it out, I have the name of a financial officer who can help us and whose fee is affordable.

Foreign territory: I don't know; I've never lived on a budget before, and I've always gotten along all right.

Empathize, and close: So did I. It's only recently that things seem more complicated. But I'm confident that we can get this squared away. And if we can't seem to do it on our own, I have the name of a financial adviser who can help us, and whose fee is affordable.

adaptations

This script can be turned on its head to be used to negotiate a higher spending threshold with a spouse who—in your estimation—doesn't allow for enough to be spent on behalf of the family.

key points

- You don't want to fix the blame; you only want to fix the problem.
- You don't deny that your spouse works hard for the money; you just want to assure yourself that the money serves your purposes.
- Be prepared to turn vague ideas about what it costs you to live the way you do into hard-and-fast dollar amounts.
- If it would be helpful, think of ways you would be willing to cut some of your own spending.

Bringing Up a Pet Peeve with a Spouse

4

strategy

The trick to this script is humility. *You* have a problem, not your spouse. It's not much, but it's something. A lot of people might not have any problem with the behavior you're complaining about. And you're more than willing to listen to your spouse bring up any pet peeve of theirs. In essence, what you're saying here is, "There's nothing *wrong* with the fact that you crack your knuckles (or leave your dirty socks at the foot of the bed, or fall asleep in the easy chair after dinner . . .), it's just that it hits *me* the wrong way. I'm not asking you to change because you're flawed, but because I react in a negative way to this one piece of your behavior." Keep it focused on you, keep it simple, and keep the conversation light.

tactics

- **Attitude:** You're very nonchalant about this. It's *almost* not worth bringing up. But you'd like to keep a minor annoyance from becoming a full-blown aggravation.

- **Preparation:** Just to make sure there's some merit to your complaint, run it by one or two close friends, and see if they understand it. If it seems as though you're making something out of nothing, maybe you need to change.

- **Timing:** Engage in this conversation shortly before the two of you are about to find yourself in a situation where the offending behavior might arise. And have the conversation when the two of you are in good moods, and getting along well with one another.

- **Behavior:** Be willing to laugh at yourself, keep a smile on your face, and keep the conversation light.

4. Bringing Up a Pet Peeve with a Spouse

Icebreaker: Boy, this may sound pretty silly, but I'm wondering if you would mind not singing along with the radio when we're in the car together. I may be strange about this, but for some reason it bothers me.

Offensive: Well, you know, there are things that *you* do that bother *me*.

Invite feedback: I'm sure there are. In fact, I'm sure there are things I do that bother a lot of people. I'd be happy to know when I'm doing something you find annoying so I can stop. Do you think you'd be willing to do the same with this?

Defensive: Well, excuse me (sarcastically). Anyway, I don't sing that loud.

Absorb the anger: Gee, I don't mean to upset you. No, you don't sing loud; this is just my little hang-up, and I'm just wondering if you'd be willing to humor me on this.

Curious: Well . . . what about it bothers you? Lots of people sing to the radio.

It's your idiosyncrasy: You know, you're right. Lots of people do. In my case, I guess my own preference is to just hear the musicians performing. It's like preferring one color over another, or one TV show over another.

Embarrassed: Gee, I feel kind of foolish now. You mean all this time I've been doing that and it bugs you?

Turn it on yourself: Actually, I feel a little foolish here too. It's no big deal, really, it's just my own little pet peeve. In fact, I hope you sing your lungs out when you're in the car by yourself!

Retaliatory strike: Well . . . um . . . You snap your gum when you chew it. *That* bugs me.

Be magnanimous: You know, I never realized that bothers you. It is a kind of pesky habit. I'll stop doing it around you, and I'd appreciate it if you would let me know if I'm ever doing it reflexively. Now, can we have the same arrangement with the singing?

Relenting: Well, it still seems pretty petty to me, but okay.

Slightly exasperated: Well, I just don't see what the big deal is.

Agree, in part: I guess that's my point. It's a little like feeling a pebble in your shoe; it's not a big deal, but you feel as though you'd be happier without it. Now, do you think you can help me out on this?

Close: Thanks; I like it when we can work out the little things like this. I really appreciate it.

adaptations

You can have an adaptation of this conversation with your spouse when you see someone else engage in behavior you don't particularly like and you fear your spouse might one day do the same.

key points

- This complaint is purely subjective; it's your problem you're asking help with.
- If the opportunity presents itself, ask your spouse what little peeves he might have with you.
- Be sure to show your appreciation when your spouse agrees to accommodate your wishes.
- This is not a marriage breaker; don't make it into a full-scale argument. Trust in your mutual ability to be reasonable with one another.

Bringing Up a Spouse's Weight Problem

5

strategy

I'm sure there's a more ticklish topic than this, but I just don't know what it is. I think the best way to approach the question of a spouse's weight is to discuss it in terms of health, and to include concerns about your own weight in the discussion. Talk about the need for the two of you to take good care of yourselves, especially as you age. Include diet, but also exercise, and point out how this may have benefited someone you know. Also, try to steer the two of you to a diet specialist or nutritionist who can offer an objective assessment of your dietary and exercise needs (This transfers the responsibility of telling your spouse that she needs to lose weight from you to the professional.). And finally, if she absolutely resists your entreaties, follow up on your own, in the hopes that you'll set a good example for her. Then, come back to the topic later as something you want her to try because you've derived so many benefits from it.

tactics

- **Attitude**: Don't be afraid to show your real concern about this. You're not sounding any alarms, but you have been giving this serious consideration, and you are urging the two of you to do something about it.

- **Preparation**: Speak to someone who has battled weight problems and gotten them under control through a diet and exercise regimen. Perhaps even arrange for them to be in the same place as you and your spouse at the same time so you can start up an impromptu conversation.

- **Timing**: You might want to present a "couple's membership" in a gym or a shared appointment with a nutritionist as an early anniversary present. But if you do, don't let it be your only gift.

- **Behavior**: Show enthusiasm for the idea, and indicate that you think you'd have a hard time adhering to a regimen without your spouse's support and participation. You might also want to hold the conversation when the two of you are out for a long, slightly strenuous walk.

5. Bringing Up a Spouse's Weight Problem

Icebreaker: Jill, I'm concerned that we're not taking very good care of ourselves. Sue, down at the office, and her husband recently went to a nutritionist who gave them a diet and exercise regimen that they're both very happy with, and I'd like for us to do the same.

Accusatory: I know what this is about! You don't like the way I look . . . you think I've gotten fat, don't you?

Suspicious: What are you suggesting? What are you *really* saying?

Shows no interest: Look, if you want to do that sort of thing, that's fine with me. But I'm not interested.

Don't lie, but don't be cruel: I think both of us have not taken good care of ourselves. We can stand to eat less, but more importantly, we can stand to eat better, more healthily. And we should be exercising more.

Be frank, but not brutal: I look at our diets, our weight, our physical condition, and it causes me concern. I want us to stay healthy for a long, long time, and right now we're not doing it—and it shows.

Be persistent: Well, I do think I'll do it, because I believe it will be good for me. But I'd like you to come too, at least to learn about our diets, because I'm concerned that both of our eating habits have gotten unhealthy.

Questions your motivation: Why such an interest in this all of a sudden?

Digs heels in: I've never exercised before in my life, and I don't feel like starting now.

Not interested: I just don't think I'm interested. You do what you want.

Half a loaf: I can understand your not wanting to get involved in a real time-consuming exercise regimen, although I also think you want us to take good care of ourselves. What I'd like to do is just make an appointment for us with a nutritionist, talk about health, and maybe find the easiest things we can be doing to make ourselves more healthy.

It's not all of a sudden: Actually, I've been thinking about this for myself for some time now, but I haven't had the discipline to do anything about it. I thought that maybe we could keep one another interested enough and disciplined enough to follow some sort of exercise regimen.

Still refuses: Nope, I don't think so. You do whatever you want; I like myself the way I am.

Close: I'll tell you what I'll do. I'll make an appointment for both of us to see a nutritionist; and if you don't want to go, I can't force you. But in the meantime, give it some thought; I really feel very strongly about this.

Agrees to a new regimen: Well, I suppose it couldn't hurt for both of us to lose a little weight. Okay.

Accepts your offer: Alright, I'll tell you what I'll agree to. I'll agree to seeing a nutritionist, but that's all. For now.

Close: That's great; I don't know if I could do this without you, but I think that together we can really make some improvements in our lives. I'll make the appointment right away.

adaptations

This conversation can be adapted for use in a situation where it is clear that only your spouse has a weight and health problem.

key points

- This is not primarily a cosmetic issue. You're concerned for the two of you; you want to be healthy.
- If you meet staunch resistance, don't push it.
- If your spouse isn't willing to commit to a new way of eating and/or exercising, at least try to get her to agree to go with you to see a nutrition counselor.

Ending a Spouse's Chronic Lateness 6

strategy

What makes this topic a little tricky is the fact that in so many instances chronic lateness is a deeply embedded habit—perhaps going back to a person's childhood—that has not caused enough grief in his life that he's felt compelled to change it. You'll often hear statements like, "Well, that's just the way I am," or "So start without me," or "I'll get there when I get there," as clues to a person's unwillingness to give up this small but potentially annoying habit. When you're punctual and he's not, you want to keep a few things in mind. First, pick your battles. It's a lot more important that the two of you get to the airport on time than it is that you get to a friend's party by 8:00. Try to be loose about those appointments for which time is *not* of the essence. Second, remind your spouse that there is much that you love about him, but this is one small piece of behavior that does frustrate you. And third, impress upon him the fact that his behavior has consequences for others. Finally, if he stubbornly refuses to change, offer to travel separately to functions to which you feel you'd otherwise be late arriving.

tactics

- **Attitude**: You don't want to blow this out of proportion, but you do want to tag it as something that has meaning for you. You want your spouse to alter his or her behavior, so you need to be frank and up-front about how you feel and what you want.

- **Preparation**: Look back on instances where your spouse has been late, especially when the lateness has caused problems (missing the first act of the play, missing the train, etc.). You don't want to throw this in his face, but if need be, you do want to be able to hold it up as a concrete example of what you're talking about. Also, find out what books your local bookstore has on time management, and what seminars might be offered at your local community center.

- **Timing**: Raise the issue a few days before a function you're both expected to attend, when punctuality is important. Offer to help your spouse to be on time for it.

- **Behavior**: You recognize that this is something that bugs you and not him, but you're not willing to simply accept it. If worst comes to worst you're at least prepared to do what you have to to ensure that you're not victimized by your spouse's lateness.

6. Ending a Spouse's Chronic Lateness

Icebreaker: You know, there are a million things I love about you. And one thing that can frustrate me. I'd like it if you could be on time for appointments and events, especially when they involve me, and I'm wondering if you'd be willing to figure out how to do that.

Doesn't think he can change: I've tried in the past, but I always wind up lapsing back into old habits. Sorry, but you may just have to learn how to live with it.

Defeatist from the start: I've always had this problem, and I suspect I always will. I just can't get myself organized, and that's that.

Can live with it: Actually, aside from missing the occasional flight, it doesn't seem to bother me. I don't mind running a little late sometimes.

Turns the tables: Did you ever stop to think that it might be your hangup about being so punctual all the time?

Offer to help: I'm really glad you recognize it's a problem, and since it does cause me frustration, I'm wondering if you'd let me help you get over it.

Explain how it affects you: I can understand that, but it affects me too. Aside from worrying about whether we'll make a flight on time, when we're expected, say, at a dinner party or a PTA meeting, it's important to me that I arrive on time because I feel as though I'm showing disrespect for others if I'm late.

Keep the focus off of you: You're right insofar as I do consider punctuality to be important; it's something I value pretty highly, not only in the case of, say, catching a movie or a flight, but because I think it's disrespectful of me to arrive late for something and keep other people waiting. I guess I'm asking you to try a little harder because it does mean a great deal to me. So can we work on this together?

(Somewhat) open to suggestion: Well, what do you have in mind?

Doesn't "get it:" Well, I don't consider it disrespectful.

Sees it as your problem: Well, maybe you need to get over your sensitivity to how other people might feel if you show up a minute or two late.

You're asking for you: I understand that it's okay for you to be late for things, so I guess what I'm saying is I'd like you to be more prompt for my benefit. I'm asking you to do this for me.

Refuses to change: Well, I'm afraid this is who I am, it's not going to change, and we'll have to live with it.

Close with a fair and modest proposal: I'm sorry you feel that way, and I guess I will learn to live with it. From now on, though, in order to avoid problems, I think when we're coming up on an event or appointment we both have to be at, I'll just go ahead and meet you there. Let's try that for a while and see how it works out.

Concrete suggestions: Actually, I was at the bookstore the other day and noticed there were a few books on time management that had chapters dealing with how to be on time for functions. I also saw a listing in the local "Y" catalog for a short seminar on the topic. I'd be happy to pick up a book that we could both read, or sign us up for a seminar.

Agrees: If it means so much to you, let's work on it together. And maybe you could loosen up a little bit about being *early* for everything!

Close: I'm glad we can work this out, and I know there are habits I have that set you off, so I hope you'll always feel free to flag them for us.

adaptations

This script can be adapted when the roles are reversed and your spouse shows an almost obsessive need to arrive hours early for functions.

key points

- Remember that he might not see his lateness as a problem.
- Be prepared to impress upon him how others might interpret it, and how it affects you.
- Have concrete suggestions on how to change, and be willing to participate in programs of change *with* your spouse.

Asking for More Input from a Spouse on Decision Making 7

strategy

Collaborative decision making between a husband and wife is crucial for what it *doesn't* yield. When you come to a consensus on something—however tortured that process might be—you avoid misunderstandings, faulty assumptions, and the possibility of resentfulness and blame. And when parents present their kids with decisions that affect them, a collaborative effort is less likely to make them want to play one parent off against another ("If I want to sleep at my friend's house, I ask Mom when Dad's not around; but when I want to go to the ball game with my friends, I know Dad's more likely to give me the green light"). However, as chores and labor get divided in a household, and one person takes responsibility for the garbage and the other the laundry, or one washes the dishes and the other pays the bills, decision making often gets doled out as well, leaving one spouse with the lion's share of responsibility. To combat this, you want to tell your spouse a couple of things. For one, you want him to know that it can be lonely and intimidating for you to make major decisions that will affect the whole family. For another, a decision made with pooled knowledge is a more informed decision. And finally, your days are full enough with responsibilities and chores; you shouldn't be expected to bear this additional weight alone.

tactics

- **Attitude**: You're not resentful for having found yourself in the position of chief decision maker, but you will be if things don't change. You're not scolding, you're asking for help.

- **Preparation**: Come up with one or two family matters that need some sort of decision to be made, and be ready to engage your spouse on them. Also, you may want to read a book or two on collaborative decision making; there are a number out there.

- **Timing**: Choose a time shortly after you have had to make a decision you think would've benefited from your spouse's input; this way you can hold it up as an example. Also, hold the conversation on a weekend, when the two of you will have a little unfettered time to make some collaborative decisions.

- **Behavior**: Don't supplicate; you're not asking for a favor. You're informing your spouse that he needs to be shouldering more responsibility. This is a good conversation to initiate over the kitchen table when the coffee's brewed and the kids aren't around.

7. Asking for More Input from a Spouse on Decision Making

Icebreaker: Sam, I wasn't happy about having to bear the full responsibility for deciding what time the kids got home from their party last night. I'm feeling like I needed more input from you, and more shared responsibility in general for making the kinds of decisions that affect the family.

Impatient: With all that I have to do at the office, I just don't have time. I know you work hard too, but I'd rather just leave certain decisions up to you.

Empathy, but without letting him off the hook: You're right, we both do work hard, and finding time to get our heads together for decision making isn't always easy. But because it's important, maybe what we need to do is set aside a few minutes each night—perhaps right after dinner—to go over any family matters that need our attention.

Compartmentalizes: Look, here's how I see it: I make decisions about how we're going to invest our money, what kind of car to buy, that sort of thing. Stuff around the house I leave to you.

Patronizing: Oh, but you make decisions so well, especially when it comes to the kids. I trust you to make the right call.

You're looking for more collaboration: One thing I don't like about that arrangement is that it puts too much weight on my shoulders to make decisions that would be better made by the two of us. We compromise the results when we don't work collaboratively.

State your reasons: I trust my judgment too, but I want to treat fairly major decisions as something we're both responsible for. It prevents me from feeling resentful for having to bear the burden myself, it makes for a more sound decision, and it lets the kids know that we're in agreement on decisions that affect them.

Needs specifics: Can you give me an example of what you're talking about?

Needs clarification: I'm sorry, but I don't know how my input is going to matter much in some of these situations; I'd probably just sign off on whatever you say.

Exasperation, abdication: Look, if it's the kids you're talking about, you're with them a whole lot more than I am; you know better than I am what they need, so you need to make those calls.

Chapter and verse: I'm not sure I gave the kids the right instructions about what time to be home last night, or whether they should've done their homework first. You might have agreed with my decision, but even just knowing that we're in agreement makes it less burdensome for me, and makes it clearer to the kids that we speak with one voice.

Be persistent: It's not just decisions that affect the kids; it's decisions that affect all of us, either directly or indirectly. Besides the kids, it's what color to paint the dining room, or where and when to plan a family vacation, or whether I should accept a promotion—which could mean more money but more travel—at my company.

Agreement: Well, you're gonna have to program the time for us to discuss these decisions, then, but if you do, I'll try to play a larger role.

Partial agreement: Well, I'll try, but I don't know that it'll do much good. I'll probably still go along with what you say, and I can't promise to devote a whole lot of time to this.

Close: Let's give it a few weeks, and see how it goes. Right now, as a matter of fact, I have two items I want your input on. Right now, as a matter of fact, I have two items I want your input on, and I'm glad we have the time to discuss them . . .

---

adaptations

This script can be adapted for use when your spouse is making too many unilateral decisions, or when there is a specific decision you want to approach collaboratively.

---

key points

- This can be one of those thankless, dreary tasks of family life; you both may need to accept it as such.
- You really value your spouse's input.
- Your kids need to know the two of you are in agreement on decisions that directly affect them.
- Learn a few tricks about how to collaborate on decision making and consensus building.
- Don't take "I'm too busy" for an answer; you're busy too.

Debating Interfamily Loans with a Spouse

strategy

A sibling is short on cash and could use a friendly loan. You could swing it, because you have the money. You're inclined to do it, but you also need to discuss it with your spouse. Chances are, however, when you first learned of your sibling's need, your immediate reaction was one of "We could probably help, but I need to think about this a little bit." With that in mind, you don't want to be in the position of putting your spouse on the spot by asking for an immediate answer. Instead, you want to present it as something you'd like the two of you to consider. Discuss all of the ramifications, both in terms of what it might cost you to put up the money and what it might cost your relationship if he has a hard time paying it back. Ask your spouse what sorts of questions come to his mind. Don't be afraid to indicate that you're inclined to make the loan, but not if your spouse isn't. Keep in mind that a partial loan is also a possibility. And above all, approach this as a business decision as well as a personal one. The loan should be secured, an interest amount attached to it, and a schedule of payments should be written down and signed off on. And finally, if all else fails, be prepared to end up disagreeing, and not making the loan.

tactics

- **Attitude**: You're intrigued at the idea of being able to help out a family member, but concerned that you and your spouse consider all the possible pitfalls.

- **Preparation**: Take a look at your own finances and be sure you're in a position to make the loan. Also, ask the family member where else he has looked to borrow the money.

- **Timing**: You need to discuss this soon after it's called to your attention, because the family member needs to know if it will be necessary to look elsewhere.

- **Behavior**: You are not supplicating or asking your spouse for approval to make this loan; you're discussing it with the idea of wanting to help out a family member *if* you both agree it's feasible.

8. Debating Interfamily Loans with a Spouse

Icebreaker: Tom, my brother has been hit with some pretty steep bills all at once, and he needs to get his hands on about $2,000. I think there are probably good reasons for us to lend him some money and good reasons not to, and I'm wondering what you think.

Concerned about repayment: No offense, but are we *sure* he'll be able to pay us back?

You share your spouse's concerns: That's a good question, and we'd have to ask him about that. We should probably think of other questions like that as well.

Wants more information: What does he need money for? He's got a good job.

Extenuating circumstances: He's usually pretty good about managing money, but they had some work done on the home last year, and then this year a bonus he was promised apparently didn't materialize.

All but refuses on principle: My immediate reaction is that I'd rather not. I don't like the thought of lending money to a family member. It can just confuse things.

Ask for clarity: Can you be a little clearer for me about what sort of confusions it might create?

Abdicates: Whatever you want is fine by me.

Won't make the decision alone: I can't make this decision myself because it affects all of us. I need for the two of us to discuss the merits and problems it poses.

Willing to discuss it with you: Well, what is it you need to know from me?

Litany of questions: I'm wondering things like how he'd pay it back, what we'd do if he couldn't pay us, whether we should charge him interest, and what we'd do if he came and told us he needed more. Those are big questions I'd need answered before I floated him a loan.

Disparaging remark: Well it was pretty foolish of him to go and spend money he hadn't actually received yet.

Wants a guarantee: I want to know that this isn't going to cost us somehow. I need some assurances.

Getting down to business: I think we'd be smart to discuss all of the things a regular lending institution would consider—whether we can afford to do this, what a payment schedule should look like, collateral, interest, and the like. But I also think we need to weigh whether this could cause a strain in our relationship with him. Do you have any thoughts on that?

Provide some context (it wasn't as foolish as it now seems): I think this is money he's budgeted for and received every year, so while he probably shouldn't have spent it before he actually saw it, I get the feeling his company led him to believe he'd be getting the money. Like a lot of us, he got hit with unforeseen circumstances.

Doesn't see a problem: I don't think it'll be a problem. Let's sit down with him and see what we can work out.

Does see a problem: Y'know, it could be a little awkward if he can't pay us back on time. I don't want to abandon him, but I don't want to threaten our relationship either.

A little more sympathetic: I suppose. So, how do you want to proceed? What do you think we should do?

Close: Perhaps we should give this some more thought ourselves. Then, in a week or so, if we're still considering it, we can draw up a list of our questions, including how best to protect ourselves if he has trouble making payments. We can talk them over with him, and see if he'd want to accept a loan from us.

adaptations

This script can be adapted for use by a couple needing to ask another family member for a loan.

key points

- Don't make any promise to a family member before discussing it with your spouse.

- Don't pressure your spouse for an answer. If anything, leave plenty of room at the outset for him to consider this and delay a decision.

- Be able to articulate the circumstances that gave rise to the family member's need for the loan.

- Insist that you discuss this together; don't be put in a position of having to bear sole responsibility for making the decision and living with the consequences.

Debating In-Law Care with a Spouse

9

strategy

It can be awfully difficult to face the prospect of our parents aging to the point where they require the kind of assistance they can no longer provide for themselves. We don't want to face their ultimate demise; we don't like the thought of their growing dependent on others; and we are anxious about whether they'll be prepared for old age. Will we be asked to contribute our time or our money to their care? And if so, will our resources be sufficient? Will I be as willing to help out my spouse's parents as I am to assist my own? The best way to approach this enormous problem is by looking at it from the standpoint of the many resources available to the parents rather than the daunting challenges posed by their aging. Sure, you may be asked to help with your father's care, but if you don't have money to contribute, perhaps you'll be able to do some shopping for him, and another sibling can help out financially. Perhaps a parent can move in with one of the siblings, either temporarily or year-round. The point is, you examine the care of your parents and your spouse's parents by considering three things: What can my spouse and I contribute, what can our siblings contribute, and what resources have the parents or in-laws already accrued in anticipation of old age? In discussing this with your spouse, what you want to do is get to a point where the two of you are willing to meet with other family members for the purpose of beginning discussions about how you will collectively care for the parents in later years.

tactics

- **Attitude**: You're concerned about this as an issue on the distant horizon, and you see it as something that affects both sets of parents.

- **Preparation**: Talk with other friends who have had to care for aging parents, and consult a gerontologist or other expert on aging to gain a sense of what the needs of the elderly are and what resources are available where your parents and in laws live.

- **Timing**: Have this conversation well before it's necessary to act.

- **Behavior**: Be a realist; raise the tough issues—even as hypotheticals—especially if your spouse is unwilling to face them. Press the need for this conversation.

9. Debating In-Law Care with a Spouse

Icebreaker: I'm not crazy about the thought, but we both have parents who are starting to age, and we need to how they're going to be cared for if they need assistance in old age.

A history of bad blood: You know how angry my father makes me. He's always been like that; he made my youth miserable, and I have no intention of helping to make his old age comfortable!

Thinking more broadly: I understand how you feel about your dad; he can be a real bully sometimes. So let's think more broadly about both sets of parents and what they might need, and not necessarily if we're going to help provide it for all of them.

Wants more information: What exactly are you getting at?

Cold facts: In about six or seven years they'll be at an age when many people begin to require things like more medical attention, physical therapy, even assistance with grocery shopping. We need to know how prepared they are for those years, and what help they might need.

Shirks responsibility: I'd like to help when the time comes, but I don't see how we can afford taking care of anyone other than our own immediate family.

Acknowledge concern: You're right; we don't have a lot of money to spend. We won't be able to do everything for them, but there may be some ways we could help.

Avoidant: Now there's no need to be an alarmist! They're all healthy, and they're going to live a long time.

Reality check: Yes, they are healthy now. But that can't last forever and we need to know what—if anything—they might need from us before that day comes.

Nervous about what this can mean: Gee, that can be a tall order. They can need an awful lot of care.

Wants specifics: How do you think *we'll* be able to help them?

Presumptuous: Oh, I'm sure they have that all figured out already.

Stubborn about the scope of assistance: I'll consider it, as long as I decide *who* we're going to help!

Appease the anger: I'm sure we can figure out how to direct our resources; if you still feel like this a few years down the road, perhaps your brothers can look after your dad. What's important now, though, is that we start talking about a plan that can be of use—if necessary—a few years down the road.

This can't be avoided: I know my parents have some resources but still may need some help, and I think your parents may be in a similar position. All we have to do now is begin to investigate what we might be looking at another few years down the road.

Outline a reasonable plan: We certainly can't handle any major problems they may have on our own. But I think it would be good to do a family inventory of resources. In other words, we should find out what plans our parents do have in place, how our siblings are in a position to help out, and what contributions we might be able to make. The entire families need to be in on this.

Hesitations are assuaged: So you see this as a team effort? Everybody involved?

Close: Exactly. What we want to do now is find out how well our parents are equipped to handle possible problems as they get older. Then, if necessary, we need to discuss with our brothers and sisters what kind of help we might be able to offer—money, transportation, time, that sort of thing. Then we can all work together to design a plan for the parents, should they need one.

adaptations

This script can be adapted for use by a family in which an adult sibling and their spouse has a child with special needs.

key points

- Give equal weight to the need to care for both sets of parents.
- Remove anxiety from your spouse by assuring him that you won't be asked to contribute more than you're able.
- Approach the problem as a team effort, involving the parents themselves, all the children, and resources that exist in the community.
- Try to get your spouse to agree to have a meeting with other family members to begin discussing the future.

Debating Relocation with a Spouse 10

strategy

There are any number of reasons why we might get the itch to pick up and move to a new locale—a better job offer for you, or for your spouse; some friends who've moved elsewhere and encourage you to join them; weariness with having lived in the same place for so many years—but regardless of your reason it is a decision that is not entered into lightly, because it's a hard thing to undo. As the old saying goes, you can't put toothpaste back into the tube. When you and your spouse sit down to discuss this, the first thing you want to do is find out what he is thinking. What's his immediate reaction? Is it the same as yours? If not, how different are you? The second thing you want to do is remind yourselves that this is just that, *an immediate reaction*. It's a starting point, a place for discussion to begin. From there you want to work together to flesh out all of the possible pros and cons the relocation poses. Finally, you want to end the conversation with an agreement to give yourselves time, to keep investigating, and to keep talking.

key points

- **Attitude**: You want to present this as an opportunity, not a mandate. You see some potential good in it, and you don't want to close any doors.

- **Preparation**: Learn a little something about where you would be relocating to—its pluses and its minuses. If this is job-related, learn as much as you can about *the job's* pluses and minuses as well.

- **Timing**: This conversation should begin soon after you have entertained the prospect of relocation in your own mind. It is best saved for a weekend, so you'll both have time to think about it.

- **Behavior**: Show a willingness to hear your spouse's fears and concerns, even if you don't share them. Restrain yourself from appearing too excited or too pessimistic; otherwise you may prejudice his thinking.

10. Debating Relocation with a Spouse

Icebreaker: Stan, I've been offered the transfer to Colorado. It's a great opportunity but it's also a big move for our family to make. We don't have to decide for another month, so I thought it would be good to start talking about the pros and cons. Do you have any immediate thoughts on it?

Does want to move: Boy, I'd love to get out of here. Let's do it!

Doesn't want to leave: You know, I'm really pretty happy here; I'd just as soon we stay put.

Doesn't know, or is ambivalent: Boy, I'm just not sure. I have pretty strong feelings in both directions.

Look for further discussion: My immediate take on it is that we really need to look at the pluses and minuses before we decide. It clearly has enough advantages that it's worth at least considering.

Reiterates a desire to stay: There may be some advantages to leaving, but I sure don't see them. I really want to stay.

Open to discussion: Fair enough. Do you want to hear my thoughts, or do you want to go first?

Need to process the issue: I understand your feelings; I know how happy you are in your work, and I think I'd have a tough time contemplating a move if you were offered a transfer. But I'd like us to at least talk about this so that we can *both* be sure we're doing the right thing.

Begin to sketch out your thoughts: Perhaps it would be good to begin with a list of the "knowns" and the "unknowns." For instance, we know the money would be much better, and we know the schools are good in the area where we'd be living. We also know you'd have to find another job. We don't know how well the kids would adjust, or how we'd feel about leaving our friends.

Only sees the negatives: All I know is that I really want to stay here. The kids seem happy, I like what I'm doing, we have friends. I don't see us upsetting the apple cart.

Accentuates the positive: All I know is that I'm tired of living here, and that you'd be making more money, so I say I'm all for it!

Adds to your list: Now that I think about it a little, I'm sure I could find work out there. But I wonder how the kids would feel about leaving their friends and going to another school. It would also be pretty far from my parents.

On the other hand, the area is awfully pretty, and the opportunity for you is a good one.

You want to proceed cautiously: I'm not quite as sold on it as you are, so I'd like us to look into it more carefully. We may well end up moving, but first I'd like to get a clearer picture of what it will mean to us.

Summarize: So for now, your feeling is that we should stay, and my feeling is that I should consider the possibility of accepting the position. I guess then, that we should look into it a little more closely to see if you might find things about it that appeal to you, or I might be able to get some clarity on whether or not I should continue to consider it.

You seem to be on the same side of the fence (or at least straddling the same fence): We both see some merits to the move and some cost to it as well. I guess that means we should explore it further, keep our options open, and keep talking about it.

Willingly agrees to hold off on a decision: All right, since we have a month, let's look into it a little further.

Begrudgingly agrees to hold off on a decision: Well, I know how I feel. But if you're uncertain, I suppose we can keep looking at the pros and cons.

Close: I can get in touch with some people from my company who work out there. I'll find out what their impressions are of living there. I'll find out what their impressions are of living there. I'll also talk to my boss and see how we can arrange to fly out and spend a few days looking around, and if the company can help you find work. We can also begin a subscription to their local paper. Maybe your boss has some ideas of where you might find work. Also, why don't we agree to keep notes of whatever thoughts come to us—either in favor of moving or against it—and talk some more in a couple of days.

adaptations

This script can be adapted for use when one member is considering leaving a job, especially if it will mean a substantial change in lifestyle.

key points

- Distinguish between an immediate reaction to the idea and a thoughtful response to it.
- Listen carefully and empathetically to your spouse's feelings about the proposition.
- Even if you are in agreement that it should or shouldn't be done, don't make an irrevocable decision on the spot.
- Remember that the aim of this conversation is simply to put the topic on the table and to agree to investigate it together.

Asking a Spouse for a More Active Social Life 11

If familiarity doesn't breed contempt, it can at least breed boredom. As couples settle into a comfortable life with one another, they can find themselves gravitating more and more to the peace and quiet of home and hearth. They work hard all day, spend a lot of time interacting with other people—some of whom they might like, others they barely tolerate—and by day's end are ready to become hermits in their own cave. And while this can indeed be restorative, it can also be an example of too much of a good thing. They fall into ruts, become bored, watch the same mindless TV shows, sleepwalk through the evening until bedtime, get up the next morning, and start the whole process over again. But what happens is that at some point one of them wakes up to the realization that they've slipped into boring habits and remain there by nothing more than the sheer power of inertia. She becomes restless, stifled, suffocated by routine, and hungers for more excitement and variety in her life. If, when she calls this to the attention of her mate, they are in agreement on the matter, then there's nothing to talk about. You get up, and you go out. You socialize more. But if the mate's dissatisfaction hasn't reached that level, then some coaxing needs to go on. In doing so, you want to get three points across: First, I don't know if you're unhappy with this rut, but I am, so let's try and do something about it. Second, What are your resistances to going out more? Late-night exhaustion? Expense? Don't like our friends? Put them on the table and let's deal with them. And third, Let's ease into this; go out a little more often than we are now. See how it goes. And then, in time, find a level of socializing that suits us both.

tactics

- **Attitude**: You're genuinely bored with your life together, and as much as you love your spouse, your needs aren't all being met by staying home all weekend. You want a change.

- **Preparation**: Check the newspapers and local magazines. Find a movie and/or restaurant you both might enjoy this Saturday night.

- **Timing**: Discuss this early in the evening, early in the work week. It's a time when neither of you will be exhausted from the week, and it gives you plenty of time to make arrangements to go out on the weekend.

11. Asking a Spouse for a More Active Social Life

Icebreaker: Boy, I sure do enjoy the time we spend at home together, but lately I've been feeling as though I'd like us to get out a little more. What do you think?

Sees a red flag: Are you saying you're unhappy with me? Should I be concerned?

Stay specific: I'm very happy with you. That's one of the reasons I want to go out more with you.

It's your problem: If you want to go out more often, go ahead. I'll just stay home.

Partial solution: That's a good idea, and I may do that. But I'd also like for the two of us to go out and socialize more.

No enthusiasm: But I like just staying here; I don't want to go out all the time.

You want some balance: I'm very comfortable here, but if I'm here too long without going out, I lose that comfort, I begin to feel stifled.

Offers a scant solution: How about if we were to go out to dinner, say, once a month?

Asks what it is you want: What do you have in mind?

No energy: But I'm so tired at night, I just want to stay here and relax.

You want to make it easy: So do I when I'm tired. But it seems as though we've even gotten out of the habit of going out or seeing people on weekends, when we do have the time and energy.

Gripes about late nights: I hate being out late; I feel tired all the next day.

Make it easy: I can understand that, and I don't think we have to make a late night of it. But if we were to, say, go to dinner and a movie, or see some friends, we could still ensure getting a good night's sleep. Especially if we did this on a weekend night.

Be specific: I'm not necessarily thinking of late nights. But I'd like to go out, say, three or four times a month, perhaps have dinner with friends, or perhaps entertain here at home. Maybe a movie or a play. Confine it to the weekend if you'd like. That sort of thing.

Not enough: I'm glad you're up for going out, but I was thinking along the lines of at least one night each weekend. How about a compromise?

Begins to come around: Well, I suppose we could try it. I don't share your frustration with being home so much, but I guess we could go out a little bit more.

Has conditions: Okay, but I don't want to go out more than three or four times a month, I don't want to spend a lot of money, I don't want to be out past midnight, I don't want to go out on a weeknight, and I'd like to have some veto power over what other couples we might get together with. Agreed?

Close: Sounds great. Thanks for agreeing to do this. In fact, why don't I make a reservation for dinner this Saturday night at a restaurant of your choice? Let me know if you want anyone to join us, and decide if you'd like to catch a movie or do something else afterward.

- **Behavior:** You are definite that you want a change, but you're quite open to listening to your mate's reservations. You're willing to compromise.

adaptations

This script can be adapted for use by an individual who would like to go out on occasion without her spouse. It can also be adapted for use by an individual who feels she does _too much_ socializing and would like to stay home more often.

key points

- By all means, you are _not_ dissatisfied with your spouse; you're only dissatisfied with the languid state of routine your marriage has slipped into.
- Have some specific ideas in mind for the upcoming weekend, and make sure they're the kinds of things that would appeal to your spouse. You may want to pick one or two daytime activities for starters, such as brunch at a restaurant or a matinee play or movie.
- If it would be helpful, you might want to ask him if he'd rather socialize with another couple, with a group of friends, or just be out with you.

Asking a Spouse for More Romantic Behavior

12

strategy

There's a thin line between a married couple growing very comfortable with one another and getting to the point where they take each other's presence in their lives for granted. The enthusiasm of the early years slowly burns off, kids come along, days get filled with activities great and small, romance gives way to familiarity. At some point you realize you've crossed the line, and you want to go back again. You miss the touching, the hand-holding, the lazy caresses in the big easy chair. When you mention this to your spouse, you probably won't get an argument, but you might find them less eager to do anything about it than you are. It can be an embarrassing thing to discuss, and they'll want to change the subject. Or they will have become so used to the way things are that they won't be feeling the same longings that you are. In any case, you want to introduce this as something you want very much to correct, even if it's something the two of you have to think about or plan ahead for. You can also come equipped with specific ideas—quiet dinners, more time away from the kids, that sort of thing—and ask that even if they're not feeling the same longing you're feeling, they go along with you on this because it will satisfy a need you know you have and a need they may have but don't know it.

tactics

- **Attitude:** You're feeling quite good about your marriage. It's strong, and it's solid. But you want to rekindle some of the early passion as a natural expression of that solidity.

- **Preparation:** Try to plan a quiet evening with your spouse for the weekend immediately following this discussion. Also, you may want to read up a little bit on this matter, so that you can cite sources who put forth the proposition that there are times in every marriage where couples have to put a little effort into that which used to come spontaneously.

- **Timing:** Have this conversation on a weeknight, after the children have gone to bed but before it's too late in the evening. A Monday or Tuesday evening is good, because at that point the rigors of the work week haven't yet begun to wear on you both.

- **Behavior:** Don't be demonstratively affectionate while you're having this conversation, for fear that your spouse will construe it as an invitation for sex rather than for discussion. But by the same token you needn't be cold or distant.

12. Asking a Spouse for More Romantic Behavior

Icebreaker: John, there's something that's been bothering me for a little while now that I'd like us to talk about. I feel as though we're not as romantic toward one another as we once were, or as I'd like us to be. I really miss it.

Doesn't share the problem: I don't know that I agree with you; I think we're just real comfortable with one another.

Identify it as your problem: I'm glad you're okay with things, and I want you to understand that I feel real comfortable with you. But even if you aren't feeling this void, I think it's important for you to know that I am, and I hope we can figure out what to do about it.

Defers to you: So, what do you want?

Misconstrues: You mean our sex life?

Clarify yourself: Not exactly, although I suppose that's a part of it. But I'm also talking about the small things, the quiet moments of intimacy, the times we'd spend curled up on the couch together, that I feel are missing for me.

Doesn't feel quite right: It just seems kind of artificial to do things like that without necessarily *feeling* like it.

Defensive: What do you mean? You *know* I love you, and you know I'd do anything for you.

Be reassuring: Of course I know we love each other. But little gestures—hugs, or kisses, or quiet dinners, things like that—have always made me feel that love more intensely and more personally. That's what I feel is missing.

Isn't feeling romantic: Geez, we're not kids anymore, you know. It's not like we're eighteen and dating.

Finds this embarrassing: I'm not exactly sure why, but I find this kind of embarrassing.

Agree: I do too. I think it's easier to *be* romantic with one another than it is to talk about it.

Not bound to age: No, you're right, and I have no interest in behaving like a teenager again. But I do believe we can still have affection and romantic interest for one another.

Gently disagree: Actually, from a few things I've read, when couples show more affection toward one another, they then tend to feel more affectionate toward one another. It's certainly worth a try. I know *I'd* like to be closer to *you*.

Break routine: Maybe we could start by setting aside one night a week for a quiet dinner alone. And perhaps take some evening walks. I've even heard it's good for couples to take their TV sets out of their bedrooms; we may want to try that for a little while.

Is okay with a modest attempt: Well, how about this; you lead and I'll follow, okay?

Still feels peculiar, but is willing to try: Well, it still feels kind of funny, but I guess it wouldn't hurt to give it a try for a little while.

Still feels peculiar about the idea: I don't know, it still feels kind of funny to me.

Press your point: I think we both feel that way to some extent. But I'm also aware of the fact that I miss having that part of our relationship, and I want it back. I believe it's important.

Close: I'm glad we're going to work on this. Why don't I send the kids to my folks' house on Saturday evening, and we can make ourselves a nice meal together.

adaptations

This script can be adapted for use by a couple when one of the two partners wants a more active sex life.

key points

- You _don't_ see this as a sign that the marriage is in trouble.
- You both may find it difficult to talk about, but that doesn't mean it's difficult to fix.
- Even if your spouse doesn't share your feelings, the fact that you feel as _you_ do is enough reason for the two of you to try and change things.
- "Romantic behavior" is a slippery term; you want to be clear as to what you mean by it.

Discussing a Spouse's Workaholism 13

strategy

In this script we make two assumptions: that this is not the first time you've discussed this (usually a full-blown conversation like this has been preceded by a couple of passing, informal observations), and that the problem isn't simply too great a workload, which your spouse has absolutely no power to control. What makes workaholism a difficult topic to get your hands around is the fact that the workaholic is not engaging in selfish, self-indulgent behavior, but the effect on the family is the same as if he was—hours away from home, neglect of domestic responsibilities, estrangement, kids growing up with just one parent. It's hard to complain to someone for working too hard. Nevertheless, the workaholic needs to be saved from himself for two reasons: not only is he hurting his family, but he's hurting himself because in all likelihood he's engaging in this behavior as a form of sublimation, or repression of some deeper, unresolved issue. Perhaps he suffers from feelings of inadequacy, or finds his marriage unexciting but is afraid to admit it. Maybe he feels ill-equipped as a father. But the real purpose of this first full conversation is not to catapult the workaholic spouse into psychotherapy, but to simply identify the behavior for what it is and give yourselves a trial period to straighten it out. During that trial period one of three things is likely to happen: either the old patterns will reemerge (in which case you then talk about seeing a therapist), the other, heretofore repressed issues will begin to emerge (in which case therapy also may be in order), or the problem will be shaken, and the workaholic will again discover that there's no need to be frightened about being away from his desk or in his own home.

tactics

- **Attitude**: You respect your spouse's dedication to work, but you're also concerned and unhappy with the effects it's having on him and on the family.

- **Preparation**: Have one or two informal conversations about this first; simply note your unhappiness with the long work hours and ask your spouse to cut back. You may want to speak with a counselor to learn more about the dynamics and roots of workaholism.

- **Timing**: Have this conversation on a Saturday or a Sunday, early in the evening, especially if the spouse has put in any work over the weekend. This gives the two of you a chance to discuss the week ahead and plan for more time together.

13. Discussing a Spouse's Workaholism

Icebreaker: John, I've become very concerned about the long hours you're spending at work. I don't think it's good for you, I don't think it's good for the family, and I don't think it's necessary to put in these kinds of hours.

Doesn't see a real conflict: But I love what I do. And I'm really good at it.

It's unintentional: I don't know what happens; I just sort of lose track of time. I'll get better.

Pleads necessity: You don't understand. I just have a whole lot of work to do all the time, and I need to stay late to get it done.

Affirm the goodness of the work: I know you like what you do, I know you're good at it, and I know it's important work. But I also know it's taking time away from the family, and I see that when you are home, you're too tired to do much of anything.

Push this point: You've said before that you would get better about this, but you still end up slipping into your old work patterns. If you really want to change, then let's talk about how we can work together to make that happen.

Not a good enough explanation: I know you work hard, and you're very conscientious about what you do. But I also know that others in your office with similar responsibilities leave earlier in the evening, and none of them work weekends. I think you're giving more to the work than you have to.

Feels powerless to change: Well what would you have me do? I need to get my work done, and the time it takes is the time it takes. It's that simple.

Anger: You think you know better than I do what the demands of my work are?!?

Defensive: What, do you think I *like* working these hours?

You see the consequences of his actions: I don't know what your workday is like, but let me be clear about what I *do* know. I *do* know that the consequences of your work schedule are being felt by all of us, and it can't continue. I think we need to be talking about how to change this so that it doesn't continue to affect the family the way it has.

There may be some credence to the idea that he wants to be doing this: I honestly don't know what the root of this problem is. I do know that there are some times when people overwork themselves because they're trying to steer clear of some other problem in their lives. That may or may not be the case with you, but whatever is going on, it has to change.

Cooperative, to a point: So what do you want me to do, quit my job? Get another one?

Promises to try harder: Look, I'll try harder. I promise. Just give me a couple of weeks.

Close: Here's what I'd like. I'd like you to work eight-hour days for the next three weeks, with no weekend work. You give some thought to how you'd like to spend our free time, and if there's anything I can do to help you. But I also want to see how we handle that as a family. I want the two of us to pay close attention over the next few weeks and see if you really can be happy not working so much, or if there's something deeper going on here that we need to look more closely at.

- **Behavior:** Keep eye contact with your spouse at all times; show that you're not going to let this pass, that things have to change, and that he is the one who has to bring about that change. By the same token, show a willingness to help out.

adaptations

This script can be adapted for use with a spouse who is working too many hours simply because of the legitimate demands of the workplace. In this case, you discuss topics like whether this work schedule is long-term, what effect it's having on you, and whether the spouse needs to be thinking about either asking a boss for some help or looking for a new job.

key points

- You acknowledge the legitimacy and importance of your spouse's work life, but you also see the need for greater balance.
- You're willing to tolerate long hours from time to time, but they can't be constant, and they must be justified.
- Mix your frustration and unhappiness with sympathy for the fact that your spouse is working so hard.
- Reinforce the primacy of family in both of your lives; if this job really does demand such allegiance, perhaps it's time to look elsewhere. Time will tell.

Discussing Potential Parenthood with a Spouse   **14**

There is no more monumental—or potentially intimidating—decision a couple will ever make than whether or not to have children. The couple who are the least bit ambivalent about this must look very closely at all the pluses and minuses, all the factors that compel them either to start a family or to beg off; they must weigh those factors, and then accept the fact that they still won't be certain what to do. It is a decision that is influenced by logic—can we afford it? do we think we'd be good at it? are we willing to do the work? etc.—but finally comes down to a "leap of faith," a decision that is reached simply because it must be reached. At that point, the one piece of advice worth adhering to is, *Don't look back!* Don't second-guess yourselves. Reconcile yourself to your decision, and move on with it. Prior to this "moment of reckoning," however, you can do a few things that might prove valuable to you. First, talk to each other and be respectful of each others' hopes, fears, and uncertainties. Second, talk to friends who may have gone through the same agonies (you'd be surprised how many did) and see what life is like "on the other side of the decision." Third, if need be, talk to a therapist trained in helping couples examine this issue. If nothing else, you may be able to get at some of the root issues that are getting in the way of your reaching a decision. And fourth, accept the fact that whatever you decide will be met with anxiety born of uncertainty. At that point, take whatever solace you can in the realization that you have at least managed to plant yourselves firmly on one side of the fence or the other.

tactics

- **Attitude:** Acknowledge that this is a conversation you may not want to have, but have to have. Also, do your best to give plenty of room for each of you to state exactly how you feel, even if those feelings are in conflict. Speak without editing, listen without judging.

- **Preparation:** Try to identify friends who have and haven't had children, and see if they'd be willing to share their stories with you. Also, identify a psychotherapist who might be skilled at exploring this issue with the two of you in a limited number of private sessions (your physician or clergy person may have a recommendation).

- **Timing:** This is a good conversation to have well before biological necessity impinges on your need to decide. Also, more particularly, it's a good conversation to have at the beginning of a three- or four-day weekend so you both have plenty of unencumbered time to mull it over.

14. Discussing Potential Parenthood with a Spouse

Icebreaker: Anita, I know we've both thought about this on and off for some time, but I think we need to give some serious consideration to whether or not we want to be parents.

Stalls, avoids: Oh, don't be silly. We have plenty of time to figure that out.

You want to press the issue: Biologically, that may or may not be true. But I think if we do want to have kids, now is the time we should make a decision. We're at a good age to become parents.

Agrees: I suppose you're right, but where do we start?

Outside pressure: Well, I know one thing. Our parents sure want us to go ahead and have a baby. Some of our friends do, too.

Wants certainty: I just wish I knew what to do! I wish we could be sure, one way or the other.

Frightened: I know, but it's just such a scary topic to me. I don't know if I'm ready to even talk about it.

Begin by getting your feelings on the table: Well, since we both seem pretty uncertain, why don't we start by talking about the different ways our feelings are tugging us. What are your thoughts about all this?

Can't get a toehold: Gee, I really don't know where to begin. I can't put my thoughts into words. It's all a jumble.

Empathize, but push on: I know; it scares me too. But we have to make a decision before too long, so I guess we have to talk about it even if we don't want to.

Ambivalence: Boy, I'm so torn. On the one hand, I see how much pleasure babies have brought to some of our friends.

They all talk about how great it is. But on the other hand, kids are awfully expensive, and the expenses don't really frighten me off. But I agree that it seems like a relentless job, and that's kind of intimidating to me. I also agree that everyone we know seems to be glad they've gone ahead and done it.

Not an issue: I don't know if we're going to decide to start a family or not, but I do know this is a decision we have to make independent of what anyone else might want us to do.

You go first: Then maybe it would help if I speak first. I think it would be great to have a child, and I think we'd be good parents. It would be tight, but I believe we could afford a child right now, too. On the other hand, I really like our lifestyle the way it is, and I don't know that I want to give that up, especially for something that's as demanding as raising a child.

State your position: I think we'd make good parents, and the expenses don't really frighten me off. But I agree that it seems like a relentless job, and that's kind of intimidating to me. I also agree that everyone we know seems to be glad they've gone ahead and done it.

Next move: Well, it sure sounds as if we're thinking the same way, but where does that leave us? What should we do now?

Close: Let's do this: Let's take the next month and talk some more to some of our friends, especially the ones who shared the same fears we have. There may be some useful information in what they say. Then, I think we need to decide either to commit one way or another, or see a counselor who can help us get off the fence. I actually have the names of a few.

- **Behavior**: You both may want to duck this issue, so be strong in encouraging yourselves to talk it through. Also, listen quietly and patiently to whatever concerns your spouse raises, even if they conflict with your own sentiments.

adaptations

This script can be adapted for use by a couple who are thinking about adopting a child. It can also be adapted for use by a single person who is considering having or adopting a child, and needs to discuss it with a close confidante. Finally, it can be adapted for use when either a husband or a wife is considering elective surgery to prevent them from being able to have children in the future.

key points

- Don't underestimate the enormity of this decision. It will literally affect the rest of your lives.
- Make yourselves immune from the pressures of others who are encouraging you to start a family.
- Have a specific plan and a specific timetable for making a decision; simply waiting a long, long time because you're too scared to make a move will *not* help clarify the issue for you.

Debating Household Chores with a Spouse

15

This is a small debate that's easily kept from becoming a big one provided you raise the issue the moment you're concerned about it. Very often couples—especially newlyweds—don't go through the task of literally dividing up household responsibilities in a way that feels equal to both partners. Instead, we arbitrarily slip into specific roles for reasons we're not always clear on. One will do the cooking, the cleaning, the laundry. The other will tend the garden, pay the bills, get the kids to the dentist. If it feels balanced, chances are it is, and couples live a long, long time repeating the same chores week in and week out. If, however, either spouse (or both) feels slighted, as though she is bearing more than her share of the load, it may be time to come up with a clear and unambiguous system for dividing the labors. Yours may be different from the next couple's—you may divide the jobs once and for all while another couple alternates responsibilities each week and still another couple puts the bulk of the work on the kids' shoulders—but in the end all that matters is that you've come up with a scheme that works for you.

tactics

- **Attitude**: You're not complaining. In fact, you're not even sure the chores are unevenly distributed. But you do want to talk about it, because it *feels* that way to you.

- **Preparation**: If you can, try to compose a list of all the jobs that require attention in your home. It can be a good starting point for discussion.

- **Timing**: Have this conversation late in the work week so that your solution can be put to the test over the weekend, when most household chores get done.

- **Behavior**: You are a team looking for the proper chemistry for your teamwork. Don't be adversarial; show as much interest in your spouse's point of view as you'd like him to show in yours.

15. Debating Household Chores with a Spouse

Icebreaker: It may just be my perception, but I sometimes get the feeling I'm doing more than my share of household chores, and I'm wondering if there's a way we could divide our responsibilities a little more clearly.

Gets defensive: Are you accusing me of not doing my share of the chores around here?

Allay fears: Not at all. You do a lot of work. In fact, I may be wrong about this whole matter. But I'm wondering if we can figure out a way to be sure the jobs are getting divided equally between us.

Doesn't see the problem: Boy, I don't know. From where I stand, I think the jobs get divided pretty equally.

You see things differently: You may be right; this may just be a perception on my part. How can we figure this out?

Shares your sentiment: It's funny you should mention that, because the truth is, I've been feeling like I do more of the work around here!

Look for an equitable solution: Maybe we would both feel better about things if we could come up with some sort of system that identifies all the jobs and then agree on who has to do them.

Has no ideas: Well, I don't know how to divide up the jobs, do you?

Could show a little more maturity: Well, I just know the jobs I *don't* want to do! I *don't* want to clean the bathroom or do the laundry, I can tell you that.

Wants balance: I don't much care what we do as long as it's fair to both of us. Neither one of us should feel as though we're doing the lion's share of work.

Close: Here's a suggestion: Let's each write a list of every job we do and every job we think the other does. Then let's put the lists together, see if we're missing anything, make one long list of jobs, and begin parceling them out one at a time. We'll see if we can agree on who does what.

adaptations

This script can be adapted for use by parents who are dividing up household chores for their children to assume.

key points

- You're just looking for an equal balance in the division of responsibilities.
- You may have some ideas as to how to achieve that balance, but you're also open to suggestions.
- You're not accusing your spouse of not doing his share; you're simply noting that it feels as if the two of you have lapsed into an unequal distribution of work.
- Remember, as with other areas of a good marriage, pretty much everything's negotiable.

Asking for a Divorce 16

Once you've committed yourself to the irrevocable decision to divorce your spouse, the hardest job you'll have will be breaking the news. And if you wait for "the right time," you'll find yourself waiting in vain. This is news that isn't delivered lightly, gently, or easily. Nor should it be delivered cryptically. When you're ready to pose the question, do so without hesitation and with no beating around the bush. Assumedly, the two of you have been trying for some time to work out your differences, but to no avail, so the news shouldn't come as a total shock to your mate. Nevertheless, brace yourself for an avalanche of feelings, accusations, guilt trips, disbelief, venom, and rage, all, some, or none of which may come your way. And as the two of you discuss it, stay cool; don't be drawn into an argument or be baited into saying something you might later regret. Convey sadness but conviction in your decision. And don't waver.

tactics

- **Attitude**: You're very unhappy but resolute. You will not be talked out of this. Maintain calm at all times, even if your spouse gets heated.

- **Preparation**: Arrange for a place to stay, either that night or, preferably, the next night. Also, begin to explore a more permanent living arrangement (even if it means eventually asking your spouse to move out). You should also have an attorney lined up, and you may want to have had an initial conversation with her.

- **Timing**: This conversation is best held on a Friday evening so you can attend to personal business over the weekend. If you have children, it's best if you can have it while they're not there, or at least while they're asleep.

- **Behavior**: Keep some distance from your spouse. Avoid contact, as that can only confuse matters.

16. Asking for a Divorce

Icebreaker: Lee, we've both tried so hard to try to make this marriage work, but I'm afraid I can't go on any longer. I want a divorce.

Wants to bargain: Look, let's give it one more chance. Maybe a nice vacation to the islands. A little more romance. I'll do more around the house. Let's keep trying.

Refusal: Well, you may want a divorce, but I don't, and I'm not going to grant you one.

Veiled threat: I can tell you one thing, I won't make life easy for you if you walk out on me.

Plies you with guilt: I can't believe you're going to end it, just like that, after all I've done for you. Obviously I take our marriage vows a lot more seriously than you do!

Incredulous: I can't believe you're saying this! I never thought it would come to this; I always thought we'd work things out. I know we can!

No use beating a dead horse: If I had any hope that more work would make things better, I'd stay and try to fix things. But after this long a time, I've become sadly convinced that it won't. I'm not happy about this, but I have to leave.

Ultimately, it's not his decision: I'll be asking for a divorce in court, and I understand you are free to contest it. I hope you'll change your mind, but if not, I guess we'll leave it to the judge to decide.

Leave it to your lawyer: I think it's a good idea for both of us to retain lawyers to work out the hard details. If there are specific issues you need to raise with me, you can pass them along to my attorney. When I hire one, I'll get you his name and phone number.

Don't get into an argument: I think we've both worked hard on this, and I know you're no happier than I am. I'm sorry if you feel I'm not taking our vows more seriously, because I am. But our marriage isn't a healthy one, and I have to leave.

Dose of reality: For a long time I thought we could work it out, too. We gave it everything we had, but I'm not happy in the marriage, and I'm sure I never will be. I have to do this.

What's the future: But where will you go? What will you do? What will I do?

How will the kids be affected: But what about the kids? How are they going to take this?

Wants to stay together for sake of children: I know the marriage has problems, but our kids are entitled to a family with two parents.

Doesn't want to involve lawyers: Let's at least work this divorce out amicably, without lawyers.

Answers may take time: I'm going to spend the night here tonight; I'll sleep on the couch if you'd like. And I plan to go to my parents' house this weekend, then find a place to live. I think we should talk to the kids tomorrow; if you want me to do it myself, I will, although I think we should do it together. It's going to take a while before things settle down, and I think we're all going to have to adjust to that.

Children aren't enough of a reason to stay together: I know that neither of us want to see the kids hurt by any of this, but the truth is, they've already been hurt by our fighting and our unhappiness. When this is over, we really owe it to them to talk with someone about how best to coparent them, even though we'll be living apart.

Protect yourself: That would certainly be easiest, but I'm in such a tense emotional state that I don't know that I could think straight. I also think there may be some complicated financial and custody issues that are best left to legal experts.

Resignation: It doesn't sound like there's any stopping you. I think you're making a big mistake, though.

Still can't accept it: This is all so sudden; such a shock. I still can't believe you're doing this.

Anger: Well, you can bet you'll hear from my lawyer! I can tell you that!

Last-ditch effort: Let's just give it one more chance; just a little longer. I know we can work it out.

Close: I wish there was more to say or do. I don't want to see anyone in our family suffer. But I have to do this, and I can only hope that for everyone's sake we'll be able to settle things down calmly and fairly, and get on with our lives.

adaptations

This script can be adapted to request a trial separation.

key points

- You acknowledge the hard work the two of you have put into trying to make this marriage work.
- If possible, avoid casting blame.
- Don't get drawn into an argument.
- Have a plan you're ready to enact as soon as you have to.
- The less said, the better; don't say anything that could come back to haunt you in family court.

Asking for a Prenuptial Agreement 17

When you go to the hospital for surgery, you have full faith and confidence that everything will go well and you'll recover as promised. Nevertheless, it is reassuring to you to sign the malpractice insurance forms, so you know you're covered in the unlikely event that something goes terribly wrong. Marriage can be approached the same way; you wouldn't be marrying this person if you didn't have full faith that it would last, but you also know that unforeseen things can happen, and in the unlikely event of a marriage failure, you want to know you're both protected. In raising this issue with your fiancé, do so rather matter-of-factly, as though your attorney is pitching it and, while it does have merit, you're simply looking at it as backup insurance neither one of you will ever need.

tactics

- **Attitude**: This is a simple formality you want to get out of the way as quickly as possible.

- **Preparation**: Prepare your reasoning ahead of time; be ready to show your fiancé that this protects both of you from any confusion and misunderstanding should you ever actually have to use it.

- **Timing**: Raise this subject after you've agreed to get married and announced it to others, but well before the wedding date.

- **Behavior**: Obviously a conversation to be held in private, try to pass it off to attorneys as quickly as possible.

17. Asking for a Prenuptial Agreement

Icebreaker: I had an interesting call from my attorney today. She wanted to congratulate us on our engagement, and asked me if we'd thought about a prenuptial agreement. At first I thought the idea was totally unwarranted, but she made a pretty good argument for just going ahead and getting one.

Trust objection: I think our relationship needs to be founded on trust, not suspicion or doubt.

Trust is still intact: I couldn't agree with you more, but I don't think this is a matter of us not trusting one another. It simply offers us both financial protection if, heaven forbid, anything unforeseen should happen.

Fear: Do you think we're not going to make it as a married couple?

Allay fears: Not at all, and I trust you feel the same way. She merely pointed out that it makes sense to sign one, get it out of the way, and then not think about it.

Angry: Well, if you think we need one, then there's something seriously wrong with this relationship that I don't know about!

Deflect anger: It's funny you should say that, because I had the exact same reaction. But she pointed out that it's something we do simply to protect us from the unknown, and that once we get it out of the way, we never have to concern ourselves with it.

Curious, if a bit suspicious: Why would we need one?

Give reasons: She made the analogy that it's like putting your seat belt on in the car. You don't anticipate any problems, and you have full faith in one another, but strange things can happen somewhere down the line that are impossible to anticipate ahead of time. This simply protects all of us from any financial problems should anything happen.

Accedes, reluctantly: Well, it doesn't thrill me, I can tell you that.

Close: Me either, which is why I told her that we should let our lawyers work this out on their own, and leave us out of it. I think we need to think of it as an insurance policy we'll never cash in.

adaptations

This script can be adapted for use by an individual who wants to maintain finances separate from her spouse or fiancé.

key points

- This was your lawyer's idea; chances are your fiancé's lawyer would agree that it's a good idea.
- Reaffirm your trust in your fiancé and your faith in the solidity of your relationship.
- Be able to present logical arguments as to why this protects both of you from any later misunderstanding.

Criticizing a Spouse's Child Care **18**

strategy

When your spouse is engaging in some form of parenting behavior that you have a problem with, you want to communicate three things. First, you want to isolate and define the specific behavior. Second, you want to reinforce the fact that your spouse is indeed a good parent, but may want to change this one specific behavior. And third, you want to be able to explain the negative (if unintentional) effect that behavior is having on your child or children. By doing this you give him something to work with, help him maintain his confidence in his abilities as a parent, and give him a way to watch for changes that might ensue in the child when his approach is modified.

tactics

- **Attitude**: Assume that critiquing one another's parenting—in a loving manner—is something you both regard as good for the family. And reinforce the fact that on the whole your spouse does a wonderful job parenting.

- **Preparation**: You may want to do a little research into the parenting behavior you find troubling. Ask a pediatrician or child psychologist whether you are in fact on target with your concerns.

- **Timing**: Have this conversation soon enough after an incident that points up the behavior you wish to critique, especially if it has clearly backfired.

- **Behavior**: You recognize that parenting is an enormous, relentless job, and you need each others' help in assessing parenting skills. Be open to asking your spouse for similar help.

18. Criticizing a Spouse's Child Care

Icebreaker: John, I'm a little bit concerned about something that's going on with you and Jason. I'm not sure you know how he hears it when you yell at him. I think it hits him harder than you want it to, and it would be a good idea to just tone it down a little bit.

Hurt: Gee, I'm sorry to hear you say that; I've always considered myself a good dad.

Offer reassurance: You're a wonderful father. You're raising a great son, and he loves you very much. This is just one piece of your behavior toward him that I think you might want to work on. If you lower your voice just a little, he'll still understand how you feel, but he's less likely to get as upset as he does.

Turns the tables: Well you know, you coddle him too much for my taste.

Reactive: I know what I'm doing; he needs the discipline, and I'm not afraid to give it to him.

You're willing to discuss his criticisms: I'm more than happy to talk with you about ways you think I can be a better mother to Jason, but for now let's stick to this one topic. I think it would do him some good if, when you reprimanded him, you didn't raise your voice quite as loudly as you do. If you soften it just a little, he'll still get your message, but he won't be so upset.

Defensive: Oh, don't be treating him like a baby. He can take it.

Where you're in agreement: I think both of us agree that discipline is important, and that may mean raising our voices sometimes. What I'm saying is that you may be more powerful than you realize, and you might sound to Jason more angry than you really are. I think that's why he gets so upset when you come on strongly.

Sarcasm: Well, then, from now on I'll be sure to whisper as if I'm talking to a little baby.

Wants clarification: Can you be clearer for me about what it is I'm doing that you want me to change, and why?

The apple doesn't fall far from the tree: Look, this is how my dad reprimanded me.

That doesn't make it right: I know this is how you were raised, but I also know you didn't like that part of your dad's behavior, and I suspect that, as good a dad as he is, he would've still gotten through to you.

Offer clarification: When he does something you want to scold him for, you raise your voice to a level that may sound fine to you but to him sounds like you're angrier than you really are. Instead of just thinking he's made a small mistake, he interprets it as being in serious trouble; as though he's let you down terribly.

Agreeable, but wants your help: I'll try to tone it down, but if I don't even know that I'm doing this, I'm going to need your help. You need to point it out to me if you think I'm yelling too loud.

Stiffen up: There's no need for sarcasm; you know that's not what I'm asking for.

Makes no guarantees: Look, I'll try, but I don't know that I can change who I am.

Close: I think it's great that you take such an active interest in your parenting, and if you'd like, whenever we have to discipline Jason, we can talk about it beforehand, and then approach him together. Let's see if that helps us.

adaptations

This may sound trivial, but this script can be adapted for use when you want to criticize how a spouse or child is treating a family pet.

key points

- Try to point out the connection between the offending behavior and the effect it yields in the child.
- Offer alternative approaches.
- Confess that you need help and ideas in your own parenting.
- Don't let your spouse's embarrassment get in the way of making your point, especially if that embarrassment manifests itself as hostility, dismissal, or sarcasm.

Confronting Actions That Undermine Your Parental Authority

19

strategy

As parents we are often in agreement on how to raise, discipline, train, and reward our children. But sometimes we're not, and when this happens, it's to the child's disadvantage. Kids need consistency in how they're raised, and they need to know that one parent speaks for both. Only then can they be clear about what the rules are, and disabuse themselves of any thoughts of playing one parent off against the other. If you come upon a situation where you and your spouse are at cross-purposes, your best bet is to cite a specific situation and hold it up as a general example of the need for the two of you to speak with one voice. And when you do this, do it with an eye toward finding some kind of compromise the two of you can both live with. This not only comforts the child by giving her a consistent picture of what is expected of her; the art of reaching that compromise enhances your parenting skills as well.

tactics

- **Attitude**: You're not saying your manner of parenting is better than your spouse's. You're only saying they're different, and the two of you need consistency so as not to undermine one another.

- **Preparation**: Read up a little bit about the need for consistency in parenting, if for no other reason than it gives your spouse something to read and mull over, and may make the case more articulately than you.

- **Timing**: Have this conversation after your child has gone to bed, but not too late in the evening. Have it shortly after your spouse has done something that illustrates your point.

- **Behavior**: Approach this as two parents on the same side of the fence, with the same goals in mind, i.e., to raise the best kids you can. Present it as a disagreement that you need to find middle ground on.

19. Confronting Actions That Undermine Your Parental Authority

Icebreaker: Jack, I'm concerned that Stephanie is getting mixed messages from us when it comes to after-school snacks. I've told her she needs to have fruit, and you're allowing her to have ice cream and candy. We need to reach some sort of agreement here.

Doesn't see a conflict: What's the problem? She has ice cream when I'm in charge, and fruit when you are. Seems like a good balance to me.

Pushes his agenda: Oh, don't be so strict. Let her have ice cream and candy after school. What's the big deal?

Looks for leeway in the rule: I know we agreed that she should have fruit when she comes home, but I think she should be allowed to "cheat" a little, just from time to time.

He's missing the point: My concern is less about what she's eating than about getting two different signals from us. When you allow her to have ice cream or candy, you're telling her that with you she can get away with something that I don't let her get away with. This makes you the "good guy" and me the bad one in her eyes. It also confuses her as to what we expect from her. She needs to be hearing the same thing from both of us.

Wants to resolve this particular conflict: So how do you want to handle this snack thing, then? I don't think she should have to forgo the stuff she really loves all the time. I think it's too strict.

Doesn't necessarily agree: Why can't we operate with two sets of rules, as long as she knows what my expectations are of her and what your expectations are of her?

Cite experts: I think that invites competition. We could talk more about this with her teacher if you'd like, but the experts I read tell me that if parents have different sets of rules, the child will gravitate toward the one whose rules are more appealing to her. It pits the parents against one another. If you'd like, I can show you some articles that can explain this much better than I can.

Doesn't trust experts: I don't need experts to tell us how to raise Stephanie. They don't know as much as you might think.

You agree to a compromise: I don't necessarily agree with you, but I'm willing to compromise. How about if she's allowed to have candy or ice cream two days a week and fruit the other three?

Still doesn't agree with you, but agrees to compromise: I'm not sure I buy all this stuff; I don't think it has to be that complicated. But all right, I'll go along with a compromise.

Close: I appreciate this, Jack. Let's agree on the compromise and then present it to Stephanie together. I think she'll understand then that we're speaking to her with one voice.

key points

- Use an example to illustrate your point.
- Don't dwell on the example; speak more about the need for consistency.
- Be willing to listen to your spouse's ideas for how to reach accommodation on points you disagree on.
- When you have reached agreement on how to handle the example you've used to illustrate your point, present it to the child together.

Confronting Inappropriate Treatment of Parents

20

strategy

If in our estimation your spouse is treating your parents poorly, your best bet is to ask her to change for your sake. Explain that you don't want to see your parents hurt, and that it only generates tension between you and your parents. There's a better than even chance that your spouse will reply that it's your parents who don't like her, not vice versa, and that if they would change, everybody would be a lot happier. You can acknowledge this part of your parents' behavior, and can even relate that you've experienced them that way too. But having done that, you then want to strategize with your spouse as to how to make things better. Offer to talk with your parents in exchange for getting your spouse to try and behave a little better. Also, offer to cut back on the visits between the families. The thinking here is that you want to demonstrate flexibility and a willingness to work things out, and you expect flexibility in return.

tactics

- **Attitude**: You can understand why your spouse might behave poorly toward your parents, but you won't tolerate it. Something has to change.

- **Preparation**: Be prepared to make concessions that will make it easier for your spouse to get along with your parents.

- **Timing**: Have this conversation a few days before you are all to be together, especially if the upcoming function will include other people as well (this takes some of the pressure off your spouse to interact one-on-one with your folks).

- **Behavior**: You're patient and willing to hear your spouse's complaints. And you show a willingness to negotiate a compromise solution. But you're also forthright about insisting that this be resolved.

20. Confronting Inappropriate Treatment of Parents

Icebreaker: Jackie, I'm not at all happy with the way you treat my parents. You hardly speak to them, and when you answer them, your answers are short and curt. It would mean a great deal to me if you would behave better when we're together.

Doesn't see the problem: I don't think I'm nasty to them; I think I treat them fine. I wonder if you're just too sensitive.

Focus on how the parents feel rather than how the spouse behaves: What I see is that they are hurt by your behavior, so even though other people might not be put off by it, they are. I'd like you to try a little harder with them because I think it would make them and me feel better.

Mutual antagonism: I'm sorry, but I've always felt that they didn't like me, so it's awfully hard to be pleasant to them.

Cites her own parents: And what about my parents? You're not exactly charming to them, either.

Acknowledge, then stay to the point: You may well be right; I may not treat them as well as I should, and not even know it. Let's talk about my folks for now, and then I'd be happy to discuss yours.

You can relate: I know they can be difficult sometimes. Believe me, they've upset me more than once. But they are my parents, and I want us to accord them some respect. Would it be easier if I had a talk with them about how they treat *you?*

Would like you to talk to your parents: I do think I'd feel better about them if you could talk to them about how they treat me.

Finds it difficult: I have a hard time hiding my feelings. I don't want to feel as though I'm playing some sort of charade, being nice to people who I don't think particularly like me.

Will make an effort: Look, I'll try to be nicer. But it won't be easy.

Doesn't see why she should change: I don't know. I'll try, I suppose, but I don't see why I should be pleasant to people who obviously aren't crazy about me.

A breakthrough: I'm happy to speak to my folks. Since we'll all be together this weekend, I'd really appreciate your making an effort to chat them up a little bit, and then I'll go and see them next week and talk about how they could behave better toward you.

Recognize the difficulty: I know it isn't easy for you, and I appreciate your being willing to put forth the effort. Let me know if I can do anything to make it easier for you.

Do this for you: The bottom line is that it makes it hard on me when there's friction between you. If you would just be a little nicer toward them—and I can see to it that we don't spend too much time with them—life would be easier for me.

(Barely) willing to cooperate: Look, I will try. But if they don't treat me any better, I can't promise how I'll react.

Will do this for you: If you agree that we don't have to spend so much time with them, and if they can treat me a little better, then I'll try to be better toward them. But I'm only doing this for you, not for them.

Close: This takes a big load off my chest. They can be a bit of a pain sometimes, so I want you to know how much I appreciate your putting forth this effort. It will certainly make my life a little easier. And maybe you and I should plan on going out and having a nice dinner Saturday night, after we leave their place.

adaptations

This script can be adapted to confront inappropriate behavior toward other family members or toward good friends.

key points

- You understand your parents' foibles.
- Ask your spouse what you can do to make things better.
- Acknowledge how hard it can be to change behavior, especially when it isn't heartfelt.
- Emphasize that this adversely affects you, so that even if your spouse has no feelings toward your parents, she will at least want to spare you any grief.

Bringing Up a Spouse's Bad Hygiene

21

strategy

This is a rare case in which you might not want your icebreaker to deliver the full force of your concern. Asking a spouse if he's aware that he's not taking good care of himself is like throwing a rock at somebody to warn him that he's in the way of a moving car. Instead, shift the focus by asking your spouse if there is something troubling him. Point out the poor hygiene as something you don't normally expect from him, and therefore perhaps symptomatic of a more important issue. That way, even if he reacts defensively or angrily, you can let him know that your real focus was his well-being, and that his appearance was only of secondary concern to you. Having broken through, though, don't dwell on this topic. Don't work the conversation until you get a "confession" out of him. Instead, be sure you've made your point and then walk away from it. On his own, in private, he will surely reflect on what you've said and take it to heart.

tactics

- **Attitude**: You're curious about his appearance and hygiene, and concerned about his emotional state of affairs.

- **Preparation**: Be prepared to let this conversation go without reaching a definitive conclusion.

- **Timing**: Have this conversation on a weekday evening, so that your spouse can pay particular attention to his appearance and hygiene on the next working day.

- **Behavior**: It's perfectly all right to be tentative and show a little embarrassment of your own. You might even consider alluding to a similar problem you yourself encountered before you met your spouse (it's okay to tell a little lie here).

21. Bringing Up a Spouse's Bad Hygiene

Icebreaker: Peter, this may sound like it's coming out of left field, but have you been feeling all right lately? I'm wondering if there's something on your mind.

Wonders what's up: Um . . . why do you ask?

Ease in gently: Well, this is a little bit awkward for me to say, but you've always been so attentive to how you take care of yourself, and it seems as though in the past few weeks your clothes have been a little disheveled, you may not be getting in the shower as often as you usually do, and it has me wondering if something is upsetting you.

Something is wrong: I didn't know it was so obvious. I *have* been feeling a little depressed lately. Maybe I'm *not* taking such good care of myself.

Embarrassed: Gee, I don't know what to say . . . this is so embarrassing. You mean you think I'm *dirty?*

Angry: What kind of thing is that to say to me? I'm really insulted!

Doesn't notice anything awry: Nope, I'm just fine. Thanks for asking, though.

Shift the emphasis: Would you care to talk about what's bothering you? Maybe it will help.

Will work on what's bothering him: Thanks. Actually, I think I'm getting it under control; I'm just embarrassed that you could tell something by my *hygiene!*

Ease his mind: Oh, don't worry about that. What's really important to me is that you get what's bothering you off your chest.

Not easy for you: Yeah, it feels kind of funny for me to bring this up too, but please don't misunderstand me. I'm just noticing that your hygiene habits have slipped a little lately, and I hope it's not because there's something troubling you.

Absorb anger: I know it must sound terribly insensitive on my part, it's just that I thought it was something you'd rather hear from me than someone else.

Wants to change subject: Can we talk about something else, please? This makes me pretty uncomfortable.

Agree to change the topic, with one last word: Sure, we can change the topic; I'm not crazy about bringing this up either, but I'm glad I did, just so you have the information.

You're perplexed, and you need to push the issue: Well, I'm glad nothing's wrong, but . . . are you aware that some of your hygiene habits may have slipped a little lately?

Caught unaware; defensive: Actually, I don't think I'm doing anything differently.

Don't press your point: Hmm. Well, okay. I guess our perceptions are different. Anyway, I'm glad that nothing's troubling you.

Close: I know this was a difficult thing for both of us to take a look at, but I'm so glad we have the kind of marriage where we can call attention to things we each can benefit from hearing.

adaptation

This script can be adapted to address the issue of a spouse's inappropriate attire.

key points

- Your main concern is your spouse's health and well-being.
- Don't expect a positive response to your inquiry; at best he will be embarrassed and want to change the subject.
- Be satisfied to drop the message on your spouse and let him deal with it privately.
- Acknowledge that it's not an easy topic for you to discuss either.

Bringing Up a Spouse's Bad Manners

22

It's extremely difficult to bring up a subject like this without making your spouse feel as though you are treating him like a child. After all, who among us doesn't remember those childhood admonitions, "Get your elbows off the table," or "Wash behind your ears"? When you're forced to say something to your spouse about bad manners, try to make it easier on both of you by keeping a few things in mind. First, focus in on particular behavior. That way, your spouse won't feel roundly condemned for his actions and can concentrate on what specifically needs improvement. Second, draw attention to how the behavior is interpreted by others. By doing this, you're not necessarily saying he is doing anything bad per se, just that it affects others adversely. Third, let him know it makes *you* uncomfortable, so that even if he doesn't want to change for his own sake, he might change for yours. And finally point out to him how it can affect *him*, by being looked down upon by others, cut out of social circles, maybe even jeopardizing his career.

tactics

- **Attitude**: You want to downplay this, but feel it's important enough that your spouse know what you've been observing about his behavior. You're pointing it out—almost casually—with the thought that it's something he might not notice about himself.

- **Preparation**: Wait for some instance of the offending behavior to occur so that you can refer to something specific when discussing it with your spouse.

- **Timing**: Hold this conversation in extreme private, on a Friday or Saturday, when your spouse doesn't have to be out in public any time immediately thereafter.

- **Behavior**: You're doing this for his own good, but you don't want to seem parental. Be objective as you point out the behavior and how you perceive others reacting to it.

22. Bringing Up a Spouse's Bad Manners

Icebreaker: Alex, this may mean little or nothing to you, but when we're out in public, I think some of the jokes you tell offend some people, and you may want to consider toning things down a little.

Personalizes things: Are you embarrassed to be with me? Is that what you're saying?

You are aware of how he is perceived: I'm uncomfortable when I think other people are being unintentionally offended or hurt by things you might say. Not everybody appreciates your humor like I do, and I'm asking you to be a little more sensitive to that.

Defensive/wants specifics: I don't know what you're talking about. Give me an example of what you mean.

Give a specific example, but don't dwell on this one instance: Well, I don't think your boss's wife was too thrilled with the joke you told her, but my main point is that it's a kind of behavior that could rub quite a few people the wrong way. And it makes *me* uncomfortable when that happens.

Resistant to change: Look, I am who I am. If people don't like it, that's their problem.

Voice of reason: You're right, in a sense. You need to be who you are, and I can admire your honesty. But I also think it can hurt *us* if people don't like some of the jokes you tell. I think it could alienate us from some of our friends, and I think it could hurt you at work if you're looking to move up in the company. And, to be perfectly honest with you, it makes me a little uncomfortable.

Defends himself: Look, my boss's wife might've taken my joke the wrong way last night. I can't help it if she's so sensitive!

Focus on yourself: I can't tell you how to handle yourself in social situations. I can only point out two things to you: It makes *me* feel uncomfortable, and it makes some *other* people feel the same way. You can be a very funny man, but I don't think you intend to do that with your humor.

Relents, reluctantly: All right, all right. If it makes you uncomfortable I'll crank things down a little. But I still gotta be myself!

Close: I hope you never lose your sense of humor, Alex. I just want you to edit it, that's all. Why don't you bring your bawdiest jokes home first and try them out on me? I can tell you if anyone might be too sensitive to hear them without being put off.

adaptations

This script can be adapted for use with a sibling, or when there is one specific person or couple who your spouse simply refuses to get along with.

key points

- Your attention is directed to how people react to your spouse's behavior, not necessarily to the behavior itself.
- It is in your spouse's best interest to change.
- Be as specific as possible about the offending behavior and what he can do to change it.
- Don't try to force him to admit that he's "wrong," but that his actions affect others negatively.

Expressing Fears about a Spouse's Health

23

If your spouse is exhibiting health problems that are serious enough for you to be concerned, and if in addition he's treating his symptoms as if they augur nothing, you can be pretty well assured that deep down inside, he's worried. He doesn't want to go to a doctor, not because he wants to minimize what might be wrong with him, but because he fears the doctor will maximize it, will tell him there is a serious problem that needs immediate attention. In this case, you have to provide the dose of reality necessary to move speculation to fact, and you have to do it directly but gently. Let your spouse know that the entire family feels *some* burden from his health problem, even if it's just the anxiety of not knowing what the problem is. Let him know also that even if he won't admit that he's nervous, you at least want him to get checked out for *your* sake. Finally, let him know that he owes this to you; one spouse has the right to know the condition of the other.

tactics

- **Attitude**: You are not alarmed, but you're not indifferent either. You are concerned, and you want answers as to the state of your spouse's health.

- **Preparation**: Be prepared to make an appointment with the doctor for your own checkup; that provides a convenient reason for your spouse to have one too.

- **Timing**: Have this conversation at a time when you can immediately call and arrange to see your doctor; don't wait until a Friday or a weekend.

- **Behavior**: If your spouse wants to complain that you're "too nervous about nothing," let him do so. The point is, you are directed at getting him to either agree with you or, at the very least, obey you.

23. Expressing Fears about a Spouse's Health

Icebreaker: Bob, I'm concerned about that cough of yours because you've had it for three weeks now. I'm making an appointment for a check-up and I'd like to make one for you as well.

Shrugs you off: Oh, it's nothing. I'm feeling better, and it'll be cleared up in a couple of days. Don't you worry about it.

Alarmist: Gee, you don't think it might be something really serious, do you? Maybe I have a massive lung infection?

Will take care of it: Ah, I'll make my own appointment. Thanks anyway.

Counsel caution: I think you're probably right. No doubt it isn't anything serious, but there are two reasons why I want you to have it looked at. First, he can give you something to speed up the recovery and maybe keep me or the kids from catching it, and second, he can tell us for sure what it is, so we don't have to speculate.

Counsel diligence and calm: I trust my suspicion that it's nothing at all to be concerned with, but I think we'll both feel better to have the doctor tell us that, and prescribe something to clear it up.

You want to go together: I'd like us to go together. The kids and I have listened to this cough of yours for a few weeks now, and I'd kind of like to be sure the doctor's going to take care of it for us sooner rather than later.

Pleads his case: Look, I've always been slow to recover from this sort of thing. Give me a little more time.

Relents: Oh, okay. You make sense. We'll go see the doc together.

Doesn't treat you seriously: You're just a worrier. I can take care of myself; just let me be.

Impose a timetable: I need to take all of our health into consideration here, including our peace of mind. I'll make an appointment for both of us for next Wednesday, and if you're all better before then, you don't have to go.

Be firm: I don't think of it as worrying so much as I do paying attention. You owe it to yourself and the rest of us to pay attention to your health, and I would like you there when I go in for my checkup next week.

Close: It means a lot to me that you can be so good about looking after your health. I'm going to call this morning and schedule the appointments.

adaptations

This script can be adapted for use by someone whose spouse is refusing to follow a doctor's orders for convalescence or rehabilitation.

key points

- Your spouse owes it to the family to take good care of himself.
- He is probably more frightened than he's letting on, and subconsciously wants you to intervene on his behalf.
- Remind him that his health problems are already affecting other members of the family.
- If need be, press the point that you won't take no for an answer.

part 6

Lifescripts

for friends

Explaining That You Don't Like Unplanned Visits

1

strategy

This can be a tricky conversation if the friend you're talking to interprets it as a repudiation of your friendship rather than simply a protection of your (or family's) privacy. If you've been playing by one set of rules for a while (i.e., impromptu visits are okay) and now impose more stringent rules, he may wonder if the friendship itself is weakening at the seams. This can be further complicated if you are still welcome at his house, unannounced, because it can feel to him like a double standard. The best you can do here is be explicit about your reasoning behind the new policy, give whatever assurance you can that you consider the friendship to be as strong as ever, and accept the fact that this new arrangement may take some getting used to. Nevertheless, however begrudging or irritated your friend may be at first, you will both slip comfortably into that new arrangement in short order, and all will be forgiven.

tactics

- **Attitude**: You are not angry about the previous unplanned visits; you simply want to set up some reasonable boundaries. You are appealing to your friend's sense of reasonableness.

- **Preparation**: Shortly before the conversation, ask the friend to give you a call to set up a time the two of you can get together.

- **Timing**: Have this conversation on or around the time you and your friend are enjoying a fair amount of activity and camaraderie in the friendship.

- **Behavior**: Don't be apologetic, because you don't want to seem as if you're sorry you're doing this. With little affect in your voice and an easy demeanor, you're conveying that this is no big deal.

1. Explaining That You Don't Like Unplanned Visits

Icebreaker: Adam, I need to ask a favor of you. I'd appreciate it if, when you feel like stopping by at my place, you just give a call first so I know you're coming. Every once in a while it's not a good time for a visit, and I like to be able to give you a heads-up ahead of time if that's the case.

Doesn't understand: I don't need a heads-up; if I come by and you're busy, I'll just take off. No big deal.

Be more specific: It would be real helpful to me if you would give a call first because there are times we just don't want the doorbell ringing at all. We're pretty protective of our quiet family time, and even if someone just pops their head in, it feels like that quiet time is broken.

Turns the tables: But you know you're welcome at my place anytime. You don't have to call *me* first. What's the deal?

You're different: Yeah, you're real comfortable about that, and I guess it's just one way we're different.

Hurt by this: We've known each other a long time. Now you're telling me you don't want me dropping by anymore?

Clarify your position: What I like is to know you're coming, because there are instances when I might be tied up with something else that's taking my time and attention. When that happens, I don't feel like I can have *any* company.

Accepts your terms: It may feel a little strange, but sure, if it works for you it'll work for me.

Feels a little irritated: Well, *if that's* the way you want it, who am I to disagree?

Feels bad: Gee, I'm sorry. I feel kinda bad. I didn't realize I'd been intruding on you all this time.

Gentle, but firm: Adam, my family and I need to have it that way because we like to have our privacy. It may feel odd to you at first, but I really hope you'll understand.

Close: I know you do things differently in your home, and I want you to know how much I appreciate your understanding on this issue.

adaptations

This script can be adapted for use with a friend who stays too long on visits to your home.

key points

- There may have been a time when you welcomed the impromptu visit, but circumstances have changed.
- The fact that you may be welcomed in his home without notice doesn't change your feelings about this.
- It may take a little while, and you both may go through a little awkwardness the first few times he calls prior to visiting.

Turning Down a Friend's Request to Be in Your Bridal Party   2

strategy

What makes weddings difficult to execute is that all the people who have a stake in them (brides, grooms, parents, friends, etc.) have their own idea as to what they should look like, so that planning for a day devoted to the celebration of the unity of two people can often include the need to somehow, however approximately, meet everybody's needs and wants. What this means is that there will be a lot of horse trading—you can have the six-piece jazz band if I can have the purple centerpiece and the veal cordon bleu. And what the horse trading means is that some people are going to be left out in the cold. Someone's not going to sit where they want, someone else isn't even going to be invited, and someone will be excluded from the bridal party. When this happens, your best bet is to paint both of you as the victims of circumstance. Try to explain two things to the aggrieved: that your hand has been more or less forced here, and that you are not at all happy about this. Then don't be in too great a hurry for them to be understanding and forgiving. Impress upon them how important it is to you that they be there, try to include them at your table to *show* them how important they are, and if need be, give them time to get over it.

tactics

- **Attitude**: You feel powerless to do anything about this, and you are extremely unhappy you've been forced into making this decision.

- **Preparation**: Make sure you have a good understanding of how you reached the decision to limit your bridal party, and be prepared to make the case that this entire wedding has been an exercise in give and take.

- **Timing**: Tell your friend as soon as your decision is reached; bad news travels fast, and you don't want her hearing it from anyone other than you.

- **Behavior**: Make sure you don't come across as if you are *asking* her to relinquish her assumed role in your bridal party. Even though you didn't want to make this decision, you are now committed to it.

2. Turning Down a Friend's Request to Be in Your Bridal Party

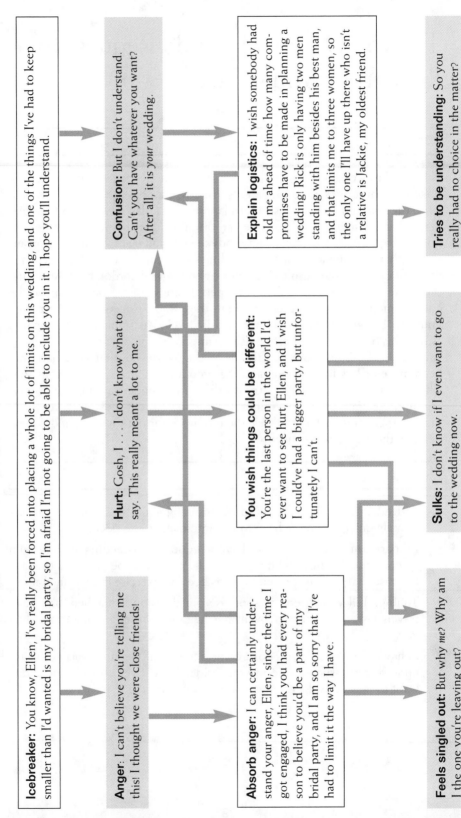

Icebreaker: You know, Ellen, I've really been forced into placing a whole lot of limits on this wedding, and one of the things I've had to keep smaller than I'd wanted is my bridal party, so I'm afraid I'm not going to be able to include you in it. I hope you'll understand.

Anger: I can't believe you're telling me this! I thought we were close friends!

Confusion: But I don't understand. Can't you have whatever you want? After all, it is *your* wedding.

Hurt: Gosh, I . . . I don't know what to say. This really meant a lot to me.

Explain logistics: I wish somebody had told me ahead of time how many compromises have to be made in planning a wedding! Rick is only having two men standing with him besides his best man, and that limits me to three women, so the only one I'll have up there who isn't a relative is Jackie, my oldest friend.

Absorb anger: I can certainly understand your anger, Ellen; since the time I got engaged, I think you had every reason to believe you'd be a part of my bridal party, and I am so sorry that I've had to limit it the way I have.

You wish things could be different: You're the last person in the world I'd ever want to see hurt, Ellen, and I wish I could've had a bigger party, but unfortunately I can't.

Tries to be understanding: So you really had no choice in the matter?

Feels singled out: But why *me?* Why am I the one you're leaving out?

Sulks: I don't know if I even want to go to the wedding now.

She's not alone: You're not the only one I had to leave out, just the most important. That's why it hurts *me* so much.

You're a victim of logistics: I wanted a much larger wedding than Rick did, and we had to make compromises all over the place. Now we're having more people than he wanted and fewer than I did. But I've learned that that's how these things go.

Don't push her: I know how hurt you are, and I'm equally disappointed. But I do hope you'll come; it will mean the world to me. Besides, I was hoping you'd sit at our table.

Understands your situation: Well, I guess the main thing is that I'm going to be there.

Close; reiterate your appreciation: I'm so grateful to have you as my friend, and I'm so happy you'll be there for me on my wedding day.

Needs time: Look, I'm going to need some time to think about this. It really did come as a shock to me.

Close; give her latitude: It was one of the hardest decisions I've ever had to make, and I can only hope you'll be there for me. How about I give you a call in a week or so? Maybe we can get together for coffee.

adaptations

This script can be adapted for use when you have to tell a friend she has not been chosen to be a godparent to your child.

key points

- You're not apologizing for this—you haven't done anything wrong—but you are deeply sorry it had to be this way. You're asking to be understood.
- Put the blame on the need for your family and the groom's family to make compromises and, if possible, give other examples of where you've had to compromise.
- Let her know she's not the only one being left out.
- Even if she seems to be leaning toward not going to your wedding, keep the lines of communication open between you. She may just be looking for you to grovel a little!

Telling a Friend He Can't Bring His Child with Him to a Party **3**

strategy

It is awfully difficult to tell even the most reasonable of friends that there is someplace where his child isn't welcomed, because for some, all the logic in the world can't cut through the pain of rejection. The one way to do this is to make it clear that your decision isn't directed at your friend's child, but at all children, and that it has less to do with the kids than it does with you. It's not a matter of your not liking kids, it's a matter of simplifying your party—making it one audience instead of two—so that you can enjoy yourselves unencumbered of the responsibility of ensuring that there are sufficient sideshow acts to keep the kids occupied and interested. And you can further lessen the blow by telling your friend you're trying to place your *own* kids somewhere else that night.

tactics

- **Attitude:** This is just a fact of life; it's a decision you and your spouse have made, and you fully expect everyone to adhere to it. You're presenting it as a logistical issue, not a personal one.

- **Preparation:** If possible, assemble a list of potential baby-sitters to make available to your friend. Also, if possible, include "adults only" on any invitation you send out.

- **Timing:** You need to have this conversation well before the party so your friend can make alternate arrangements for child care. Also, because meanings and intentions are often misunderstood in phone conversations, it's a good conversation to have face to face.

- **Behavior:** You *sincerely* hope your friends can come to your party, and will do whatever you can to help them make necessary arrangements. Your behavior shows that you're "going the extra mile" to see to it that they can be there.

3. Telling a Friend He Can't Bring His Child with Him to a Party

Icebreaker: Nick, Julie and I are really looking forward to seeing you at our party. I just wanted to give you a heads-up to let you know we're asking everyone not to bring their kids.

Hardship: Well . . . then, I don't know that we can make it. I don't know about finding a sitter. You might have to count us out this time.

Confused: I don't understand. Jimmy's always come with us to parties at your house.

He's the exception: Yeah, I can understand you not wanting kids there, but surely Jimmy's the exception. He can take care of himself. He won't be a bother.

Insulted: Well, if Jimmy isn't welcome, maybe we shouldn't come either.

Make some suggestions: That's why we wanted to give everyone notice ahead of time. If you can't find a sitter, I have a list of responsible kids who might be available and I'd be happy to give you their phone numbers if you'd like.

Explain your reasoning: We've always enjoyed having entire families here for parties—especially you folks—because the kids have a good time here too. But we've also come to realize it makes us realize that they have things to oc- cupy themselves, and that gets to be com- plicated for us. It makes it harder for us to fully enjoy the adults' company without thinking about whether the kids need anything. In fact, we're trying to arrange for our kids to sleep over at their friends' house that night.

It's nothing personal: I love Jimmy, he's a terrific kid; we're only doing this be- cause when any kids are here, we feel it's important that they have things to oc- cupy themselves, and that gets to be com- plicated for us. It makes it harder for us to fully enjoy the adults' company without thinking about whether the kids need anything. In fact, we're trying to arrange for our kids to sleep over at their friends' house that night.

Accepts your request: Well, it may be a pain in the neck for us, but I suppose we can work something out.

Appreciation: I want you to know how delighted I am to know you're going to be there.

May not come: Well, this changes things. I don't know if we'll be able to make it. I'll have to let you know.

It's up to him: Nick, we really hope you can work something out, and you'll let us know if you want the name of some sitters. It will mean a great deal to have you here if you can possibly make it.

Last ditch plea: Do you think you can make just one exception for Jimmy? I can assure you he won't be a bother.

Wouldn't be fair: If we were to make an exception for anyone, it would be for Jimmy. But we don't want any of our other guests to feel slighted, so we're asking that all the kids stay home.

Close: We don't have these get-togethers often, but it means a great deal for us to be able to gather our friends this way. I really appreciate your trying to work this out.

adaptations

This script can be adapted for use with siblings, or when you're just inviting one other couple over to your home for dinner.

key points

- You and your spouse have already decided this, and you are now trying to give everyone advance warning.
- You recognize that this may signal a change in tradition, but you have your reasons for making it.
- Emphasize how fond you are of the friend's child, and that you're trying to take his well-being into account here too.
- If he insists he may not be able to make it, tell him how much you want him there, but don't pressure him for an answer.

Asking a Friend to Repay an Outstanding Loan

4

This is one of those areas where familiarity can breed contempt. You're close friends with someone who's in a bit of a financial fix. The side of you that cares about him wants to help out, but the side of you concerned with your financial stability is wary, and with good reason. If a bank lends him the money and he doesn't pay, the bank has clear recourse. But what of a friend? How do you make sure you get your money and at the same time do everything in your power to protect the friendship? One answer is to have a clear contract beforehand, with everything spelled out and a list of collateral he is willing to offer you. A second strategy is to show a degree of flexibility by asking for installments that you find acceptable and he finds workable (be willing to bargain a little). And a third strategy is to impress upon him the fact that he may need to cut out certain monthly expenditures in order to pay you back, and that's *his* problem. Don't make it yours. In the example, we will assume $3,000 was borrowed, a vague understanding was reached between the two friends as to when the money would be paid back, and the loan is now overdue.

- **Attitude**: You don't want to bully your friend, but you want to be straightforward with him. He needs to pay the money back (or at the very least, begin to pay it back), and the two of you need to figure out how he is going to do that.

- **Preparation**: Come up with terms of repayment that would be acceptable to you; then, in discussion, present more stringent terms and be prepared to ease up on them.

- **Timing**: Wait until the loan is a week or so overdue, and if possible have this discussion early in the month, when most checking accounts are a little fuller.

- **Behavior**: You're cooperative but businesslike. You're prepared to negotiate. But, if necessary, you're also prepared to speak to a lawyer for advice. In other words, you are determined to come away with an understanding of how this debt will be retired.

4. Asking a Friend to Repay an Outstanding Loan

Icebreaker: Greg, I need to talk with you about something. I'm going to need to have you repay our loan by the end of this month (three weeks hence), and I was wondering if you wanted to handle it in a lump sum or if you'd like to handle it in smaller payments.

Wants your trust: I'll get you your money; you know I'm good for it, don't you?

Can't pay you now: Gee, I'd love to, but I'm afraid I can't swing it right now.

Wants to make a deal: I can't really do it now, but how about if I start paying you off a little each month, starting next month, but at a slightly higher interest rate than we first agreed upon?

Can pay you, but it will be difficult: Well, I'm still awfully low on cash. I guess I could scrape some money together, but do you think you could give me a little more time?

You have faith, but want proof: I put my faith in you when I loaned you the money. Now that I need it, I have faith that you'll return it to me. How do you want to do that?

Ask for specifics: Why don't you explain your financial situation to me so we can see what we can work out that will be acceptable to me and workable for you?

Push for the deal you want: If we do that, I'll need some specific figures and specific guarantees. Are you prepared for that?

Offers terms of repayment: How about if I pay you $100 a month and end up paying you an extra $200 as interest?

Gives you a (bleak) financial sketch: Right now I'm spending about as much as I'm making, so I'm not really able to put anything aside. That's my problem.

Agrees to pay you on time: Sigh. All right, I'll get your money to you by the end of the month. I'll get you a check.

Close: Great. I'm happy I could lend you the money and I appreciate your conscientiousness in paying me back on time, especially if it's a bit of a stretch for you.

Don't make his problem your problem: Sounds like you're going to have to cut back on some of your expenses. I was expecting you to pay me back by the end of the month, but I'd be willing to take $400 a month for starters, with interest.

Counterproposal: I'm afraid that's not enough, Greg. I could work with $400 a month, with an additional 1 percent interest.

Asks for leniency: Can you possibly make it a little less? How about $200 each month?

Final offer: I will accept $300 a month from you, with an additional 1 percent interest. I am not in a position to accept anything less.

Agrees to your terms: All right, I suppose. I'll make the monthly payments to you.

Can't do it: I just can't make those kinds of payments. I'm sorry.

Be firm but flexible: Greg, I don't want to put you on the spot. I need my money, and you need living expenses. I want to be flexible with you, but I need a reasonable amount of money from you each month, and I need assurances that you'll pay me regularly and on time. With that in mind, I'll accept $300 a month, with an additional 1 percent on the interest, and if you choose not to agree on that, I'm afraid I'll have to consider speaking with my lawyer about how you and I can clear this up.

Tries to lay on the guilt: Boy, I thought our friendship was worth more than this. You're really disappointing me.

Close: Greg, this has been difficult for both of us. I'm sorry you couldn't make the payments we originally agreed to, but I'm glad we could work something out. I'll write up a little note of understanding and get it to you tomorrow.

adaptations

This script can be adapted for use when a sibling has borrowed money or when a friend has borrowed something else of value to you and neglected to return it.

key points

- If at all possible, be clear ahead of time regarding how the loan will be repaid.
- If your friend says he can't repay it, let him know you're willing to discuss how he *can* repay it, but you're not going to accept his premise that there's nothing he can do about it right now.
- Be prepared for hard feelings, and don't be blackmailed by guilt.
- If he has a problem, help him to figure out how he can solve it; don't make it your problem.

Asking a Friend for a Substantial Loan

5

strategy

This is a request you only pursue if you know the friend has the money to lend, you can justify the expense, and you can offer repayment terms that benefit both of you. In other words, make it as easy and reasonable as you possibly can. But even after doing that, you're really not asking for the money; you're only asking that she consider it. Be very clear that you're not asking for an answer on the spot, because otherwise that's exactly where you'll put her—on the spot. Then, if she sounds reluctant, encourage her to voice her concerns and then back off.

tactics

- **Attitude:** This is both a favor and a business proposition, so present it in a matter-of-fact matter. Also, begin by telling the friend you wouldn't make this proposition unless you felt fully confident that she'd say no to you if she wanted to.

- **Preparation:** Prepare by looking into the terms and interest rates offered by banks so you can propose terms that are easier for you but will still benefit your friend. Also, be prepared to explain what you want the money for, and make it compelling.

- **Timing:** Ask your friend at a time of leisure, when the two of you are relaxed and she can give it some uninterrupted thought.

- **Behavior:** Show extreme patience. Make this a soft sell. Show no urgency or desperation.

5. Asking a Friend for a Substantial Loan

Icebreaker: Shellie, I only want to ask this of you because I honestly believe you'll say no if you want to. I'm wondering if you'd be willing to consider loaning me $5,000—with interest, of course—so I don't have to go to a lending institution.

Needs time: Hmmm . . . I'd really need to think about that. It's a lot of money.

Skeptical: I'm a little nervous about lending money. It can really cause problems between friends.

Wants to know why you're coming to her: Why not go to a bank or a credit union?

Wants to know why you need the money: What's the money for? Are you in debt or something?

Let her take her time, and give her details: I agree, which is why all I'm asking is that you mull it over. Lending money can cause misunderstandings between friends, which is why, if you consent to this, I would want us to have a legal contract that included collateral, terms of payment, and an interest rate we can agree upon.

Why you are asking her: There are two reasons I'm asking you. For one thing, I think we can execute this more quickly than a bank, and for another, I think I can pay you a higher interest rate than your savings account is earning and at the same time pay less interest than I would if I borrowed the money commercially.

Give your reasons for wanting the money: We have an opportunity to do some renovation on our house that would *finally* give the kids a playroom. We really want to be able to do this, but we'll need to borrow to make it happen.

Wants time: Look, I really need to think about this. When do you need an answer from me?

Leaning against giving it to you: Gee, I don't know. I just have my doubts about this.

Wants to know that you've done your investigating: Well, where else have you looked?

Is leaning toward helping you out: Well, it does sound reasonable. We may be able to do something.

Give a reasonable timetable: What I'd like to do is call you back in about a week, if that's enough time for you to consider this.

Don't pressure: I certainly don't expect an answer from you right now. How about if we give it a week for you to think about it, and maybe even jot down any questions or concerns you might have. I'm more than happy to address them.

Show that you've done your homework: I've looked at rates and terms at three lending institutions, and we've asked our parents if they could help out, which they're really not in a position to do.

Agrees to give it consideration: All right, all I can promise is that I'll give it some thought. Give me a call next week, and we'll talk some more.

Close, show appreciation, but don't make it look like a done deal: It's awfully good of you to consider it. How about if we touch base early next week, and you can let me know if we can work out a contract?

adaptation

This script can be adapted for use by an adult child who wishes to ask a parent for a fairly substantial gift of money.

key points

- You recognize the problems an arrangement like this can cause between friends, and you've tried to account for them.
- If she says she wants to think about it, take it as a good sign, back off, and offer to get in touch with her in a few days.
- Have compelling reasons why you need the money and why it is mutually beneficial for your friend to lend it to you.

Suggesting That a Friend Get Psychological Counseling

6

This can be an exceedingly risky conversation to have; not only is there the chance your friend will reject your overture outright, it's also possible for the exchange to put a real strain on the friendship itself. There are a couple of things that you can do to minimize this risk, however, not the least of which is making it clear to your friend that you're not suggesting she's in need of serious help, only that she appears to be having a hard time coping with life right now, and talking it over with someone could be of use to her. Also, you have a great deal more credibility if you yourself have seen a counselor and can relate the benefits firsthand. If you haven't, perhaps you can encourage a mutual friend who *has* to initiate this conversation. Finally, let her know you'll do whatever you can to help her hook up with a counselor who's a good fit for them.

- **Attitude**: Your concern for your friend is not a casual thing; while you're not alarmist, you are worried enough to put the friendship on the line over it.

- **Preparation**: Have the name of at least one referral for your friend. Also, be prepared to cut the conversation short if your friend makes it clear she does *not* want to discuss it.

- **Timing**: Have this conversation in private, at a time when the two of you will not be disturbed and, if possible, at either your house or hers.

- **Behavior**: You bring this up with great reluctance because of your respect for this person's privacy, but you are looking straight in the eye at her, speaking in a slow, modulated voice, and impressing upon her the fact that her situation needs some kind of intervention.

6. Suggesting That a Friend Get Psychological Counseling

Icebreaker: Maryanne, there's something that's been of concern to me that I felt I needed to talk with you about. It's clear that you haven't been yourself lately, that things are troubling you. When I've been in a situation like yours, I've always found it helpful to spend a little time with a counselor, and I'm wondering if you've thought of that for yourself.

Stoic: It's nothing, really. I'll be fine in a little while, don't worry.

Doesn't want you interfering: I appreciate your concern, but I'll thank you to stay out of my business.

You recognize you're taking a risk by raising this topic: It's not easy for me to bring this up, particularly because I do respect your privacy. Now, you're going to do whatever you choose, but I feel I owe it to you as a friend to point out the pain I see in you. My own experience is that talking to someone about it, even for just a few sessions, can give us a whole new perspective on how to tackle whatever's bothering us.

Won't budge: I said, I'll take care of this myself. Now let's drop it.

Curious about your problems: Why did you see someone?

Doesn't want to be stigmatized: I'm not crazy; only crazy people see shrinks.

You're not suggesting drastic action: All a counselor would want to do is help you to find ways of managing whatever stress or other difficulty you might be feeling.

Doesn't know where to find someone: I wouldn't even begin to know where to look for someone.

Doesn't believe in it: To be perfectly honest with you, I've never put a lot of stock in all that psychological mumbo-jumbo.

Fearful: I don't know. It seems kind of scary. What if I don't like it? What if I don't like the therapist? What if there's something really wrong with me?

Calm the fears: All you need to do is see someone once. If you don't feel comfortable, you can find someone else. And I'm sure you're going to find that there's nothing seriously wrong with you—that you simply need to get a handle on things, like we all do from time to time.

Offer to help: I'd be more than happy to give you some suggestions. Your doctor or clergy might have some ideas as well.

Give some background: I was just overwhelmed with work responsibilities; I didn't feel like I could cope. The therapy really helped me to sort things out and get some perspective on them.

Close; back off: I'll certainly respect your wish. Just please understand that if you do change your mind, I'm quite happy to talk with you about my own experience. And I appreciate your willingness to hear what I had to say.

Will consider it: I'll give it some thought, that's all I can promise right now.

Wants your help: You'll help me find someone, and maybe help me get an appointment?

Close: I think it's wise of you to keep an open mind. Let me just give you the name of the person I was so happy with, and if you ever feel like it, you can give her a call. I'll also be in touch with you next week.

Close: I'll do anything I can to help you. In fact, here's the name of the person I saw, who I highly recommend. Let's give her a call right now.

adaptations

This conversation can be adapted for use when you think a sibling or a friend's spouse should get psychological counseling.

key points

- You're not suggesting intense psychotherapy.
- You'd only like the friend to commit to going to an initial session.
- Counseling is quite common; many people use counselors, especially for short periods of time.
- Recognize when your friend is shutting down, and don't go any further. Just reiterate your concern for her and your availability to her, and close the conversation.

Asking a Friend to Drive More Safely

7

strategy

The best way to approach this conversation is out of a sense of caring for the other person rather than a need to criticize him. Don't bring up his own reck-lessness unless it's blatant. Instead, point out how difficult it is for even good drivers who drive aggressively to watch for everyone else on the road. Also, vaguely indicate that you'll consider not riding as a passenger in his car unless he slows down. If nothing else, he may agree to be more cautious when you're in the car with him. Finally, don't press him; what you're doing with this conversation—at the very least—is letting him know his driving habits haven't gone unnoticed. If nothing else, he'll give more thought to how he drives in the future. And with this in mind, you *may* want to consider then asking other friends if they would make similar requests of him.

tactics

- **Attitude**: Keep the mood light. You're concerned, and it's genuine. But don't come across as preachy. And don't hold your own driving habits up as an example of what you expect from your friend.

- **Preparation**: You may want to gather traffic accident statistics from your local police precinct to drop into the conversation at a propitious time. Also, be prepared to no longer be a passenger in his car.

- **Timing**: Have this conversation before the two of you are about to go out somewhere, but not immediately before. It's a good conversation to have in the afternoon if you'll be heading out in the evening.

- **Behavior**: Keep a conversational tone of voice and, if he jokes about his driving, try to maintain a mood of levity but at the same time stick to your point.

7. Asking a Friend to Drive More Safely

Icebreaker: Ted, I'm glad we're such good friends, because it makes it easier for me to ask you to please drive more safely, not only when I'm in the car with you, but for your own sake as well.

Mildly insulted: Hey, I'm a good driver. I know what I'm doing out there, and to tell you the truth, there are a heck of a lot of people who might drive slower than I do but who can't be trusted behind the wheel!

Embarrassed, wants to change the subject: Um, yeah, sure, whatever. Wanna go grab a burger or something?

Makes light of it: Yeah, okay, I'll stay in the right lane and drive five miles an hour from now on. And I'll use my blinker three miles before I'm ready to turn. Anything else, Grandma?

Reinforce his abilities, if not his judgment: The truth be told, Ted, I think you're an awfully talented driver. Your reflexes are a lot quicker than mine, and I think you have a real feel for the road. All I'm asking you to do is take it a little more safely, if for no other reason than the need to look out for other drivers who *aren't* so alert. Remember, even race car drivers have collisions.

Reinforce your point, gently: At the risk of sounding like an old nag, yeah, I'd love to grab a burger . . . but only as long as you promise me you'll take it easy out there. I don't want to see either of us hurt, or anyone else on the road for that matter.

Pick up on his mood; don't get too serious: Actually, four miles an hour would make me feel better, but, hey, I'll live with five. Look, I don't mean to make a big deal of this, and I appreciate the spirit in which you're taking it. I'm just aware of how easy it is even for good drivers like you to wind up bending a fender because someone else might not be as alert or aware as you are. Thanks for agreeing to slow down.

Still resists you: I'm sorry, but I'm a good driver. I know my abilities and my limitations. I'm not gonna change.

You won't ride with him: I was hoping you'd give it some thought just for safety's sake, and I still hope you will. But in the meantime, I guess when we're headed out together, either I'll drive or we'll have to take separate cars.

Still won't budge: I think you're making a lot out of nothing, but if you want to drive us, I'm not gonna fight you on it.

Close: Well, I'm still glad we had this talk, and I appreciate you hearing me out.

Humors you and offers half a loaf: Look, I'm not going to agree with you, not for a minute. But if it'll make you feel better, yeah, all right, I'll be careful, at least when you're in the car.

Close: Great. Like I said, this kind of conversation is one of the things that makes me really appreciate your friendship. Now let's get outta here.

adaptations

This script can be adapted for use with a friend who takes unnecessary risks while engaging in sports or hobbies, such as sailing, dirt biking, or mountain climbing.

key points

- When you're in a car, you value safety above all else, so don't be afraid to stand on that principle.
- You're not debating his skills as a driver, only his judgment.
- You're not insisting he drive more safely, you're asking. But you can insist that you won't be a passenger in his car.

Deflecting a Friend's Inappropriate Personal Questions   **8**

What can make this conversation tricky is that what one person regards as opinion, another regards as fact. If you're uncomfortable talking about certain private matters, you run into trouble when your friend wants to convince you you're being unnecessarily closed-minded, let alone close-lipped. When she tries to transform her opinion ("*I* feel fine talking about these things") into fact ("*I* feel fine talking about these things, therefore everyone else should as well"), she runs the risk of being intolerant of the boundaries you have set up to protect your privacy. At that point you want to do two things: remind her that there is no "right" or "wrong" answer to the question of what is or is not appropriate to discuss among friends, and assure her that you're going to keep certain things to yourself.

- **Attitude**: You want to approach this with understanding. Your friend didn't realize she was wandering into unwelcome areas, so you're merely trying to be clear about your boundaries.

- **Preparation**: Be prepared to accept a somewhat diminished role in the other person's life—at least temporarily. If these discussions are important to her, an alternate outlet for them will be sought.

- **Timing**: You want to address this issue as the questions arise, unless they arise in a public setting where you don't feel comfortable launching this conversation. If this is the case, ask your friend to come aside and sit where you can talk uninterrupted.

- **Behavior**: You neither want to castigate your friend for her feelings about this topic nor apologize for yours. You have hit upon a place where the two of you are different, and that is neither good nor bad, but simply a fact of human relationship.

8. Deflecting a Friend's Inappropriate Personal Questions

Icebreaker: Wendy, I think we have different levels of comfort about what we're willing to talk about with one another. I'm a pretty private person, so I'm a bit ill at ease when it comes to answering some of the questions you're asking.

Holds herself up as an example: Well, I *certainly* have nothing to hide. I'd tell you anything you wanted to know about *my* personal life.

Acknowledge the difference between you: We are different in that regard, aren't we? It's like a left handed person and a right handed one. And I hope you'll respect my wish for privacy as much as I respect your openness and candor.

Tries to egg you on: Oh, c'mon, don't be so old-fashioned. It's just a few harmless secrets among friends.

The issue for you is how it makes you feel, period: I'm sure they are harmless, and perhaps you *do* see me as old-fashioned about this. But I know I need to act in accordance with how I feel, so I hope you understand if I choose not to answer some of the questions you might ask.

Feels put off by your reluctance: Well, I *certainly* didn't mean to sound nosy! Never mind, then! I won't ask you anything personal.

Discuss reasonable limits: I think we all have limits to what we're comfortable talking about, and yours and mine are just different. There are some personal things I'm quite comfortable talking with you about. In fact, I often value your input. I'm just asking that we stay within each others' limits.

Feels as though this creates a gap between you: I'll back off from asking personal questions, but I have to tell you, it's important to *me* to be able to discuss these sorts of things. This kind of drives a wedge between us.

You can accept the limits this might impose: I understand what you're saying, and I think you're wise to realize that this *is* important to you, and that you may well need to have these discussions with someone else. I'm just glad our relationship has enough else going for it that we can still be close.

Judges you: Look, this isn't the Victorian era. You need to lighten up and accept this kind of stuff. Everyone talks about their personal life now, and you need to get with it. Believe me, in time, you'll find it liberating.

You need to do what works for you: I'm glad you find it liberating to discuss these kinds of things, and maybe I'll change some day. But I know who I am, I'm comfortable with who I am, and it would mean a great deal to me if you would agree to respect that.

Decides to "humor" you: Well, I have to tell you, I don't necessarily agree with you, but if it makes you uncomfortable, I'll lay off, okay?

Close: I don't know about you, but I think it's the sign of a strong relationship when two friends can have a difference of opinion and style like this and be able to talk it out. And I appreciate your honoring my feelings, even if they're not in sync with yours.

adaptations

This script can be adapted for use when a friend is telling you jokes you find offensive.

key points

- Your feelings needn't require justification; they are what they are.
- If your feelings about this topic are going to change, it's not going to be as a result of your friend's wanting to pressure you to change them.
- You respect her attitude toward this as much as you expect her to respect yours.

Deflecting a Friend's Inappropriate   9
Personal Conversations

strategy

Sometimes people assume that whatever they're comfortable talking about, you're comfortable listening to. One person loves to discuss his religious beliefs, and another wants nothing more than to keep his private. One person likes to talk about his love life, his domestic quarrels, or his child's police record, and the other wants no part of such a conversation. When you encounter this situation, the first thing you want to keep in mind is that you owe the other person no explanation or logical reason for not wanting to engage in such a conversation. You simply feel uncomfortable—for whatever conscious or unconscious reason—and you want your friend to respect your feelings. In addition, you want to make it clear to your friend that there's nothing inherently wrong in her wanting to raise a certain topic, no more than there is anything wrong with you not wanting to discuss it. This is a matter of personal taste and preference. And finally, if necessary, you may need to make it clear that not only do you not intend to divulge any personal information from your life, you don't want her to divulge her secrets to you.

tactics

- **Attitude**: Feel free to show your friend this bothers you, and you won't feel comfortable until it stops.
- **Preparation**: Be ready for her to ask you to defend your position with logic, and be ready to tell her that shouldn't be necessary if you can't.
- **Timing**: You need to raise this issue the moment your friend raises a topic of conversation that doesn't suit you.
- **Behavior**: Look your friend straight in the eye; show her that you care for her, and that there are plenty of conversations the two of you have that *are* extremely valuable to you.

9. Deflecting a Friend's Inappropriate Personal Conversations

Icebreaker: Betty, I need to tell you that I don't feel comfortable discussing family finances. I'm not interested in the details of your finances, and I prefer to keep mine private.

Slightly angry/hurt: I thought we could confide in one another about anything.

Be clear about the issue you're raising: I'm sorry if you feel as though I'm closing you off, because I'm not. I'd like to believe we could talk with one another about anything that was *important* to either of us. If money came up because one of us needed cash, for instance, I would hope we could talk it out. But there are certain topics I like to keep private unless there's some urgency to discussing them. I hope you understand.

Doesn't see a problem: What's the big deal? It's only our money we're talking about here. I have nothing to hide—why should you?

Misses your point: Are you embarrassed because you know we make more money than you do? I certainly don't mean to flaunt that.

Reiterate your principles: I choose not to have conversations about finances with *anyone*, regardless of whether I think I might have more, less, or the same amount of money as they have. I simply don't discuss it, and I hope you can honor that.

You know what you want, and that's all that matters: I suppose I can understand your candor, but I'd rather not hear about your specific money ups and downs. I don't know that I can explain it any better than that, but I don't know that I should have to, either.

Accepts your wishes: Well, if that's how you feel, I guess there's not much for me to do about it.

Wants to be able to talk with you: I'll tell you what. I won't ask you about your finances, but from time to time I may want to bring up mine. I just like talking about them, especially when I'm doing well.

Gently reject the proposal: I don't think I want to have that conversation with you, Betty. If it's important for you to be able to talk about it, perhaps you can find someone else to be able to discuss it with.

Close: I guess this is one of those things we'll always feel differently about, but I'm glad we can have those differences and not let them get in the way of our friendship.

key points

- You aren't passing judgment on *her* wanting to talk about things that you deem too personal.
- You would like her to understand why you feel the way you do, but if not, you simply want her to respect it.
- You may appear to your friend as if you're "shutting her out" of a part of your world. Assure her that the relationship is very valuable to you.

Confronting a Friend's Inappropriate Treatment of His Spouse

10

strategy

My assumption here is that your friend's inappropriate treatment of his spouse does not involve any form of physical abuse, which would require its own discreet form of intervention that wouldn't involve talking directly to your friend. A less drastic form of inappropriate treatment—such as ridiculing a spouse or making her the butt of jokes—can be dealt with head-on by letting your friend know that you feel uncomfortable when subjected to this, and that your hunch is the spouse does too. But be aware that the success of this conversation is largely dependent upon the flexibility of your friend; if, say, a husband is unwilling to yield an inch on whether he thinks he should treat his wife differently, you need to decide how far you're willing to go with your confrontation. You may be testing the durability of this friendship.

tactics

- **Attitude:** Don't be afraid to show your friend that this behavior annoys you. On the other hand, be charitable and let him know he may not be aware of how his behavior is being received or perceived.

- **Preparation:** Decide how important this is to you. Are you willing to risk losing this friend because you won't tolerate his inappropriate behavior? This will help you decide how far you'll push the topic.

- **Timing:** Have this conversation when the two of you are alone, immediately or shortly after you have been privy to the inappropriate behavior.

- **Behavior:** Make and sustain eye contact with your friend. Keep your voice level, but let him hear your concern in it.

10. Confronting a Friend's Inappropriate Treatment of His Spouse

Icebreaker: Alex, I hope you don't find what I'm about to say impertinent, but I sometimes wonder how Betsy feels when you make fun of her in public. I get the feeling it bothers her sometimes.

Thinks the behavior is appropriate: Look, she's so gullible, she practically asks for it. I love my wife, but she's just not all that bright, so I poke fun at her a little bit.

Remind him how his behavior affects others: I don't think you mean to make her feel uncomfortable, but I suspect she does. I know I certainly do when I see you treat her that way. I feel badly for her.

Refuses to budge: How we are with each other is our business. You should really stay out of it.

Doesn't see problem: Oh, don't be so sensitive. She likes to be kidded as much as anyone.

Encourage more sensitivity: I know I don't like to be kidded so frequently, especially in front of my friends. Don't you think it might be useful to ask Betsy if she minds it at all? Because she certainly seems to. I may be all wrong here, but on the other hand, she might surprise you.

Angry at your "intrusion": Hey, look, I hate to sound impertinent, but why don't you mind your own business?

This is your business: I understand your being angry at me; I guess this is pretty personal stuff. But I brought it up because I care about both of you, and I think Betsy might be getting her feelings hurt here.

Agrees to talk to spouse: I know what she'll say; she'll tell me it's no problem for her. But okay, I'll talk with her about it.

Won't agree with you, but will consider what you're saying: I don't think you understand Betsy like I do, but I'll tell you what; if you're uncomfortable when I pick on her, I'll be sure not to do that when we're together. How's that?

Focus on your concern for spouse: I'm sorry if you feel I'm invading your privacy here. If I thought you were being hurt by something Betsy was doing, I guess I'd talk to you about it, and if you told me to stay out of your business, I would. So perhaps I should speak with her, and if she wants me to butt out, I'll gladly do so.

May end friendship: If you say anything to her, I may just need to end this friendship. You really need to stay out of our affairs.

Give him a chance to change things: I hope you'll give this some serious thought, Alex, because I think our friendship means a great deal to all of us.

Close: We're both very fond of the two of you, and I hope you give some thought to what I've said. Whatever you do from here truly is *your* business, and you can be sure I won't interfere.

Reward "encouraging" behavior: Well, I'm asking you to be gentler with her for her sake more than for mine, but I guess that's a start. I'll be anxious to see if she doesn't perk up a little bit when you're in my company.

Softens his stance: Well, if it bugs folks, I guess I can lay off her a little. I just mean to have fun with her, you know, not hurt her.

Close: I think that's great. Give her my best, and let's get together soon.

adaptations

This script can be adapted for use when you feel a friend is treating another friend inappropriately.

key points

- You're raising this topic because you care about both your friend and his spouse.
- Let your friend know how you feel when you're treated in a like manner.
- Don't be afraid to communicate the strength of your displeasure, but at the same time don't be afraid to communicate how important the friendship is to you.

Bringing Up a Friend's Bad Hygiene

11

strategy

Elsewhere in this book I've discussed how best to have this conversation with family members, but friendships pose their own unique challenges and opportunities for a conversation like this one. Friends don't always assume or invite the same level of intimacy as family members, and are often less likely to allow you to comment on their more private habits. On the other hand, a topic like this can be addressed with a certain frankness not often found in families because the history of the friendship is less likely to be marked by the complications of past hurts, envies, and angry times that often punctuate long-standing family relationships. To a friend it can be easy to say, "I see this in you," without triggering the same visceral reaction you might get from, say, a brother or a sister. One way to go about this ticklish subject is to address it as a fact of life that you're concerned about both for yourself and for your friend. Point out that as we age our bodies change and may require more diligent hygiene, that you're wondering if your friend has any ideas as to how to manage this, and that you're aware this is something you both should be thinking about. Steer the conversation in the direction of your desire to ask a professional (perhaps a dermatologist) for ideas, and gently remind your friend that he is in the same boat. In the end, if you've only given him something to think about, you'll have succeeded.

tactics

- **Attitude:** You want to treat this casually and somewhat tentatively. Don't be afraid to show that you're a little embarrassed by the topic, and that you're looking to get help as much as you're looking to give it.

- **Preparation:** Spend just a little time with a dermatologist or internist learning about hygiene and our bodies' changing chemistry. Also, be prepared to shift the conversation to another topic when you feel this one is exhausted.

- **Timing:** Hold this conversation at a time when the two of you will be alone for a while, preferably away from the home.

- **Behavior:** Don't discuss this in hushed whispers, as though it's a topic that shouldn't see the light of day. Look relaxed; speak in a normal tone and volume, and with little affect in your voice.

11. Bringing Up a Friend's Bad Hygiene

Icebreaker: You know what, Jack? I think you and I have come upon the same problem. As we get older, I think we're having a harder time just keeping clean, eliminating our body odors. I'm thinking about talking to a dermatologist, but I was wondering if you had any ideas on how we can manage it.

Doesn't notice the problem: To tell you the truth, you may have a problem, but I don't think I do.

Feels invaded by your question: Hey, that's kind of a private subject, isn't it?

Embarrassed: Um, can we not talk about that? I mean, do what you have to for yourself, but this is kind of embarrassing for me.

You had the same experience: It's interesting you should say that, because that's what I thought too, until my wife mentioned it to me and explained how we can be pretty unaware of how our body's natural odors are picked up by others. You might want to run this question by your wife as well.

Play upon the depth of the friendship: It is, which is why I was hoping you and I could talk about it. It's something we both share, and I don't feel comfortable talking about it with any of our other friends.

Sympathize: I'm embarrassed by this too, which is why I was hoping we might be of help to one another. Because you're probably the most open and honest friend I have, I figured you'd be willing to talk about it.

Is somewhat incredulous: We need better hygiene as we get older?!? That doesn't sound right to me. I think we're just fine.

Doesn't show much interest: Well, you do whatever you think you need to do. Don't worry about me.

Keep him informed: That's fine, but I might want to learn what I can do about it, give it a few weeks, and ask you if you think I'm having any results.

Substantiate your claim: I know it sounds odd, but a doctor explained to me how our body's changes can include change in the rate we develop bacteria, and a bunch of other stuff I didn't understand. But the upshot of what he said was that this is one of a good many areas our bodies undergo change, and I think that's what's going on with the two of us.

Shows limited interest: Well, if you learn something from your dermatologist, I suppose you could let me know.

Close: It really helps to have a friend like you to discuss this sort of thing. I'm going to look into how we can stay on top of this, and whatever I learn, I'll pass on to you. You can do whatever you want with it.

key points

- You've noticed this problem, even if your friend hasn't. You want to relate that you went through the same thing.

- This is not something you like talking about, but you consider yourself to be close enough to this friend that you feel comfortable broaching the subject with him in particular.

- Your aim is to give him something to think about, which he can then rectify on his own.

Bringing Up a Friend's Inappropriate Attire

12

By and large adults feel free to dress any way they see fit, regardless of how well- or ill-suited it is to a particular context, and there's nothing inherently wrong with this. But this makes bringing up a friend's dress a topic that's probably not worth broaching unless your friend's inappropriate attire somehow negatively affects you. In other words, if you don't think she dresses right for work, there's nothing much you're going to do about it, and if you try, you run the risk of creating an unnecessary breach in your friendship. There are times, however, when her disregard for fashion, custom, or protocol can reflect poorly on you, and at those times you want to appeal to the strength of the friendship, the willingness you both have to do charitable things for one another, and her desire to protect you from any discomfort, and hope that that will carry the day. The example I cite here is of a woman who is staging a formal party and is asking her decidedly informal friend to dress uncharacteristically nice for the party.

tactics

- **Attitude**: You're asking for a favor, and you want your friend to understand why this is important to you, even if it's not important to her.
- **Preparation**: Be prepared to suggest compromise outfits that might meet—or at least approximate—both of your needs.
- **Timing**: Hold this conversation well in advance of an occasion when your friend will need to dress appropriately.
- **Behavior**: You're asking but not begging. Discuss this matter-of-factly. Make it clear that you do have expectations for how your friend will dress, and you're hopeful she will meet them.

12. Bringing Up a Friend's Inappropriate Attire

Icebreaker: Jane, the party I'm throwing next week is semiformal. I know how you dislike getting dressed up, but it would mean a lot to me if you would pick out a nice dress for the evening.

Doesn't see a problem with her attire: What's wrong with the way I normally dress?

"Makes a statement" with her attire: I'm comfortable with what I wear, and I don't think anyone should get hung up on appearances. If others want to wear dresses, that's fine with me, but I don't want to be judged by them if I don't.

Stresses discomfort: Look, I'm sorry, but I'm really not comfortable in a dress. I have to go casual.

Will consider it: (Icily) If it means that much to you, I'll give it some thought.

You simply want her to dress in accordance with the context: It's not a matter of "right" or "wrong." I just find that if you dress too casually, so that you look so different from everyone else, it tends to draw unnecessary attention to you. It becomes a distraction.

You don't want to politicize your party: I know we all have our hangups, but I'm just trying to ensure that even my "hung up" friends enjoy themselves, so I hope you'll indulge me just this once.

Does she see a solution?: I understand your feelings about dresses. I'm asking people to come fairly dressed up and you'd rather not wear a dress, so I'm wondering if you can suggest some sort of alternative that would work for both of us?

Reinforce this decision: I know this is a pretty unusual request, so I really appreciate that you're willing to give it thought. I hope you can find an outfit that works for you and fits with the tone of the party.

Threatens not to come: Look, if I'm going to be such a distraction, maybe I should just stay home that night.

Doesn't see the value in dressing appropriately: It all just seems so superficial to me.

Is willing to try: Well, I suppose I could put together *something* that would keep me comfortable and satisfy you.

Ask her to be reasonable: Jane, I really want you there next week. It means a lot to me to have you there. Do you think you can find a way to do this for me?

You don't necessarily disagree: You know, you may be right. I'm not trying to tell you that the right clothes should be important, I'm only trying to point out how people react, and what makes them comfortable or uncomfortable. I want to avoid that so people can just enjoy themselves at the party, and I'd really appreciate your help with this.

Close: I'm very grateful to you for this. Tell you what, how about I throw another party in a few months and make it "come as you are"?

adaptations

This script can be adapted for use with an office colleague who is dressing inappropriately, particularly when that colleague's demeanor reflects on you.

key points

- You're not judging your friend's dress to be "right" or "wrong." You're simply asking that she conform with your wishes.
- Be willing to give a little to get a little.
- If she agrees to do something about this and indicates anger or frustration in her voice, don't address her feeling, just applaud her words.
- If possible, find a way to *show* your gratitude, perhaps by returning the favor.

Trying to Stop a Friend's Foolish Action   **13**

As difficult as it can be to stop a friend who is about to do something stupid, you may have some leverage that her family does not, because the constant, daily intimacy of family life can breed a kind of resentment that many friendships can avoid. You're a fresh voice, a voice of reason, an alter ego. You have the license to say things to one another that a husband or wife, parent or child, does not. You can take risks with your friend. When a friend is on the verge of foolish behavior, what you want to do is threefold: acknowledge the legitimacy of the dissatisfaction that is giving rise to this temptation, show her the problems and dire consequences of going through with the foolish action, and open her eyes to alternative ways of solving her problem.

- **Attitude**: You're concerned for your friend, for her family, and for the unforeseen consequences of what she is contemplating doing.

- **Preparation**: Gather one or two alternative avenues of solution to her problem and be prepared to present them to her.

- **Timing**: Have this conversation as soon as you can, at a time and place that guarantees complete privacy.

- **Behavior**: Show sympathy for her plight but be strong in insisting that she's running the risk of making a huge mistake. Look her in the eye at all times, and don't let the conversation get off track.

13. Trying to Stop a Friend's Foolish Action

Icebreaker: Diane, I know things aren't going well with your marriage right now, but having an affair is only going to cause you and your entire family a whole lot of grief down the road. I think you and John have to take a good hard look at whether or not you want to stay together and just deal with that right now. You owe that to each other, and to your kids.

Wants you to stay out: Thanks for caring about me, but this is my business, not yours. You need to keep out of this.

It is your business: Diane, this is my business insofar as I care about you and your family and don't want to see you do something that's going to hurt any of you. I particularly don't want to see your kids stung by this.

Seeks short-term pleasure: All I know is that I've been unhappy now for a long time, and I'm happy when I'm with Ted. I'm entitled to that.

First things first: It may well be that your marriage can't be saved, but you need to figure that out first. Then, if the two of you do decide to separate, you're free to pursue other relationships. But you can't figure out what's best for you and John if you're getting involved with someone else at the same time.

Spite: John's been selfish and preoccupied for months now. He's neglected me and taken me for granted. So let's see when I start neglecting *him*.

Empathize: I can understand your being angry enough to want to get back at him, but you'd be smart to steer that anger directly toward John so that it doesn't involve anyone else, especially your kids. You shouldn't use another man for retaliation.

It's too late, so there's nothing wrong with what she's about to do: I'm afraid my marriage is all but over anyway. Yeah, I may jump into this affair with Ted, but he and I would just end up together in the long run.

Counsel patience: You may well be right, but if you end your marriage in this way, you may end up regretting the unnecessary pain it caused the rest of your family. If you're sure the marriage is over, then you and John need to see a counselor to negotiate an amicable separation. This needs to be done cleanly.

Poor impulse control: I'm sorry, but I feel like I've been patient for years. I can't sit around waiting for something right to happen in this marriage anymore.

Rationalizes: Look, I can be discreet about this. And besides, this is a harmless affair. It doesn't have any effect on the problems John and I are having.

It's difficult to do the right thing: You're probably right, but it's so *bad*. All I know is that I've been so starved for happiness and now I'm getting some, and it feels good.

Steer her impulses: Clearly you're feeling miserable in your marriage and you want to do something to make you feel better. I think that's where counseling can help you, even if it turns out to be directed toward ending the marriage.

Bring her back to reality: I know you're smarter than that. We'd both like to believe that an affair wouldn't hurt anyone else, but you know better.

Understand, but focus on primary responsibilities: I know how good it must feel to have someone show that they care about you, especially when you've felt neglected for so long. But you need to finish what you started with John before you move on to anything else. If your marriage is going to end, it needs to be a clean ending. You'll feel better for it in the long run, and your kids will handle it better as well.

Doesn't know where to turn: You make sense, I suppose, but I don't know *what* my next move should be.

Agrees with you: I suppose you're right, but I really don't hold out much hope for my marriage.

Will think about it: Look, I'll give this some thought. Okay?

Close: I'm going to send you the names of some counselors tomorrow. You can see any one of them any time you want, confidentially, and, if you wish, alone. I'm also going to keep in touch with you to find out if there's anything I can do to help you through this. I'm keeping my door open to you.

adaptations

This script can be adapted for use when a friend is failing to take any action in a situation that requires some kind of change.

key points

- Your friend is acting on impulse; try to show her that the consequences of her actions will long outlive the feelings that gave rise to them in the first place.
- If necessary, remind her that one of the jobs of friendship is to say the things that the other doesn't want to hear.
- If applicable, remind her that her children might be affected by what she is contemplating.
- Offer to be present for her in whatever capacity she needs and you can reasonably handle.

Turning Down a Friend's Request for a Loan

14

In the "you can't get blood from a stone" vein, it's easy to turn down a friend's request for a loan if you don't have the money. What's difficult is when you *do* have the reserves but have personal reasons for choosing not to lend it out. In so many words, your friend will call you selfish, unfeeling, untrusting, and disrespectful of the long and trusting relationship the two of you have built up over the years. This is why your best bet is to take the position *that lending money is a relationship buster,* that you've had bad experiences in the past, that you don't want anything to come between the two of you, and that you will help him out *any other way* the two of you can think of. You *do* care about him, and you tell him as much. You *do* want to see him get the funds he needs, and you tell him this as well. You're not so much turning your back on him as you are partnering with him to find a solution that meets both of your expectations, and you tell him this. And finally, having offered to help, leave it up to him to take or leave your proposal and to live with the consequences. Don't force your help upon him or appear too eager to offer it, as though you're buying off your guilt for not giving him what he wants. Leave the door open. It's his choice to either come in or stay out.

- **Attitude**: You're sorry you can't do this, but you feel no guilt. You want very much to maintain and protect the friendship.

- **Preparation**: Be prepared to offer your friend alternative ways you can be of assistance. Also, be prepared for an onslaught of anger and/or guilt-tripping.

- **Timing**: You owe it to your friend to inform him as soon as you've made your mind up. And do it face to face.

- **Behavior**: Avoid getting into a debate about whether or not you should rethink your position (you shouldn't) by keeping the two of you focused on the fact that this is a fait accompli, and the best you can do now is decide what he is going to do next.

14. Turning Down a Friend's Request for a Loan

Icebreaker: Bill, I've had a number of bad experiences lending money to friends, even when they've offered collateral, so I'm going to have to turn you down. In fact, we've decided not to loan money to anyone anymore. But I'm wondering, isn't there some way I can help you look elsewhere for the money you need?

Plays for pity: I don't think there is any other way to get this money. I don't know *what* I'm going to do now . . . I guess I'll have to forget the whole project. (Sigh.)

Bargains with you: Please, tell me what the problems were before, and I know we can work them out. Do you want a higher interest rate? Different terms? How can we make this happen?

Angry: Boy, and I thought we were friends! I'd help you out if you needed it! Never mind, I'll find the money myself. Somehow.

Show sympathy, but don't change your position: I'm sorry you're going to have to find some other way to fund this thing, Bill, but maybe I could be of some use to you in identifying how you can do that.

Stick to your principles: I'm afraid I can't loan you the money. I've just run into problems too many times. But think about whether there might be some other way I can help you.

Absorb anger: I understand your being angry at me; you feel like I've let you down, and I'm sorry that my position on this may cause you some problems. I hope you'll let me see if I can help you out some other way, though.

Resents you: I think you just want to help me because you feel guilty about turning me down. I don't want your help.

Wants to know what you think you can do: How else could you possibly help me? What I *need* is money.

Premature despair: Never mind. I didn't need to do this project anyway.

You do care about this friend: I can see why you might question my motives here, Bill, but I simply want to help because you're my friend and I care about you. I'd be delighted if you'd take me up on this, but if you don't, I'll understand.

You've already thought about how to help: I've talked to some financial people and come up with a list of possible loan sources for you; everything from commercial institutions to government programs to family members. Let's find some time to take a look at it together.

Don't take responsibility for his feelings: Bill, it's up to you whether or not you want to try and go ahead with this, with or without my help. My door is open. If I can assist you in some other way, I'm eager to do so. So when you're ready, you just let me know what you've decided to do.

Wants to mull it over: Well, I don't know *what* I'm going to do next. I guess I'll just think it over.

Is open to your ideas: Well, I guess it can't hurt to put our heads together on this.

Thinks he wants to look elsewhere: I think I'll just look around for another way to do this. Thanks anyway.

Close: Let me give you this list of alternative forms of financing, and I'll call you in a few days. Whatever you decide to do, I'll do whatever I can to assist you, and I hope it all works out.

adaptations

This script can be adapted for use when a friend wants to come and visit for an extended period of time—perhaps to vacation in your city or town—and you don't want him to.

key points

- Be straight about the fact that your refusal is not predicated on a lack of funds, but on a fear of what would happen if the loan went bad.
- Reiterate your concern for your friend's well-being, and look for genuine ways to express it.
- Let him know that this is not a problem with him per se; there is no one you _would_ lend money to.

Notes

Notes

Notes

Notes